With admiration, appreciation & best wishes,
to Jean & Barry
Masters extraordinary of Balliol

John

Oxford   28 June 1993

Treasures of the
Library of
Congress

Treasures of the
Library of Congress

Revised and Expanded Edition

Charles A. Goodrum

Photography by Michael Freeman and Jonathan Wallen

Harry N. Abrams, Inc., Publishers, New York

Revised Edition 1991

Editor: EDITH M. PAVESE

Designers: NAI Y. CHANG and ELLEN NYGAARD FORD

All photographs in this book, with the exception of those reproduced from Library of Congress negatives, were taken by Michael Freeman and Jonathan Wallen.

Library of Congress Cataloging-in-Publication Data

Goodrum, Charles A.
    Treasures of the Library of Congress/Charles A. Goodrum; all photography for the revised edition by Jonathan Wallen.—Rev. and expanded ed.
        p.   cm.
    Includes bibliographical references (p. 335) and index.
    ISBN 0-8109-3852-9
    1. Library of Congress.   2. Library resources—Washington (D.C.).   3. Libraries, National—United States—History.   I. Title.
Z733.U58G66   1991
027.573—dc20   90-1147
                                            CIP

The design of the Library's original building started as a prosaic, unadorned, working government city block. By the time they actually began to build, they had decided to make a building "Just like they would in Europe—only better!" In 1888, Congress and the designers would show how artistic the nation had become.

Page 1: *Roland Hinton Perry's fountain stretches fifty feet across the face of the Library at street level. It contains twelve bronze figures, dominated by Neptune (who would be twelve feet high if he stood up).*

Page 2: *One of three bronze entry doors, this one The Art of Printing, by Frederick MacMonnies.*

Page 3: *One of Philip Martiny's sculptures, bearing a newly invented electric light.*

Pages 4–5: *The Great Hall of the Library with the Minerva mosaic by Elihu Vedder on the opposite wall.*

Page 6: *Some of Philip Martiny's cherub sculptures, here above a bust of Thomas Jefferson, whose books formed the Library's nucleus.*

Page 9: *The Rotunda of the Main Reading Room.*

Page 10: *John Flanagan's bronze clock over the entrance to the Main Reading Room.*

Page 11: *The ethnological heads ornamenting the keystones of the windows were, according to a contemporary guidebook, "the first instance of a comprehensive attempt to make ethnological science contribute to the architectural decoration of an important public building." There are thirty-three heads modeled from data gathered after six months of research into racial types. The sculptors duplicated careful measurements and relationships of facial features the scientists had generalized for each race.*

CONTENTS

Foreword

The Library of Congress is different from other libraries, not just in size but in kind, as this new edition of *Treasures* makes clear. It is, in fact, an information conglomerate with two separate identities: a *collection in Washington* and a *service center for the nation and the world*.

Let's talk about the first part just briefly. The Library of Congress houses the largest and most diverse collection of recorded knowledge ever assembled on earth. We will soon cross the 100 million mark in terms of items—we get 31,000 items a day, in all languages and formats, of which we keep 7,000.

This collection is important to our democratic legislature, and this pattern of attaching a national library to a legislature was followed by the Japanese and Koreans after World War II. Our arrangements have also recently been studied as a model by many in Eastern Europe who are trying both to open up their national libraries and to build congressional research services.

In addition, the collections are important for scholarship since this Library is a place where the variety and scope of the collections make connections possible that cannot easily be made elsewhere. The importance to democratic citizenship is that it provides open access to all interests and all parties at a location in the center of power with materials that are almost all located in one place.

We have remarkably little of our materials in remote access—much less than many great university libraries have. The Library is housed in three buildings. Over the next decade, we are trying to give each of these buildings a distinctive character that will illuminate—and facilitate access to—the full range of our collections.

The Jefferson Building is the place for the humanistic study of the past. It is being reconstructed to have reading rooms for all the major cultures of the world. It will, in effect, be America's living museum of the written word: perhaps the closest thing anywhere to the world's memory. It will be the entry point for studying the diversity of human experience as represented in the 470 languages that make up our collections.

The Adams Building will be the place for the scientific study of the present. We have reading rooms here for both the social and natural sciences in addition to our unique reading room where one finds machine-readable software and other data banks, as well as rooms for technical analysis. Here we hope also to get our 4 million scientific and technical reports, as well as related material in many languages, out to the public in more usable fashion.

Finally, the Madison Building, the administrative headquarters of the Library, is the place to probe the multi-media future. The collections of the sound and pictorial world are concentrated here.

So the three buildings represent a kind of a past/present/future focus as well as a humanities/science/multi-media division. Part of the challenge is to make the Library a more usable, creative place for both the government and the scholarship of a free people. This Library offers a visible statement of the importance of the pursuit of truth, of objectivity, and of memory, in a city of power, advocacy, and present-mindedness.

The second role of the Library of Congress is not as a place, but as a national service center in the information age: the spark plug for the emerging new electronic library without walls of the twenty-first century.

The Main Reading Room.   13

The traditional office of the Librarian of Congress, properly embellished with ceiling frescoes, plaster trumpeters, and carved panelling, sits just off the Great Hall. Librarian Ainsworth Rand Spofford designed it for himself, and it proceeded to serve seven successors until a new Librarian's Office was built in the James Madison Memorial Building.

Opposite: *Librarian of Congress James H. Billington, photographed in his office atop the James Madison Memorial Building.*

Our service to the nation has its origin in the cataloging for libraries. We recently put the entire bibliographic record of the Library of Congress on-line experimentally with fourteen very different kinds of libraries throughout the country.

There should be more such on-line networking to serve the nation in the future. But the biggest, most interesting challenge is to make textual material as well as the bibliographic record available—and to find ways of mediating the collections to ordinary people. The national library should aspire to provide the extraordinary amount of foreign-language materials, jargonized information, and general data we process, not just to academic scholars and productive Research and Development, but to a wide range of people. All this requires the warehousing that we and other large research libraries do.

Information technology alone should not determine what we do for the future. We must decide as a free people, as a rational people, as a discussing, contending people, variously and collectively, how to use it all. The rapid pace of this technology's advance only increases our need to make important decisions. We at the Library of Congress have already decided that we are going to network with schools, libraries, and other institutions. Some technologists say we should bypass such intermediaries and go directly into people's homes. But that seems to us not consistent with the values of our society— and particularly with the idea of being a diverse, pluralistic people. It is important to get things out to reinforce local institutions, not for sentimental or traditional reasons, but because we want to make sure that technology brings our materials into those institutions that are close to the people—and helps reinforce those institutions.

Our pilot program in this area is called American Memory. It is designed to get our unique materials out to a broader audience—initially through optical disks but eventually in digital form and on-line. We want to provide permanent additions to other libraries around the country and to use new technologies in ways that stimulate curiosity and the active mind. Ideally, at some time in the twenty-first century, all our unique materials will be widely available in the new highly compressed, largely digitized files that will be emerging in libraries.

Libraries have provided, from the very beginning, part of the mise-en-scène for our unprecedented effort at critical self-government. Both the first Continental Congress in 1774 in Philadelphia and the first meeting of the Congress of the United

States in 1789 in New York took place in buildings that housed major libraries. The Library of Congress that Thomas Jefferson created for our new nation grew up around his own 6,487-volume collection.

Libraries are places of authentic pluralism. Browsing requires physical effort, interaction with other people and with the creative extensions of other people, which is what books really are. The moral imperative of reading came from the simple fact that our type of democracy depended on knowledge and grew through books, which by their very nature foster freedom with dignity. Books do not coerce, they convince. They speak the private voice of reason to the active individual. They do not shriek public authority to passive crowds. Books have historically been the companions of a responsible democratic citizenry, and books have also tended to bring things together for a widely scattered people. Libraries bring books together for people, books that disagree with one another and require an active, individual response. Books distill information into knowledge and, at the same time, slowly inculcate wisdom and humanism among the people who live with them, in them, and around them.

One preserves books, then, not just out of an instinctive clinging to the artifacts of memory, but as a check against the dangers of the new electronics. We keep books so that the individual will always have a portable, affordable link with the rest of humanity, a link that no central authority can easily control.

Books are the best guides we have for the exploration of our own humanity, for the world within as well as the world without, for the messy middle state in which we live as human beings—somewhere below the angels but above the animals. We are a fallible species on a fragile planet, living at the intersection between the natural and the supernatural, forever seeking mastery and yet always confronting mystery. In such a situation we need all the guidebooks we can find for our inner discoveries as well as our outer explorations. Beyond the value of the book in making democracy dynamic lies the individual enrichment that books provide as each of us seeks to obtain the mastery of self necessary to sustain the mystery of creation.

The unleashed, unlimited pursuit of truth may be the last frontier and the ultimate proving ground for our American ideal of freedom. In a world of increasing physical restraints and limitations, it is only in the life of the mind and the spirit that the horizons of freedom can remain truly infinite. We must discover what we should have known all along, that the pursuit of truth is the noblest part of Jefferson's pursuit of happiness. It is a non-competitive enterprise in which one person gains from another's discovery. In a dangerous, complex world, where new, powerful forces are being released by new technologies, the pursuit of truth can help keep us from the pursuit of one another. The reader of *Treasures* will see how important the Library has been—and will be—to this great endeavor.

James H. Billington
The Librarian of Congress

Opposite: *This, the original Office of the Librarian of Congress, is now used for ceremonial functions.*

Pages 18–19: *The original building of the Library is now almost one hundred years old, and the Architect of the Capitol has undertaken to renovate it to its appearance of 1897. Re-gilded, the frescoes refurbished, the rooms are now recovering their original brilliant appearance. Here, the rehabilitated Southwest Corridor including a view of the Capitol through a western window.*

CHAPTER I

Just What Is This Place?

We're about to walk through the Library of Congress. Practically every literate American has heard of the Library, but almost no one knows exactly what it is. If it does nothing else, it collects superlatives the way a magnet draws filings. "The Library of Congress has one copy of every book ever printed." Not true. "It has one copy of every book ever printed in the United States." Not true. "It has more Shakespeare Folios and Gutenberg Bibles than any other library anywhere." Not true either.

But the superlatives that *are* true boggle the mind: It *is* the largest collection of stored knowledge in the world. It does have more maps, globes, charts, and atlases than any other place on earth. It *has* accumulated more books from England and America than anywhere else—but *mirabile dictu*, less than half of its collections are in English! It does have—almost—every phonograph record ever made in the United States, the largest collection of motion pictures in America, more Civil War photographs, more personal letters in Sigmund Freud's handwriting, more Stradivari violins, more flutes, more handwritten copies of the Gettysburg Address in Lincoln's own hand, more...et cetera, et cetera, than any other institution in the world. But in this book we will try to keep the superlatives to a cabined few—and indeed, if I can fight back the statistics, we may see no more numbers either, for we are approaching the Library by a different door.

What we are seeking here is the unique, the very important, the astonishing. The Library is indeed the storehouse of the national memory, and in its totality becomes in fact the world's greatest encyclopedia of everything known by Western man to date. But such broad sweeps will not concern us here.

Our search is for tightly focused significance. We will try to find the vastly valuable, the gems that should be known about, the individual pieces that should be used or appreciated.

Before we plunge in, however, a decent respect for rational minds does suggest that we get some general feel of what the Library of Congress is. The confusion we all share comes about, of course, because it *is* Congress' library. No law or appropriation bill has ever called it the *nation's* library or the *national library*. It was designed by the Legislature to help it govern and it is the oldest legislative library anywhere. Governmental? Legislative? Then why does it have the watercolor portrait that George Gershwin painted of Arnold Schoenberg? Why does it have Houdini's self-filling punch ladle, and Percy Bysshe Shelley's holograph review of *Frankenstein*—the one its author kept with the dead Shelley's heart in a casket in her bedroom? Not to mention Jefferson's rough draft of the Declaration of Independence (with Franklin's marking-outs to make it more readable and Adams's interpolations to make it more legal). Handwritten; brown ink.

So let's begin with a very fast look at what the institution is and how it got to the point where such treasures are quite "necessary and proper." Like a questionable song title, it started in Philadelphia.

The Founding Fathers were book-oriented from the very first. Being mostly lawyers, they were trained to look everything up in a book before they did anything, and then to write more themselves so that they could look it up in a book the next time. With such antecedents, it was logical that at each step in the creation of the government, they managed to locate themselves within arm's reach of a sizable collection of books. In 1774 they used the volumes of the Library Company of Philadelphia—housed at the other end of Carpenters' Hall, where the Continental Congress convened. In 1787, as the Constitutional Convention, they used the same collection. In 1789, now organized as the First Congress of the United States, they secured access to the four thousand volumes belonging to the New York Society Library—shelved upstairs from where they were meeting in City Hall. In 1791, back in Philadelphia as the Second Congress, they were again on the Library Company's rolls with "free use...to the members of both Houses...." The point: from the very beginning of the government the legislature had been accustomed to having a library at hand—and indeed for nearly twenty years they had it there without having to spend a penny of appropriated funds.

It was not that they were unwilling; it was the constituents who were unsympathetic. In 1790 a committee had suggested the purchase of $1,000 worth of books with $500 a year additions thereafter. A typical response came from the *Independent Chronicle* of Boston:

> The late motion respecting the "Library" for Congress is truly novel—could it be supposed that a measure so distant from any thing which can effect the general purposes of government, could be introduced at this important period?...How absurd to squander away money for a parcel of Books, when every shilling of the Revenue is wanted for supporting our government and paying our debts?
>
> ...It is supposed that the Members of Congress are acquainted with history; the laws of nations; and possess such political information as is necessary for the management of the affairs of the government. If they are *not*, we have been unfortunate in our choice....It is supposed that the members are fully competent for these purposes, without being at the expence of furnishing them with Books for their improvement.
>
> ...The people look for *practical politicks,* as they presume the *Theory* is obtained previous to the members taking their seats in Congress.

Hamilton and Jefferson finally struck their famous Compromise and in 1800 the Congress was moved to the new Federal City laid out in a swamp south of Georgetown, Maryland. There was a bill passed to pay for the transfer of the three branches, and the fifth section permitted the purchase of $5,000 worth of books with the "fitting up of a suitable apartment for containing them." This was the official beginning of the Library of Congress. The volumes were to be selected by the Secretary of the Senate and the Clerk of the House and were to be available to all Members of Congress—but not to the executive branch or the judiciary. It was strictly Congress' library.

What kind of a library was it to be? Since this is an argument that is still being debated every year, it might be of interest to note the three choices the first committee thought it had. Some of the members believed the money should be spent for a small group of working tools—the kind of books the Members would have known back in their home law offices and the kind of books needed to make laws. A narrow, restricted collection. A second group thought it should be a "public" library. Public was defined in those days as being a subscription collection which was available to a local elite such as a college faculty or a mercantile group; in this case, the members of the legislative establishment and their staffs. The people who used it should pay for it, but it should be a collection that reflected both their professional and their leisure literary interests. The final third wanted a national library that would serve all the federal government, but would also be a cultural and historical archive for the whole country. Such an institution was an accepted ornament of statehood—almost all of the major European countries had one, although the European versions belonged to the kings, not to the parliaments.

The committee chose the first option—a simple, functional set of working tools. In June 1800, they sent to London for books on law, political science, history, and any map that could be found describing the New World. (The map question is intriguing. The book orders for the first quarter century are saturated with map purchases. At first glance they would seem to relate to the need to develop an unexplored country, but if you read the justifications it is apparent they were to be insurance against international litigation. It is clear that the early leaders all assumed the North American continent would be balkanized and ultimately end up as several different nations—either colonies or client states of their European parents. The legislators wanted all the proof they could get of where land claims had been made, borders set, settlements established—geographic precedents in ink and *dated*.)

The first shipment of books arrived packed in eleven hair trunks. The British bookseller, sensitive to the needs of a developing nation, explained he "judged it best to send trunks instead of boxes, which after their arrival would have been of little or no value." The Senate took him at his word and instructed the Secretary "to make sale of the trunks in which the books lately purchased were imported."

Jefferson appointed one of his closest friends as first Librarian of Congress—one John James Beckley—and at two dollars a day salary Beckley set out to build his collection. He asked for recommendations from everyone, and the list of titles that President Jefferson himself sent was clearly the most thoughtful and the most useful. My own favorite came from Senator Samuel Latham Mitchill, who was characterized by his fellow legislators as a "living encyclopedia," a "chaos of knowledge." Mitchill urged the expansion of the Library to "enable statesmen to be correct in their investigations and, by a becoming display of erudition and research, give a higher dignity and a brighter luster to truth." Sublime justification for a library card.

The Library grew routinely in a second-floor room of the Capitol until it reached some four thousand volumes, and on April 27, 1813, a series of three events was tripped that were to be the most important episodes in the life of the Library. On the April date, a column of American troops marched into the Capital of Upper Canada (then called York, now Toronto), and set fire to the Parliament Building. They destroyed the archives, burned the parliamentary library, and carried off the plate from a nearby church.

On August 24, 1814, a column of British troops marched into Washington and took prompt revenge by setting fire to the Capitol Building. They destroyed the national archives and reduced the stacks and reading room of the Congressional Library to ashes. Barely four weeks later, on the 21st of September, ex-President Jefferson sent in his suggestion for rehabilitation and repair. Assuming the total loss of the book collection, he noted that it was going to be exceedingly difficult to replace the Congressional Library "while the war continues, and intercourse with Europe is attended with so much risk." He then described his own collection of

"between nine and ten thousand volumes," presently housed in his study at Monticello, and noted that the contents mainly "related to the duties of those in the high concerns of the nation."

He explained that it had been his intention to give Congress "first refusal" of his library at its own price on his death, but in view of present difficulties, this might be "the proper moment for its accommodation." He offered to sell the books in annual installments but was ready to make the complete collection available at once. "Eighteen or twenty wagons could place it in Washington in a single trip of a fortnight."

By November the books had been counted and found to number 6,487 volumes appraised at $23,950. The Senate passed a bill to buy them in December, and the House reluctantly agreed in January. (The entire New England delegation—including Daniel Webster—voted against the idea.)

The volumes had been shelved at Monticello in long pine boxes that Jefferson had designed as modular bookcases so all that was needed was to put a plank across the face of each unit and load it into a wagon. The tenth and final wagon arrived in May of

A rare-book librarian uses one of the original volumes from Thomas Jefferson's personal collection which formed the nucleus of the present Library of Congress.

1815, and when the face-boards were removed, the routine, quite ordinary collection of the previous year had been "instantly" replaced by the largest, most sophisticated library in the United States. As Jefferson said, "I do not know that it contains any branch of science which Congress would wish to exclude from their collection; there is, in fact, no subject to which a member of Congress may not have occasion to refer."

It would be hard to overstate the importance of the Jefferson connection to the life of the Library. The Jefferson antecedents have affected selection policies, the catalog scheme, access, user audiences. In 1815 Jefferson was recognized as the leading humanist in America and his library reflected his personal interests: architecture, philosophy, art, literature, and science, as well as his political and social concerns. The Congressional Library Committee understood this, and they were fully aware

that they had a national treasure in the volumes. They therefore instructed the Librarians to see that the Jefferson collection was perpetually reinforced and that whatever additions were required to keep it current, catholic, and comprehensive should be secured.

Jefferson had organized his collection around a philosophical scheme devised by Sir Francis Bacon. He had taken Bacon's concepts of Memory, Reason, and Imagination (the "three faculties needed to comprehend knowledge") and developed forty-four interlocking subject divisions to form a classification schedule. When the Congress inherited the volumes, it was decided to continue the scheme with only minor modification, so that as late as Theodore Roosevelt's time, tens of thousands of volumes were flowing in and being assigned one of the original forty-four classification numbers. (The result was so chaotic that when they tried to apply Dewey

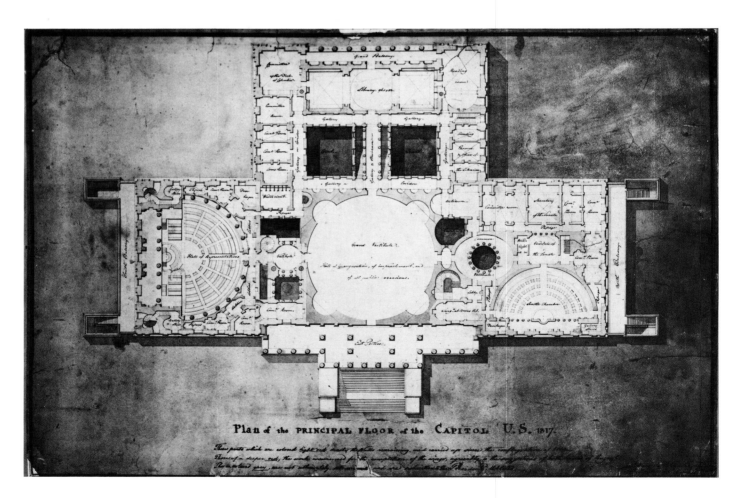

Benjamin Latrobe's plan for the Library of Congress in its original home in the Capitol Building. At that time, before the present House and Senate wings were added, the Library overlooked the Mall and occupied space roughly equivalent to that given the House and Senate chambers.

24

decimal numbers in 1901, it proved overwhelming, indeed impossible; the Librarian of the time gave up and devised the so-called Library of Congress Classification Tables with nearly 20,000 subdivisions essentially to fit the books simply sitting on the shelves—no great thesaural hierarchy or philosophical system.)

Given such an extraordinary collection, Congress found itself perpetually guilt-ridden over its denial of access to the nonlegislative public. As a result, as the years went by, it grudgingly gave the Supreme Court, then the executive branch agencies, the diplomatic community, and ultimately the general citizen the right to use this expanding collection.

After the Jefferson episode, the Library grew in size and service; but this is not the place to detail such elements as the creation of a separate law library, survival of two more fires, the establishment of complicated exchange agreements with foreign governments, and various questionable practices that resulted in the turnover of several of the Librarians of Congress. (Indeed *every* Librarian in the nineteenth century had his appointment terminated either because of politics, patronage, or peculation!)

Like most successful institutions, the Library benefited from major innovations of single, larger-than-life individuals, not programs or legislation. Jefferson's mind gave us the *shape* of what has become the largest library in the world. Ainsworth Rand Spofford gave us the *size* (some feel the enormity) of the institution; Herbert Putnam gave us the *use* of it—its purpose and application. Mr. Jefferson needs no comment. Spofford was a huge, dynamic Cecil Rhodes figure, and Putnam was a little pink-haired bantam of protean impact. Both of the latter deserve our attention for a few paragraphs.

Spofford was Librarian of Congress from 1864 to 1897. He came on after Lincoln's appointee (a physician) had been fired for shortchanging booksellers, juggling accounts, and engaging in war speculation. Spofford was professionally spotless. His only flaw was a Napoleonic desire to build the largest library in the world. Comparisons to Alexander and the Alexandrian Library would have been appropriate and he would probably have agreed with them himself—very solemnly.

Recall the scene of his challenge. It is the close of the Civil War. The Library has approximately eighty thousand volumes and is the fourth largest in the country. It is located in a huge, three-floored, cast-iron room sitting across the Mall side of the Capitol, and it has been going along peacefully as a quiet place in the city, universally recognized as Congress' library made available to the serious public. Until Spofford arrives.

Congress' library? There was no such confusion in Spofford's mind. From where he stood, it was the *nation's* library and too much time had been wasted already. His first challenge was to get as many books as he could, as quickly as he could, and as cheaply as he could. He opened his campaign on all fronts.

First, the Copyright Law. There had been copyright legislation since 1790 with the law calling for deposit to the State Department and then to the Interior Department and then to the Patent Office, but few people gave it much attention. What books were deposited (after paying a dollar to the clerk of your nearest district court) were stacked in damp basements all over Washington. Spofford saw the concept as a potential gold mine. It took him four years of brisk lobbying, amendments, and general legislative exercises but by 1870 he had a law that read: "All records and other things relating to copyrights and required by law to be preserved, shall be under the control of the librarian of Congress." Anyone claiming a copyright on any book, map, chart, dramatic or musical composition, engraving, cut, print, or photograph or negative thereof must send two copies to the Librarian within ten days of its publication. Penalties were spelled out, and the Librarian could demand compliance.

It worked beyond Spofford's wildest dreams. In the next 25 years the Library received 371,636 books, 257,153 magazines, 289,617 pieces of music, 73,817 photographs, 95,249 prints, and 48,048 maps. Each one had to be acknowledged, recorded, and preserved somehow, but Spofford was at least consistent. While the stuff was pouring in, he carried on complicated negotiations with the Departments of State and Interior to recover all the deposits he'd missed back to 1790!

He took on the Smithsonian Institution. The Smithsonian, under the physicist Joseph Henry, had initiated a series of publications as far back as 1848 which first were used to draw together the major scientific writing produced in America, but soon were used to establish exchange agreements with scientific societies all over the world. The idea had been to keep up on what was being done abroad, but the scientific revolution exploded and the result was that papers, series, reports, journals, "contributions," studies began to pour in from every-

By 1876 library space within the Capitol was exhausted, and Librarian Spofford (at right above) was starting his twenty-year campaign for a new, separate building. When this drawing appeared in Harper's Weekly *in 1897, library materials were stored from one end of the Capitol to the other, and the clutter in the library itself made most of the collection useless.*

where and the Smithsonian was being overwhelmed with paper. Spofford wanted everything; the Smithsonian was only too happy to make an agreement "so long as we have access to it when we need it…," and Spofford took over both the past receipts and ongoing agreements.

He begged entire private libraries and got himself listed as beneficiary in wills and legacies. He absorbed the Toner collection of medical history and persuaded Congress to buy him the Force Library of Americana which brought in 40,000 pamphlets, 1,000 early maps, 1,000 volumes of bound newspapers going back to the 1700s, and 429 volumes of manuscripts covering the Revolution and the founding of the Republic. He began buying documents in European archives through London booksellers, and he scooped up unwanted government holdings ("January: 3,000 volumes of bound newspapers from State; 3,000 govt. docs. from the War Department; February…").

The outcome of all this was not hard to predict.

He ran out of room. Paper and the printed word were pouring in relentlessly and, recall, he had only the rooms within the Capitol to work with. There *was* no other office building on Capitol Hill and there would be none before 1908. The copyright law alone was bringing in wagonloads with every mail. He persuaded Congress to convert two nearby "wings" to stacks and he filled these. He put up wooden shelves in the corridors and filled them. He filled the Capitol attics. He filled the crypt under the Capitol dome. Material was piled in the halls between committee rooms and through the working space of both houses.

In 1880 they are worrying that "Fire may break out at any moment in that dark upper loft, where gas has to be lit.…The very dust of decomposing paper, and of the friction induced by constant handling may become inflammable." In 1882, the Capitol engineer reports that "a proposed plan for raising the dome of the Capitol 50 feet, in order to secure additional space in and near the rotunda for

The Main Reading Room has 45,000 volumes on open shelves for quick reference and easy access.

In 1873, Congress staged a design competition for a new Library. Here is the Second Prize winner, a Greek temple reflecting the style of the Capitol across the Plaza.

the Library...[is] a dangerous and perhaps fatal enterprise."

There was clearly no alternative but to build another building. It was a classic case of mixed emotions. On the one hand, Congress was becoming desperately eager to move the Library out so the legislators could reclaim the Capitol for legislation. On the other, they knew that their proprietary claim to "Congress' books" would be forever lost. It would become the nation's library in strong competition with their own daily needs, and they would have sacrificed much of the purpose of having an arm's-reach library of their own. For a century they had been able to walk off the House or Senate floor, seize a book or document, and take it straight back into the debate. No longer. But on the third hand (!) the legislators felt a genuine pride in the enormous cultural treasure they had in the collections of the Library and wished to give it the housing and prominence it deserved. (While the argument ebbed and flowed, the traditional services of a library disappeared under the avalanche: periodicals were no longer shelved in series; there was no card catalog; the Jefferson classification scheme was producing as many as ten thousand books with the same call number on the spine; aisles were clogged, books unshelved.)

And so we come to the building of "The Library of Congress" that we all know today. Conceived in 1873 as a simple, functional library building, by the time it was completed twenty-five years later it had become "a new national Temple of the Arts." As John Y. Cole, the institution's leading present-day historian has said, "More than 50 American painters and sculptors 'proved' that the United States could surpass any European library in grandeur and devotion to classical culture." Contemporary guidebooks made it clear: "It has been designed and executed entirely by American art and labor [and is] a fitting temple for the great thoughts of generations past, present, and to be."

This book is concerned with the treasures of the Library of Congress, and surely one of the primary treasures is the building itself—the jewel box that houses the collections. It is recognized as being the preeminent expression of American Victorian architecture in the nation, which is precisely what its builders intended it to be.

It began with the obligatory "open competition for a design." Twenty-seven of the nation's leading architects submitted plans. On December 22, 1873, the firm of Smithmeyer and Pelz won the contest with a strong and effective Italian Renaissance facade. Congress didn't like it and reopened the competition. A new dozen competitors joined the first twenty-seven and Congress now had Romanesque, German Renaissance, French Renaissance, and thirteenth-century Gothic to choose from. While the committees were bickering about styles, an argument broke out over sites. The contest had been run predicated on a tract across the Capitol Plaza from the Capitol front. A new group appeared demanding that it go at the foot of Capitol Hill beside the Botanic Garden, another wanted it halfway to the White House on Judiciary Square. The influential Senator Conkling headed a group favoring the extension of both Capitol wings "so as to form an enclosure something like that embraced by the colonnades at St. Peter's at Rome."

The American Library Association got into the argument; President Hayes discussed it in each of his State of the Union messages. The local papers

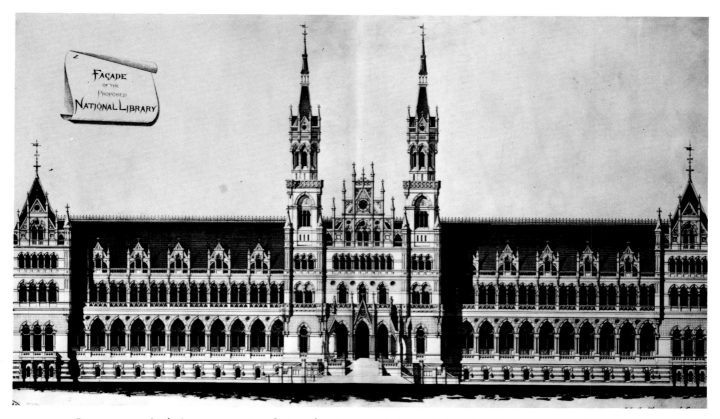

Congress required sixteen years to select and approve a design. During that time, some Members felt the Library should be built on Judiciary Square; the above building was designed for that site, reflecting the Victorian Gothic style of the Houses of Parliament.

The final winner by Smithmeyer and Pelz, "a national possession, an example of a great public building monumentally conceived, faithfully built, and worthily adorned." It opened on November 1, 1897, with a staff of 108. When the Madison annex was opened in 1980, the original building (above) housed 2,100 employees.

Construction took eight years. **Right:** *The keystone is placed in the southwest clerestory arch of the Main Reading Room.* **Below:** *Many of the plaster decorations were created on the spot by artisans working in impromptu studios in unfinished space in the new building.*

OCT. 16. 1894

The building is drenched in symbolism; here, Commerce and Art.

and eastern cultural magazines took sides on both style and place. Not until 1886 were the necessary decisions made to start building, while poor Spofford was being buried ever deeper in more copyright deposits, Smithsonian exchange receipts, international government document agreements—all rising relentlessly like water around the sorcerer's apprentice.

But the delay caused major changes in what the building would look like. When it had been conceived in General Grant's time, it was being funded by a nation still staggering from the Civil War. By the time it was actually built, the Gilded Age was at its height. The nation was rich and wanted to flaunt its culture. The functional library had become a museum.

Construction started in 1889. By 1893 the dome had been redesigned, raised, and covered with 23-carat gold leaf. Various art schools and academies were asked to nominate American artists to decorate it, and twenty nationally recognized sculptors

plus twenty-three painters were committed to the task. There were dozens of portrait sculptures to be created in bronze, marble, and plaster at a flat $5,000 each, 18 months from contract to delivery. All the major names were involved: Daniel Chester French, Augustus St. Gaudens, J.Q.A. Ward. (James Whistler was originally to "oversee the murals," but he reneged, saying that he "once worked for Uncle Sam—as a draughtsman in the Coast Survey—and didn't want any more of it.")

In fact, the building was built by the Army Corps of Engineers under Brigadier General Thomas Lincoln Casey, and he did a splendid job. He brought it in well under contract, returned a substantial part of the original appropriation to the Treasury, and made all his deadlines! He also rode herd on every detail as seen in this letter to sculptor Paul W. Bartlett: "There is no improvement to be suggested concerning the figure of *Law*, but I want to say regarding *Columbus* that, while it is very good and has a good deal of character the figure is so

The collar mural around the top of the dome in the Main Reading Room is by E.H. Blashfield, and represents the evolution of civilization. The twelve ten-foot-high seated figures symbolize the twelve countries that have contributed the most to the development of civilization. The figures range from the East (Egypt—written records) to the West (America—science). Blashfield used, among others, the young Lincoln sitting on an electric dynamo to represent America and the actress Ellen Terry for England (literature).

Right: One of four medallions in the corners of the Pavilion of Discoverers, each designed and sculpted by Bela Lyon Pratt. Each contains a female figure representing a season of the year.

Opposite, top: The rooftops of the three-building complex of the Library as seen from the dome of the Capitol. Although covered with 23-carat gold leaf when originally built, the dome of the Main Building was replaced with copper in the 1930s and now wears the patina of aging copper green.

broad or *large round,* and the coat so short comparatively as to seem a little droll, a tendency however that you certainly will have no difficulty in correcting.... How soon may we expect to receive your sketch of *Michaelangelo?*" The building was drenched in allegory, and uplifting mottoes appear in cut marble and painted plaster.

It opened in 1897 and is now approaching a hundred years of hard use. It has worn very well. Generations have found it almost as inspirational as the founders hoped.

The patterns of arches, the brilliant color everywhere, the really splendid proportions have made tedious and repetitive tasks far easier to bear, and it is an interesting tribute to the beaux-arts designers that of the now *three* Library of Congress buildings this is the overwhelming favorite of the staff. The great Jefferson Building was filled up in 1935, and an even larger art deco Adams Building was built behind it. That, in turn, was filled by 1965, and the Madison Memorial Building was designed in General Services Administration Moderne and opened in 1980. It is larger than the first two buildings combined, but a vote by the present five thousand employees would be overwhelmingly for Mr. Spofford's building as the sublime place to work.

They started moving Spofford's mountains of paper out of the Capitol, across the Plaza, and into the new building in 1897. The building opened in splendor on November 1, and for the next five years visitors poured through its halls as if it were a world's-fair exhibition. It was an enormous success and achieved everything Spofford had hoped for and more. Regrettably, Spofford himself had been fired four months before the new building opened.

And equally regrettably, he probably should have been. By the close of his career, he appears to have lost all track of what his library was there for. There is only one justification for a research library. It is *use.* Most libraries are for use now; a few can justify their being for use in the future. But there is no excuse for next to no use at all. When his successors started to dig through the mounds of unexamined, unprocessed materials they had inherited, they found 230,000 pieces of music, over 50,000 maps, 59,589 prints, "many tons of periodicals and newspapers," and literally hundreds of thousands of untouched books that had lain in dead storage throughout the back reaches of the Capitol. What had Spofford thought he was doing? "I fought to bring us oceans of books and rivers of information," he said. In classic Victorian style, he was committed to the belief that reading had a positive moral value per se. He was convinced that if he brought all the world's literature into a single place, it was bound to benefit the American people—just how this was to happen was a detail that could always be faced tomorrow.

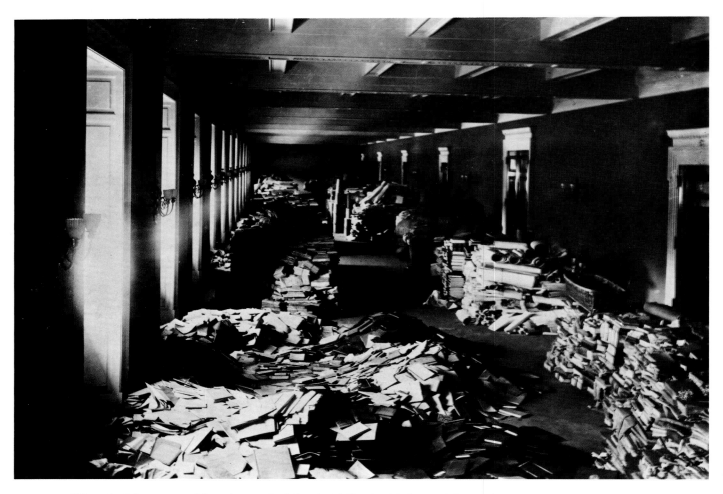

When the Library moved into the new building in 1897, classified material went directly to the shelves—leaving over 800 tons of books, pamphlets, maps, manuscripts, and pieces of sheet music, which Librarian Spofford had not had time to process. It required decades to absorb the materials into the collections. The above were copyright arrearages.

So what had gone wrong? Librarianship is based on a tripod of three equal supports: you *get* the material (acquisition), you *organize* it for use (processing), and you *use* it (reference and research). Poor Spofford had built his first leg higher than anyone had ever tried before—and forgotten the other two almost completely.

Our fathers believed that God looks after fools, drunkards, and the United States, and if this is so He certainly blessed the Republic with Spofford's two successors. The first was a newspaperman by the name of John Russell Young. Young's role was to get Spofford's materials installed, sorted, and made ready for handling. His real contribution was the assembly of the finest staff of librarians in the country. Young offered the profession a chance to carve a national library out of the mountains of material Spofford had assembled, and librarians responded from everywhere. The State Librarian of New

Hampshire joined the staff, the head of cataloging of the University of Wisconsin, librarians from the Boston Athenaeum and the Boston Public, copyright specialists from Macmillan and the publishing world, the archivist of the Department of State, et cetera. Young brought order out of chaos, worked eighteen months, and dropped dead at the age of fifty-eight. It was 1899. Now what?

President McKinley turned to the American Library Association and asked who was the most innovative, service-oriented librarian in America. The answer was surprisingly unanimous (considering the contentious tradition of the organization): Herbert Putnam, the thirty-eight-year-old librarian of the Boston Public Library. He agreed to take the job and moved into the Library of Congress' "Mahogany Row" where he held forth for the next fifty-six years.

He was incredibly successful and a moving viola-

tion of every tenet of public administration and management the textbooks have yet devised. He was so short that he avoided standing in public—but prevented any subordinate from sitting in his presence. His thirty-six division chiefs reported directly to him—marvelous span of control; there was no hierarchy. His successor, the poet Archibald MacLeish, said the Library hung from Putnam "as the miraculous architecture of the paper wasp hangs from a single anchor." When the managers were assembled for their daily hour-and-a-half directive sessions, they were required to commit his instructions to memory; Putnam would tolerate no note-taking within his line of sight. His administrators worshiped him.

His staff was receiving wages of a dollar a day as late as World War II yet people pleaded to be taken on at their own expense. After forty years of his leadership, the Library of Congress was the only agency in Washington that had no form of civil service, no tenure, no promotion scheme, instant hiring and firing, and a loyalty that awed the personnel experts who came to study the phenomena.

What did he do with this staff—and Spofford's mountains of books? He drove both of them to near-manic activity. He created a national program for the blind, distributed talking books, and spread free Braille across the country in order to use the "embossed books" being deposited for copyright. He got a donor to give five Stradivari violins, another donor to build an auditorium to play them in, and started the oldest, most active chamber music program in America—in order to get the sheet music off the shelves and into use. He invented a special classification system to fit the largest library collection in the world and began to print and sell the resulting catalog cards at cost so that every library in the West could get instant cataloging for pennies. He published endless bibliographies so that scholarly institutions would know what the Library had, and then built the largest interlibrary loan system in the country so everyone could borrow these books through their own local libraries. He designed a legislative reference service (leading to the one which now answers two thousand Congressional inquiries a day, served by hundreds of legislative specialists and supported by the largest computerized information system in the world). He created one of the earliest science information programs in the country, and built the largest collection of Oriental literature (and the staff to serve it) outside the Far East. He created the first...

But enough. You get the idea. An absolutely astonishing figure. There was not a corner of the Library which Putnam did not galvanize into a frenzy of service, either making the professional skills of the staff available to a nationwide audience or pulling the books off the shelves and pushing them into users' hands. When someone expressed concern that if Putnam kept loaning books out of the city some might be lost (and declaring that "You have an obligation to posterity to preserve them"), Putnam snapped back, "Nonsense, we are ourselves a posterity. Some respect is due to the ancestors who have saved for *our* use." He stormed around with almost no diminution of energy until his ninety-fourth summer, when he was injured in a boating accident while sailing alone off Cape Cod.

And thus with Spofford and Putnam the Library of Congress was formed into the institution that we know today. Since Putnam's time, four respected Librarians have used the instrument, emphasizing what each saw as the Library's greatest need in their own day. The poet Archibald MacLeish was Librarian from 1939 to 1944, and he was preoccupied with re-organizing the Library and jerking it into the shape of a twentieth-century governmental institution. (The staff described his tenure as "living in the tail of a comet"; and Franklin D. Roosevelt, who had appointed MacLeish on the advice of Supreme Court Justice Felix Frankfurter, was so impressed with what the poet had done at the Library that he transferred him across from the White House and made him an Assistant Secretary of State.)

Luther Evans was next (1945–53), and he emphasized the Library's activities in the international field, expanding international exchange agreements, and sending Library staff to advise Third World countries on how to establish their own library systems. Evans became so involved in these international programs that he left the Library to become Director General of UNESCO in Paris.

L. Quincy Mumford followed (1954–74). Mumford had been a very successful librarian at the New York and Cleveland Public Libraries, and he represented the plea of the American Library Association to have a real, professional librarian in the office for a change. Congress was equally fatigued with the pyrotechnics of MacLeish and Evans, and settled down to a more temperate twenty years of simply running the library as a library. Mumford's tenure came at the same time as Sputnik and America's fear of losing its educational and technical edge. As a result, the Library set up acquisition offices in the major capitals of the world, and Library employees based throughout Africa and Asia pursued comprehensive—near-total—collecting which in turn brought in tens of thousands of foreign-language volumes air-freighted every week from every continent. In order that the major universities and research centers might know what these materials were, the Library converted its cataloging to digital form and distributed the information on weekly reels of computer tapes. As time passed, the so-called MARC tapes were supplemented by microfiche and ultimately optical disks so the research institutions could choose the format most appropriate to their own data storage system.

When Mumford retired, President Ford selected the eminent historian Daniel J. Boorstin to head the Library (1975–87). Boorstin let his Deputy run the Library as a librarian, and he himself concentrated on introducing the scholarly world to the Library's riches and vice-versa. He sponsored seminars, set up councils of scholars and centers for book promotion, staged social functions honoring creative Americans, and in general "opened up" the Library more extensively than any of his predecessors, emphasizing the institution in its role as a national library (although still without using the forbidden words). Somewhat to the staff's surprise, the Congress, rather than fretting over this distraction from its being primarily the Congressional Library, seemed to take pride in the broader definition, and endorsed the new activities with both personal and appropriations support.

And this brings us to today. In the final years of the Reagan Administration, the President selected James H. Billington to be the thirteenth Librarian of Congress. Dr. Billington was a long-time and internationally recognized Russian scholar and Director of the Smithsonian Institution's Wilson Center. He has only recently inherited the controls, and what his particular emphasis and purpose for the Library will be is about to unfold.

I have now spent all the words I dare on the Library as a functioning program. It is not what the Library does but what it does it *with* that concerns us in this book. There are, however, certain oddities about the Library which stem from its history and which we should be aware of as we go along:

One. The result of its past leaves us with a library of staggering variety. What's in a library? Books, of course—but in this case, just barely. In this library scarcely one *fourth* of the collection is books. Frequently the books are only the road maps to the seventy-five million other things within the collections, and this leads us to:

Two. The great strength of the Library of Congress is its linkages...cross specializations...cross formats. Someone comes in to study the Battle of Gettysburg. He starts with books but is quickly led to maps carried on the field, to original photographs made on the scene. He is shown original pencil sketches sent weekly to *Harper's* or *Leslie's* by field artists. He sees daily dispatches sent back to the London and Edinburgh papers by British correspondents. He sees the diaries and letters of hundreds of officers and men who participated in the action.

Someone comes in to analyze the convulsion in Tiananmen Square. She studies the verbatim tapes of the ATRA archives—minute-by-minute coverage of both television and radio, all networks, day in and day out—as the events occurred. As the personal papers of American statesmen are deposited, she can see the reports and correspondence of ambassadors, military figures, legislators linked to the event. And all of the Library of Congress material is freely available to anyone who comes in the door. Which leads us to:

Three. Whose library is it? What should the Library's proper role be? Is it a vast, tax-supported public library where high school students...undergraduates...tourists...anyone can come, skip the inadequacies of their local libraries and find in one place the knowledge of the world as a one-stop reference center served by general librarians? Or should it be a court of last resort, available only to the serious scholar who has first exhausted the resources of his own campus or public library, and then in the Library of Congress be served by highly skilled specialists who know more about each specialized collection than any visiting scholar can ever know—but who are very scarce and very expensive?

So we turn to the Treasures of the Library of Congress. Let's see what they are, and try to get some idea of why.

CHAPTER II

The Book

Let's begin with books. Oddly enough, this is the only chapter in this book where we will look at books, but let's start there. The Library has twenty million books cataloged and on the shelf—which we'll forget at once. The ones we want are in the vaults. The rare and the unique. When most people think of rare books, what is the first thing that comes to mind? The Gutenberg Bible? Probably, and that's fine for our purposes. We can begin there. The Library has a Gutenberg Bible; it is one of the three perfect vellum copies in existence, with the other two just where you would expect them to be: the British Museum and the Bibliothèque Nationale. The Gutenberg is the most valuable book in the world. When one came up for sale in 1978 it went for $2,400,000 and it was "only" a paper copy at that.

The Gutenberg Bible deserves all the attention it gets. It is a sublime piece of bookmaking in itself, but it is even more awesome for all the things it represents. Let's consider it for a moment.

First, what does it look like? It is huge. It has 1,282 pages and when it is opened it is almost as wide as a card table. It is so thick that it is usually bound in two volumes, but the Library of Congress' copy is in three with thick, leather-covered boards for covers. The first astonishing thing about it is that the pages look quite new. The sheepskin pages are white and smooth, and the ink is jet black with brilliant red capitals sprinkled about. It has none of the feel of an ancient book; the type rather than being old, broken, and primitive is precise and highly detailed, with delicate serifs and hairline diacritical marks. The spacing is perfect, margins crisp and straight, and the inking absolutely uniform. It is difficult to imagine how it could possibly look "newer" which, of course, is astonishing in view of the fact that it was completed in 1455 and is the first book ever printed with movable metal type.

The very first try at printing may well be absolutely perfect. There was no slope-up as they worked out the bugs of the invention, and this, too, is astonishing when you think of the technical problems Gutenberg had to solve: he first had to invent a means of getting every piece of type carved, duplicated, and exactly the same height and square so it would print evenly in the chase; he had to create a metal hard enough so that it would not mash down yet be soft enough so that it could be melted and poured. He had to invent an ink stiff enough so that it would not simply run down through his letters (recall, the only ink they had was soot in water for quill pen inkwells); he had to find paper hard enough to take the ink cleanly (the paper of the time was soft like blotting paper); he had to build a press that would press the paper smoothly across a form of type the size of a newspaper yet not damage the delicate typeface nor leave unprinted space (he adapted the local winepress for this task). Yet given all of these hard-edged technical problems to overcome, he still designed a page so sublimely proportioned, the distance between the lines, the width of the column, the set on the page so perfect that when you look at it you have the sense: it simply could not be improved.

Before we look into how it came about and what it represents, let's finish talking about the Library's

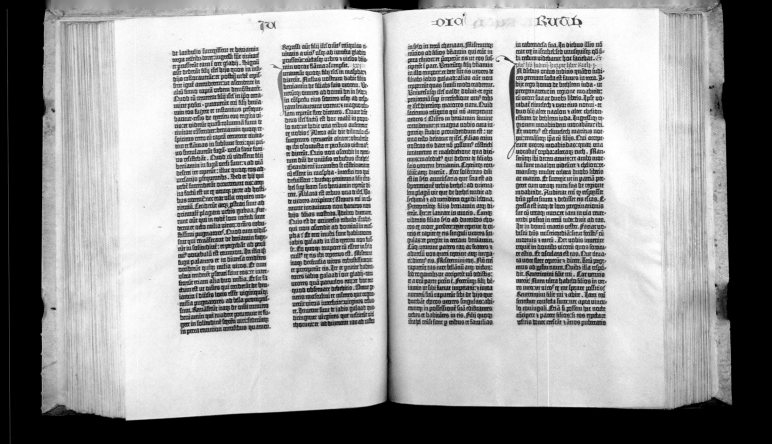

The Library's copy of the Gutenberg Bible is one of the three perfect vellum copies extant. Frequently called the 42-line Bible, the Gutenberg was the first book printed with moveable type. The design was intended to make the book look hand made, and the first examples of printing were called artificial writing. The decorations seen here were added by hand after the letters were printed.

own specific copy of the Gutenberg—how it happened to end up in Washington in the very teeth of the Great Depression.

The Library's copy was one of those that Johann Fust, Gutenberg's partner, took with him to Paris in 1458. He sold copies to the king of France and to the archbishop of Paris—and he sold the Library's copy to a group of Benedictine monks, who carried it home with them to their abbey at St. Blasius in the Black Forest of Germany. There it stayed until the French Revolution, when French troops flowed into Baden and the monks fled with their Bible to a monastery at Einsiedeln, Switzerland. The French armies kept coming so they moved from one place to another, and by 1808 they were holed up in a shelter in a mountain pass at Spittal-am-Pyrhn in the Alps when the emperor of Austria heard of their difficulty. He offered them an abbey at St. Paul, they accepted, and took their Bible there—staying on for well over a hundred years.

Following World War I and the breakup of the Austrian Empire, the abbey became increasingly desperate for funds, and finally in 1926 the monks were driven to put the Gutenberg on the market, offering it for $150,000. A German book dealer named Otto Vollbehr took advantage of the situation and bought the piece which, by the time he had paid duties, fees, and what-not, cost him $370,000.

Dr. Vollbehr brought it to this country and in order to give it a setting appropriate for such a rarity added some three thousand other volumes printed before 1500 which he had collected through the years. He then offered all these incunabula to Librarian Herbert Putnam for $1,500,000 cash. If he could get anyone to pay that much at one time, it would be the largest book sale ever made up to that date.

By the time Putnam was ready to try the idea on Congress it was 1930, the stock market had crashed, and the country was sliding ever deeper into the world's worst depression. Putnam seems to have gulped and with a nothing-ventured-nothing-gained attitude went to the appropriate committees of Congress and asked for the money to buy the unlikely collection of books. Apparently no one was more astonished than Putnam when the Congress voted him the money with only a gesture of debate. After the triumph, Putnam was returning to the Library across the Capitol Plaza when he met an arch-conservative member from an agrarian state who had voted in favor of the measure. Putnam

thanked him and then asked, fairly timidly for him, "Why?" He was told: "Mr. Putnam, we are a young country. We have no monuments. If we know where they are and can be got we ought to get 'em." And so the splendid vellum copy came to the Library of Congress and is now housed in the Library's Great Hall "right out there" where anyone coming through the front door can walk up and look at it. It stands almost upright in a special, air-conditioned case, and the displayed page is changed at regular intervals so that the volume ages equally throughout. Immediately facing it across the hall there is another case which is identical except that it holds the Giant Bible of Mainz—according to many experts one of the finest examples of early Renaissance manuscripts in the West. Its presence there, only forty feet from the invention that sealed the doom of all illuminated manuscripts, is drenched in irony. For that story, we need to go back a bit.

This is neither the time nor the place for a history of books and bookmanship. That is a fascinating story in itself—and I personally find the nomenclature one of the most interesting things about it. Do you know how many of our "ordinary" words come from classic bibliophilia? The first books were papyrus rolls and the Latin for roll is *volumen*, from which we get "volume." The roll was rolled around a stick to keep it from sagging and the Latin word for the stick was *umbilicus*, the navel of the book. The scrolls were stored on shelves in bins and a tag hung off each umbilicus. In Latin the tag telling what the scroll was about was called a *titulus*—obviously our "title."

The scrolls were very long (some still exist which are over 100 feet), which was fine for epics, but clumsy for laws, mathematical tables, and tax records. So the rolls were subdivided and we get "tome" from the Greek word for cutting. Incidentally, somehow we have been given the idea that the ancient volumes were terribly rare in their own day—quite wrong. The Romans had many publishers who kept whole galleries, or "factories," of slaves, all of whom were copying the same book at the same time. Cicero's publisher, Atticus, would release hundreds of copies of his works simultaneously, each produced by teams of slaves and contract workers. The increasing use of books in church services (where they were needed for specific passages, not read seriatim) killed off the scrolls, which were then cut into folded leaves and kept between boards (a *codex*)—and the codex

This page and opposite: *This, the last great hand-illuminated Bible, was being made in the same town at the same time as the Gutenberg. Traditionally called the Giant Bible of Mainz, the book is decorated with magnificent initial letters and marginal designs of birds and flowers. The pages were dated as they were finished, so we know the book was started on April 4, 1452, and finished fifteen* months later. The Bible was seized by King Gustavus of Sweden in 1631 and given to the Dukes of Gotha from whom it was purchased by Lessing J. Rosenwald of Philadelphia. Rosenwald gave it to the Library on the 500th anniversary of its creation. Scholars believe the lettering, the initial letters, and the marginal hunters and animals were designed by three different artists.

Anno 1566 Henric. a Stockpeim cantor magunt. posteror. mem. prodidit

Above and opposite: *The Nekcsei-Lipocz Bible was completed about 1342 and belonged to the Count of Bacs, a prominent official in the court of Charles Robert of Anjou, King of Hungary (1310–42). The vellum sheets are unusually thick, the embellishments strong and filled with fantasy.*

became the bound book as we know it from A.D. 500 on.

This gets us like a skipping stone to the medieval manuscript, where we should pause for a bit. The Library of Congress has cuneiform tablets, a second-century A.D. papyrus of *The Iliad,* and a similar fragment of Isaiah from the fourth century, but the Library's early holdings really start with substance in the High Middle Ages.

By this time the handwritten, illuminated manuscript had been perfected and had gone from being a simple communication device to an art masterpiece. These great books were as frighteningly rare as we have been led to believe, and they were desperately precious even in their own time. Centuries had passed during which those able to read had shrunk to a minute portion of the society, and the common books of the classic period had either been destroyed or crumbled from age. Our picture

of written learning being guarded in fortress-like monasteries during the Dark Ages is quite valid. There the monks did indeed spend their whole lives laboriously drawing one letter after another, but in so doing they distilled techniques and conventions that we accept without thought today. The keepers of the written tradition, the creators of the beautiful books, started with the Irish in the 600-800 period, moved to the Anglo-Saxons in 900-1000, and came to rest in France in the thirteenth century. (Scribes were held in such honor in Ireland that the penalty for killing a scribe was the same as that for killing a bishop.)

The product for all this period was the vellum manuscript. Vellum is dressed skin, usually from sheep, goats, or calves. It is washed, stretched, scraped, and then rubbed smooth and makes one of the finest materials ever used in book production. It takes ink beautifully, it ages soft white, it is

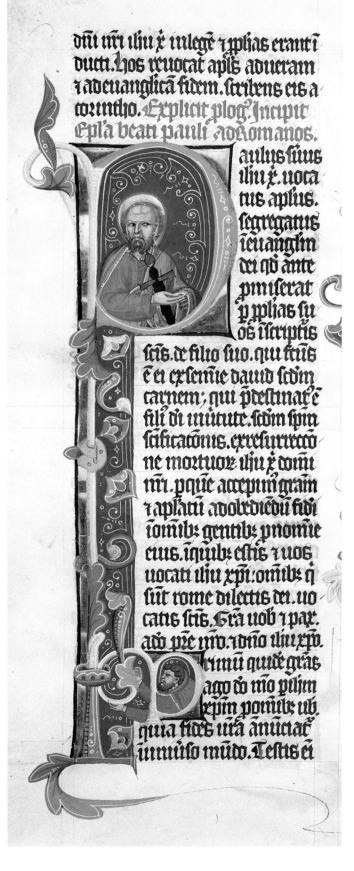

tough and long-lasting. Its only drawback is the time it takes, and therefore the high cost of making one leaf. A typical book of the day had about three hundred pages and required the skins of at least a dozen sheep. (Incidentally, the delicate Books of Hours are made on a vellum so thin that when you blow on a sheet it ripples like tissue paper yet is so tough it will hold beaten gold for centuries; this is called uterine vellum and came from the skin of stillborn lambs.)

Most religious houses had scriptoria, where tilted desks were set beside windows and the copyists worked in absolute silence to reduce the chance of losing their place. They had a horror of introducing an error into a text, a fear that far exceeded the simple difficulty of correcting mistakes on vellum. The whole system of book distribution was built on the loan-copy-return of the master texts. Once a text was copied (frequently taking many months if not years), the old copy was returned to the parent house, the new copy was loaned to another house for them to make copies from, which in turn was loaned…et cetera. If a line were dropped, a word misread or miscopied, the error would be both perpetuated and proliferated across whole countries. Considering that almost everything they were copy-

Opposite and below: The Warburg Book of Hours is an astonishing manuscript from the late 1400s which, although smaller than a man's hand, contains 45 brilliant, detailed miniatures. Its tissue-thin vellum pages carry pictures of delicate flowers interspersed with grotesque creatures suggestive of the school of Hans Memling.

Above: *A French Book of Hours manuscript on vellum. Four and a half centuries after it was created, the book appears to be as beautiful as the day it was first opened.*

Right: *Hand-illuminated missal, 1451. A beautifully lettered and decorated manuscript whose extraordinarily uniform and graceful script has led some scholars to believe that the product of this scribe—possibly even this particular book—was the model for Gutenberg's type. When the Gutenberg letters are compared piece by piece, they more closely duplicate the alphabet of this volume than any other still existing.*

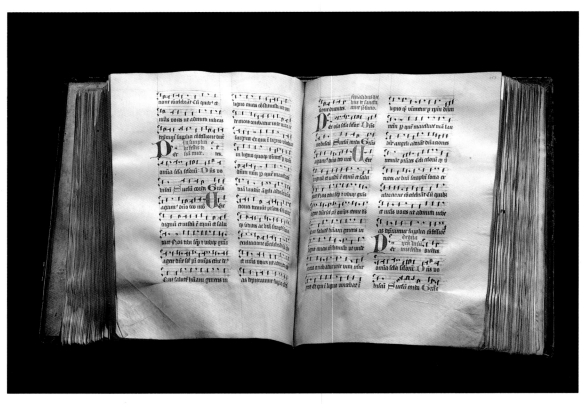

Above and right: *Two decorated initial letters from the 1451 Missal, demonstrating the variety of treatment that can be found in a single volume.*

This 1494 French edition of Giovanni Boccaccio's biographical tales, De casibus virorum illustrium, *is sumptuously illustrated. Interestingly, the illuminator painted large miniatures related to the text over several of the woodcuts, exactly as though blank spaces had been left for the purpose.*

ing had itself been copied and passed on for a thousand years, the purity of the texts was a serious matter. Almost none of the material was new. The manuscripts were the Bible, missals, Psalters, the writings of the Church Fathers, and in some few monasteries, the rare classic texts of philosophy, literature, and medicine. Some of these ancient works appear in many houses across Europe, while others, like those of Catullus, existed for a thousand years in a single manuscript until the Renaissance.

A manuscript page was created by first taking an awl and pricking the spaces down the left margin. It was then ruled across with a blunt scriber that made a hollow on the front and a ridge on the back. The letters were then drawn on the rules so if any ink showed through, the space between lines would be clear on both sides of the sheet. The pen was a reed or a quill cut crosswise with a pen knife.

The script they used reflected both the individual and his religious house, and it developed very logically through the ages. Our sense of a "religious" page versus an "ordinary" page came at the time of Charlemagne. The rich, thick, black letters of Gothic lettering were reserved for sacred texts; thin, light, "clean" letters were used for literature and philosophy. When the scribes began to proliferate the Greek and Roman texts, they wanted a script that "looked Roman," so they copied the capital letters off their local ruin and modified their Gothic small letters to match. (Have you ever thought about how many of our capital letters are quite different from the same letter lower case? A capital a is not a large a but A; a capital g is not a g but G. Likewise d's face the other way, e's become E's, r's are R. Reason: Charlemagne's scribes tried doing the whole line in Roman capitals large *and* small but it took up too much space. They solved it by keeping most of their narrow Gothic lower case, making them look Roman in treatment, and saving the classic for the capitals.)

Medieval manuscripts have no title pages. It is not clear whether this is simply because no one thought of it, or it seemed such a waste of vellum. Without a title page, and without page numbers, which hadn't been thought of yet either, you can tell if you have the complete book by the first and last lines. The texts will start with the word *Incipit*, meaning "here beginneth," and end with *Explicit* which means "here is unfolded" or "rolled out to the end"—carried over from the days of the rolled scrolls. (Oddly enough, if a leaf were missing in the interior of a volume, there was no way to detect its absence if it happened to start and close with a complete sentence.)

The illumination—the painting, gilding, and elaboration of the pages—became more and more ornate until the minature work alone seems to defy belief. The details and margins of local scenes, portraits of patrons, saints, flowers, and animals are so minute that they literally were painted with a single eyelash for a brush. At the same time the initial letters became so complicated a single design could require weeks to execute. The next time you come on a medieval manuscript turn straight to the first line of the Psalms. David set the illuminators up with a splendid "B" to play with in *Beatus vir qui non abiit in consilio impiorum.* (This is known as the Beatus Page and the medievalists are forever grateful David spoke Latin.)

Before we leave these great pieces of art which were so carefully and so painstakingly made, I can't help recalling the instructions I had from my own teacher in bookmanship, Hellmut Lehmann-Haupt. Dr. Lehmann-Haupt used to plead with us to "give the manuscript a chance." Picture it as it was created, he would say. Think of it slowly coming into being, a sheet at a time, in a darkened, low-ceilinged room with soft light coming in through gray-green glass off the cloister. Then imagine it complete and opened on a lectern in a gloomy abbey crypt where the gold illuminations catch the flicker of thick candles and the crackle of the vellum is absorbed by the damp vault overhead. Or think of it triumphant, tilted back on the high altar of a cathedral with beams of sunlight from the stained-glass clerestory slanting down onto the pages. One senses that in the world where they were made and used there was no question but that the words came straight from God.

By 1300 the making of books had left the monasteries and gone commercial. Paris was filled with professional copyists who duplicated magnificent Bibles and missals for the rich, and made plain, unadorned volumes for students and the working clergy. With the coming of the Renaissance, the thirst for the "new" books—the great texts of the classic period—was so great that a whole industry developed across Europe just lettering books. These two trends come together in the Giant Bible of Mainz, now facing the Gutenberg in the Great Hall of the Library of Congress. The Bible is huge, it is drawn on the finest of vellum, and it represents the quintessence of all the illuminators had learned about making books beautiful.

Now the market and demand were there. Money was available. The texts of the Renaissance (Dante, Boccaccio) were appearing; reports of explorations were coming in (Marco Polo, Vasco da Gama); religious arguments were creeping closer (Erasmus, Luther, and More). The need for fast, accurate duplication of printed words was building and Johann Gutenberg set out to exploit it. As the scholars say: In the Middle Ages men had more time than they had vellum; in the Renaissance they had more paper than they had time.

Gutenberg was not trying to print books. He was trying to make machine-made manuscripts. The early descriptions of Gutenberg's invention all refer to it as "artificial writing." Thus all his efforts were to make a page so like the Giant Bible of Mainz, for example, that the buyer could not tell the difference. This attempt to duplicate manuscripts, this reluctance to recognize a new thing in its own right, went on for decades. And this gets us to incunabula.

Incunabula is the shorthand word for things printed between the invention of printing and the end of the fifteenth century—roughly 1450 to 1500. It refers to the early, sturdy volumes produced while the craft was spreading across Europe, the time when the fonts of type were being designed, presses built, and the early printers were getting the feel of their trade.

The first one, by definition, was the Gutenberg Bible itself. We know only bits and pieces about Gutenberg the man, but he came from a family of goldsmiths, most of whom worked for the arch-

This is one of only two known copies of an Italian translation of Epistolae et Evangelia, *the gospels of the New Testament. The book has been called the finest illustrated book printed in Florence in the fifteenth century. Shown here is one of the 500 woodcuts in the volume, the moneychangers being chased from the Temple, and the elaborate title page.*

episcopal mint in Mainz for most of their lives. Gutenberg seems to have gotten the idea for his invention about 1435 and began to borrow money to develop it at once. He kept borrowing money for twenty years and went through a great deal of it.

He did all his work in secret and even melted down his type on occasion when he thought events were going to reveal what he was up to. In 1450 he borrowed eight hundred guilders from Johann Fust, a local lawyer, and put the invention itself up for security. Eight hundred guilders would buy "100 fat oxen" or several sizeable farms at the time. A few years later he borrowed another substantial sum from Fust, and by 1455 had run up a debt to the sum of 2,026 guilders and still had produced nothing. Fust, who had himself borrowed some of the money he'd loaned, threw up his hands and foreclosed to find that Gutenberg had been "just about to start" on the Bible (always referred to in the trade as The Forty-two Line Bible, there being that many lines of type to the page). There is some evidence that Gutenberg had been at this point for some time and that Fust feared he would be at the threshold forever.

The point of this story is that although Johann Gutenberg invented the process, the Bible itself was actually printed and sold by Fust with the help of Gutenberg's type designer, Peter Schoeffer. Gutenberg turns up as a member of the local court and drops out of our story for good.

Fust and Schoeffer deserve a great deal of credit themselves. For one thing, they stayed with the production of the great Bible, which was no small feat in itself. It took them three hard years to print it, most of the time running six presses twelve to fourteen hours a day. The material costs alone are frightening. We know of at least thirty vellum copies printed and these required over 1,500 sheepskins for the pages. Paper wasn't a great deal cheaper (having to be made by hand a screen at a time) and the two printers are known to have done at least 180 copies of these. But the product was a triumph. The Bibles were sold as manuscripts; there was no bragging about the printing idea, and they promptly went on to produce smaller Bibles and Psalters of equally high standards and even more beautiful type, presumably designed by Schoeffer as time progressed. (Schoeffer ultimately married Fust's daughter, and both families passed on a thriving publishing house at the end of prosperous lives.)

Passing on is important here. There were no patent laws in those days, so considerable effort was made to keep the process secret, but this proved hopeless. Even by the time the first book was finished, their work force would have exceeded two dozen men, and the natural leakage of skills plus a battle between two archbishops fighting to bring Christianity to Mainz resulted in the sack of the city, with the smoking ruins driving even more of the printers to other towns. Thus in no time the idea had spread down the Rhine to Holland, across to England; it went up the Rhine to Switzerland and down to Italy. By 1500 Rome had dozens of printing houses, and Venice, as a shipping and trading center, had over 150 full-time presses in operation. These were the days of the pioneers in the trade, and each individual made his own contribution to what we know as the book.

Nicolas Jenson gave us the Roman typeface which still dominates our present books and newspapers. Erhard Ratdolt created the first book with a title page (in Venice and not until 1476). William Caxton introduced printing to England, produced 103 known different titles, and himself translated twenty of the texts into English so "plain" people could read them. He printed the first edition of Chaucer's *Canterbury Tales* and did more for English spelling in one year than anyone in the previous one thousand. As their printing houses took on

Each page of a block book like the Biblia Pauperum *(c. 1470) was cut from a single piece of wood. The illustrations served as sermon texts for the unlettered, provincial clergy.*

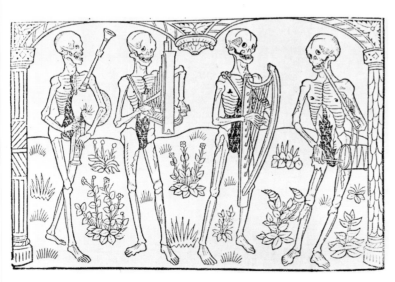

Above: *Only six copies of this first Latin edition of* Danse Macabre *are known. The 24 illustrations have been called the finest examples of French woodcuts in the fifteenth century.* Right: *Sebastian Brant's* Das Narrenschiff (Ship of Fools) *was a best seller of the fifteenth century. The design of the 114 woodcuts, which contributed greatly to its popularity, has generally been credited to Albrecht Dürer.*

Bernhard von Breydenbach

PEREGRINATIO IN TERRAM SANCTAM

(Journey to the Holy Land)

1486

The two woodblocks shown here come from the first travel book ever printed and are the first travel pictures ever reproduced of a real scene drawn realistically, and were also the first known foldout inserted in any publication.

Bernhard von Breydenbach was a member of the German nobility and also the Dean of the Cathedral at Mainz. As he explains in the book, he fears he "had lived somewhat freely in his youth," and in his later years "resolved to undertake a Pilgrimage to the Holy Land in hope of obtaining the salvation of [his] soul." He resolved to do it in style with a full retinue—including his own artist to make pictures of what he saw. The draftsman selected was Erhardus Reuwich, a recognized woodblock designer of the time, and with his arrival the party set out for Jerusalem on April 25, 1483. On the way they visited the principal cities of the eastern Mediterranean, saw the Holy Land, and went on to the Monastery at St. Catherine, Mount Sinai, Alexandria, and Cairo. They returned at the end of January 1484.

The trip appears to have been a total success and when they had all returned to Mainz the Dean resolved to share the experience with the community. Breydenbach wrote the text; Reuwich borrowed a font of type from Peter Schoeffer and designed the complete book with the

first illustrations ever made deliberately to accompany a text. (Previously illustrations had been either a design, a generalized tower or castle, or some similar convention.)

The book became an instant best seller. Reuwich tinted some of the pictures by hand "in several colors"; he had his printers paint red initial letters on many pages; and he translated the text from the original Latin to German four months after publication (1486), into French and Dutch (1488), and it appeared in Spanish in 1498. It went through eight editions and became the most popular travel book in Europe up to the discovery of the New World.

The two plates reproduced are: (on the front of the foldout) a detailed, factual picture of Venice as it appeared in 1483 showing all the landmarks (most of which are still standing) and (on the back) a generalized "tourist map" of Jerusalem noting the major sights in the city plus day trips in various directions. The illustrations are divided among pictures of whole towns, single buildings of interest and importance, and maps of the areas. Present-day travellers to Venice will recognize that the artist drew the scene as it would appear from the point where the church of S. Giorgio Maggiore now stands.

personalities of their own, each of the great printers took "marks" or "devices" which they affixed to the ends of the volumes, saying with pride, "I did it."

The shields of Fust and Schoeffer, Caxton's firm initials, and the splendid dolphin and anchor of Aldus Manutius remind us of one of the most interesting of the early figures.

Aldus started as a scholar, not a craftsman. He was born in 1450 and spent his early years teaching the sons of the Prince of Carpi, during which time he became increasingly incensed at the degradation of the classical texts he was forced to use. Convinced that the manuscripts he was teaching from would have outraged their original authors, he set out to clean up the errors. He begged, bought, and borrowed texts from all over Europe and compared, traced, and sorted out the various strains, trying to get as close to the original as was possible fifteen centuries after the fact. Having finally gotten back as far as he felt he ever would, he decided to go into the printing business to share his solutions. He bought a press in Venice and between 1494 and 1515 managed to print the first Greek editions of Aristophanes, Aeschylus, Aristotle, Herodotus, Plato, Sophocles, Demosthenes, and Pindar. (The money for the press, incidentally, came from his pupils, who are reported to have worshipped him.) He then moved into broader areas and published the first popular editions of Dante, Petrarch, and Erasmus from his own time.

But the act of printing was just the start. Aldus was the first to reject the idea that a book had to look like a manuscript. He was convinced that the invention was being applied in the wrong direction. Instead of huge, wood-bound lectern folios, he believed a book should fit in a saddlebag so it could be moved and read at leisure. He shrunk the pages, invented cardboard covers to be used instead of pine, decided that the Roman type would never squeeze together enough to make a hand-holdable volume so he invented italics which take up much less space yet retain their legibility.

Finally, he was committed to making the book as beautiful a piece of hard print as the manuscript had been as a work of hand art. He designed clean, austere pages that have never been surpassed for their grace and visual harmony. He selected his famous colophon from a coin of the Emperor Titus, using it to illustrate his motto: Hasten Slowly. Present-day book designers are still trying to achieve his sublime combination of balance, readability, and

Three famous printers' marks from Library first editions. Left: Aldus Manutius' dolphin and anchor (signifying his motto "Make Haste Slowly"). Center: William Caxton's initials. Right: Fust and Schoeffer's shields.

Johannes de Spira introduced printing to Venice in 1469, completing this second edition of Cicero's Epistolae ad familiares *in that year. The elaborate interlaced border and initial "E" illuminate the opening page of the work, the earliest Venetian imprint owned by the Library of Congress.*

Printed by Aldus Manutius in Venice at the very end of the incunabula period, Francesco Colonna's Hypnerotomachia Poliphili *is among the most beautiful printed books ever made. The harmony between the superb woodcuts and the handsome type made it a masterpiece of Renaissance bookmaking. As George Painter noted, "Radiantly and graciously Italian, classic, pagan, renascent," in contrast with the Gutenberg Bible, which "is sombrely and sternly German, Gothic, Christian, and medieval," these two masterpieces of the art of printing mark the opposite ends of the incunabula period.*

that graceful, open feeling that makes a book a delight to hold and return to. (This reminds me of the printer Cobden-Sanderson's remark four hundred years later: when a customer complained that C-S was charging an awfully high price for a very plain book, C-S responded, "Madame, I charge as much for my restraint as for my elaboration.")

Let's move up to the present day to ask, How did the Library of Congress get all these gems of the fifteenth century? The Library actually owns over 5,600 pieces of incunabula, an incredible number when you consider their rarity and value. The answer is that the Library and the nation are deeply indebted to a few dedicated book collectors who invested their time and fortunes to accumulate the collections and then leave them to this public institution, where scholars will have perpetual access to the treasures. The treasures were *given* to us.

While the single Vollbehr purchase provided a broad base to start with, the John Boyd Thacher collection was a gift of 904 incunabula heavily focused on the difficult and the unusual, and the later gift of 600 more from Lessing Rosenwald brought in the illustrated and most beautiful of the fifteenth-century beginnings. And these are literally only the beginnings.

As you walk through the vaults looking at the astonishing pieces lying there row after row, you are seeing the gifts of specific benefactors to the nation. Here is the Massachusetts Bay Psalm Book, the first book to be printed in North America and one of three known perfect volumes in the world— the gift of Mrs. Adrian Van Sinderen. There is the most complete collection in existence of Walt Whitman first editions, diaries, personal letters, notebooks, and unpublished manuscripts, the nucleus a gift of Carolyn Wells Houghton. The Jean Hersholt Collection of Hans Christian Andersen manuscripts, drawings, and first editions. The Leonard Keblers' gifts of Cervantes, including *Don Quixote.* The McManus and Young collections on magic, the Katherine Golden Bitting Gastronomic Library, Colonel Fabyan's collection of books on cryptography and the Bacon-Shakespeare controversy. Another vault has the Clarence W. Jones comprehensive collection of Henry James, the Frank Hogan collection of rare early American children's books, one of the finest collections of William Blake in the world, the Hugh Walpole collection, Sinclair Lewis.

These individual targets, which frequently represent a lifetime of patient collecting on the part of some individual, yield the kind of totality that no

A million dollars worth of books. Books need not be incunabula, of course, to be of great value. The five above are newer but costlier. Their value comes from a combination of rarity and what they represent.

    Lying at right is the Library's Massachusetts Bay Psalm Book, *the earliest surviving book printed in what is now the United States. It was made in 1640 by the printer Matthew Daye of Cambridge, Massachusetts; there are eleven known copies in existence. At the center is a first edition of John Bunyan's* Pilgrim's Progress. *One of the rarest books in all English literature, it was printed in 1678. Lying at left is Juan Zumarraga's* Doctrina Breue, *printed in Mexico in 1539–44, and considered the first existing book printed in the Western Hemisphere. Although it is believed three other titles may have preceded it, no copies of these have ever been found. (The type of the Zumarraga is beautifully cut and strongly sophisticated; there is nothing primitive about it.)*

    The two books standing are: right, John Eliot's Indian Bible, *Cambridge, 1663, and, left, Caxton's* Mirrour of the World, *1481. The Indian Bible was laboriously translated word-by-word into the language of the "New England Indians." It would be eighty years before an English Bible was first printed in America. Any single title of Caxton would be vastly valuable and in this instance four Caxton titles are bound together in a single case.*

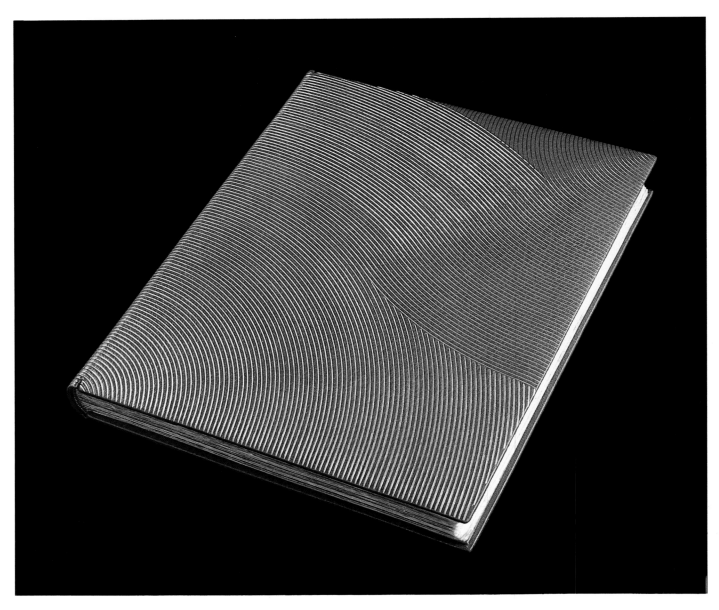

institution can ever get by itself. It is a healthy progression: the individual collector starts with a deep interest, usually in an individual or format. The casual collecting at the beginning grows into a driven, near-compulsion to "get everything." Enormous quantities of time and money are invested in the chase, and the ultimate result is near-totality—which thereafter makes serious research far more efficient.

The Alfred Whital Stern Collection of Lincolniana is an excellent example. Through the years he assembled six thousand pieces relating to Lincoln: writings by and about, memorabilia, photographs, broadsides, sheet music, prints, cartoons, contemporary newspapers, autographed letters from, to, and about Lincoln. The materials then brought to-

Above: *One of the by-products of a fine collection of rare books is that it tells the story of bookbinding from the earliest medieval manuscripts to the beautiful limited edition books of today. Shown on these two pages are striking examples of modern bookbinding from the 1930s. Sweeping lines of gold fan across this volume of Charles Baudelaire's* Poèmes *on a binding created by Henri Creuzevault in 1933.*

Right: *This 1931 Paul Bonet binding, of Paul Fargue's* D'Après Paris, *is a superb example of the marriage of bookbinding and art deco design.*

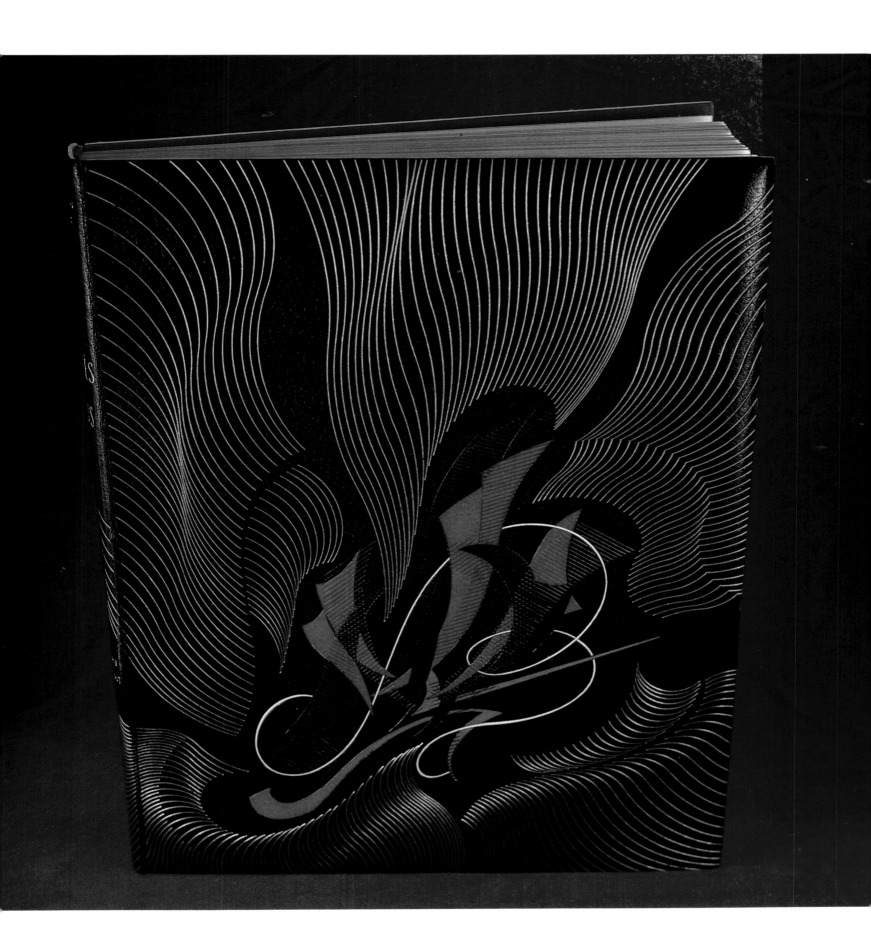

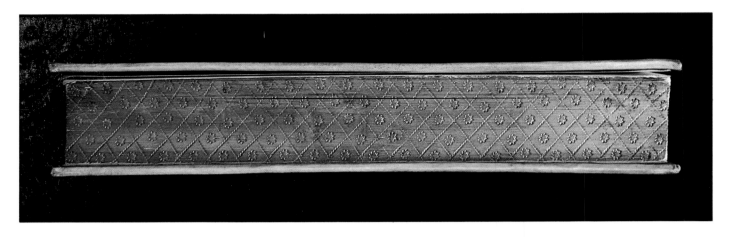

Fore-edge painting was a technique frequently employed during the nineteenth century to decorate fine books. The gold embossing on the fore-edges of the pages of this 1844 volume, Illustrations of Baptismal Fonts *by F.A. Paley (above), helps to conceal the painting of Waltham Abbey which is visible once the pages are fanned. An even more detailed painting can be seen on the memorial volume (opposite),* The Life and Remains of Henry Kirke White, *1825.*

Top: *Five manuscript and printed texts are bound together in this fifteenth-century German binding of leather and oak boards.*

Above: Ancient of Days *by William Blake, the frontispiece to Blake's* Europe, a Prophecy, 1794. *The Library's collection of Blake materials is exceptionally strong due to Lessing J. Rosenwald's personal interest and generosity.*

gether in a single room explain themselves. Item A becomes more meaningful in the presence of Item B, C suddenly has a significance never seen without the background of D and E. Similarly, the carefully assembled Rosenwald collection is far more valuable than the literally millions of dollars it is worth in sale value. Rosenwald sought to trace book illustration from ancient, Oriental xylography to the most modern of contemporary design. It is the cumulation of styles, the borrowings, the modification and development of an idea through these long runs of time that make the whole greater than the parts.

Let's conclude our look at books with a glance at two single volumes which fill every requirement for a "treasure" under anybody's definition: the Warburg and 1524 Books of Hours. They are stunningly beautiful and they were intended to be just that—fantasies, gems of bookmanship that were to the castles and châteaus of the High Renaissance what Fabergé eggs were to the Imperial Russian court. There were also everyday, hard-use Books of Hours, but these have literally been worn out and discarded through the centuries. The deliberate gems, the barely-to-be-touched miniatures are still with us and still serve the role they played in their own time as tiny pieces to be shown to guests, given as precious gifts, used to celebrate major events in the lives of their owners.

The earliest Book of Hours that has survived is one drawn by William de Brailes, an illuminator who worked in Oxford around 1250. A Book of Hours was a devotional handbook which carried its user through the proper prayers of each day, matching for the laity many of the devotions of the religious orders and clergy. The Horae used the so-called "Little Office of Our Lady" as a text and concentrated on the episodes in the life of the Virgin Mary.

Each Book of Hours starts with a church calendar which identifies the appropriate days for celebrating the feasts of the Church and the saints. The great Church festivals such as Christmas and Easter were always written in red ink and from this we get the phrase "red-letter days." Lesser festivals and saints' days were in black, and anniversaries of the local saints and churches were inscribed in blue. A trained medievalist can scan the calendar in a Book of Hours and immediately tell what region (and in many cases, even what town) its owner lived in from the saints celebrated.

Of the hundreds of Horae known to exist, no two

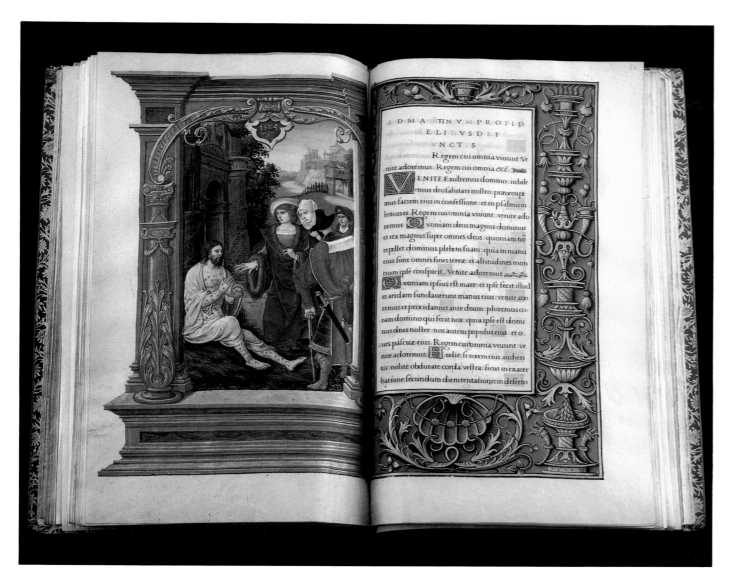

are alike, and many were painted expressly for specific individuals. The latter have scenes familiar to the patron worked in as background for the holy pictures or they have individuals from the owner's households drawn in the crowd scenes. The margins are filled with flowers and animals and some, like the Warburg, have tiny, grotesque creatures that provide a startling contrast to the idyllic figures around them.

The Horae are drawn on thin vellum, and the embellishment involves the ink of the letters, the beaten gold of the illumination, and the paint pigments of the miniatures. As a rule, each of these three tasks was performed by a different artist. The pictures are referred to as "miniatures" but the reference does not necessarily imply size. The word

Above: *One of the sixteen full-page miniatures from the 1524 Book of Hours,* Horae Beatae Mariae ad usum Romanum. *In addition to these fully developed embellishments, there are twenty-six small portrait miniatures of the evangelists and saints in the book and sixteen illuminated borders.*

Overleaf: *The 1524 and Warburg Book of Hours. Most of the rare-book treasures in the Library of Congress are protected by special, handmade slipcases which in turn hold silk covered chemises that protect the rare bindings— in this instance one of handtooled leather and the other (the Warburg) of scroll metal with metal clasps.*

Page 74: *A portion of a page from the Warburg Book of Hours enlarged almost four times to show the detail of the decorations. (The distortion of the page is the result of having to photograph such items hand-held with no flexing of the spine nor glass-flattening the pages in order to avoid any possibility of damaging the centuries-old pigments.)*

comes from the Latin *minium*, which was the red color used to point up the capital letters. *Miniare* meant to paint in vermillion, and as the years passed the painter of manuscripts branched out from initial letters to marginal embellishments to full-page pictures.

The creation of Horae extended well past the invention of printing. It was the last occupation of the scribes and illuminators once the routine preparation of books had been taken from them, and a few of the volumes extant came as late as 1550. Even as a live orchestra has more status than re-cordings and painted portraits more appeal than photographs, for the people who could afford a vellum Horae there was nothing the printing press could do that approached the beauty of these gems. It is intriguing to consider, though, that thanks to five-color separations and computer-driven presses, the printing press has given us the pages we are holding in our hands. We can cling to the thought that it took a human mind and hand to create them in the first place, but Gutenberg's machine has come a long way in a remarkably short space of time.

CHAPTER III

Oklahoma!

I've been claiming that the Library of Congress' great strength lies in its overlaps—everything means more because of what's on either side of it. It occurred to me there might be some merit in a demonstration (this could also be a way of answering the traditional "What's all the stuff good for, anyway?"). But let me show you how vast diversity in format has an impact on research techniques. Suppose you wanted to do a real, in-depth, everything-there-was-to-know study about the nation's great folk-musical, *Oklahoma!* Using the Library's resources, what do you find?

You'd probably start by asking, Where did it all come from? How did a couple of super-sophisticated Easterners like Richard Rodgers and Oscar Hammerstein manage to make a million-dollar blockbuster out of a Territorial box supper and a farmer's smokehouse? (Hammerstein himself used to say the first half of the play "wrestled with the question, 'Which boy would the girl go to the dance with?'")

You begin in the nearest almanac or encyclopedia and find that *Oklahoma!* started as a short-lived, straight play from the Depression called *Green Grow the Lilacs*. This was written by one Lynn Riggs, so we'll begin our search there. And that means the Copyright Office.

Most libraries start any research the first time something by, or about, an individual appears in print. The Library of Congress starts *before* it appears in print—frequently years before in the case of the unknown, unpublished playwright, and much of the Library's unique treasures are buried in the Copyright vaults waiting to be asked for. The unknown sheet music of Jelly Roll Morton was buried there for decades; the early unpublished Sinclair Lewises lay there until his later fame exhumed

them. (Did you know Lewis' first published work was *Hike and the Aeroplane*, a children's book, 1912?)

So we explore the archived Lynn Riggs deposits and find a dozen early plays, including such titles as *The Lonesome West*, *Knives from Syria*, and *Reckless*.

Above: *Oscar Hammerstein's copy of the holograph score of the song "Oklahoma!" with music written by Richard Rodgers and lyrics by Hammerstein.*

Opposite: *The program cover for the Broadway show.*

In *The Lonesome West* we find a hated stepmother with three sons trying to get out from under her heavy hand and off a failing Oklahoma farm. In *Knives from Syria* we find a widow trying to force her daughter to marry the hired man, with the daughter wanting to marry an itinerant Syrian peddler. (The peddler is trying to sell a collection of knives "good for cutting the throats of men," and a confusion in the night ends up with the daughter marrying the peddler and the widow marrying the hired man!) In *Roadside* we have a swaggering, footloose cowboy falling in love with a girl who reduces him to a subdued and proper member of the farm community. But suddenly in 1928 we find a play being copyrighted that seems to have a Syrian peddler named Ali Hakam selling knives to a threatening hired hand named Jeeter Fry who works for a widow named Aunt Eller who has a beautiful young niece named Laurey in love with a swaggering, footloose cowboy called Curly. This, of course, is *Green Grow the Lilacs*, and our running jump at the target has shown us the early antecedents of the *Oklahoma!* characters. The now familiar figures came out of Riggs' unsuccessful tries at plays that never made it, but he had the skill to see which figures "worked" and he salvaged these to make a play that flew. The Copyright holdings contain millions of unplayed songs, unpublished poetry, unacted plays. In most cases the marketplace was right; they deserved their interment. But undoubtedly there are also masterpieces in there which—because of timing, timidity, or simply because they were never seen by the proper eyes—have been lost, probably forever. They are interesting tailings from the nation's intellectual mines. Intriguing but tragic.

But, you ask, doesn't everything that's copyrighted become part of the Library's collections? No. Each year about six hundred thousand items are deposited for copyright; about four hundred thousand of these will be transferred to the Library and made available to the visiting public. Of these, 250,000 are trade books, the kind you see in bookstores; 250,000 are magazines; and the final 100,000 are sheet music, tapes, maps, motion picture reels, computer programs, and the electronic array of compact disks, optical disks, and all the material needed to support the nation's VCRs. (Oddly enough, the copyright archives used to overflow with homemade hand-drawn music staffs from annual thousands of unpublished songs. The latest Copyright Law revision permitted the substitution of taped casettes, which turn out to deteriorate faster than the earlier paper format.)

The remaining two hundred thousand are put into storage and kept indefinitely, simply arranged by registration number. These are stranger still. The Library keeps no textbooks, no commercial catalogs, no books of sermons; it catalogs none of the beach balls, ash trays, Snoopy paperweights, designs for lingerie lace, carnival dolls, or matchbook covers—all of which are *copyrighted* as objects of creative art, not *patented* as "useful designs." Most printed music and printed plays go on to the Library shelves. The handwritten, the typed, await discovery in the copyright warehouses.

Getting back to *Oklahoma!*, we have "established" Lynn Riggs. He is now under "bibliographic control," as the librarians say, and we can explore him through the road maps that are the Library's catalogs. We find a growing list of his plays, we find him in books about Southwestern playwrights, and he turns up in proliferating doctoral dissertations throughout the microfilm collections.

We learn that Riggs was a regional playwright who, like Will Rogers, grew up in Claremore, Oklahoma, and, also like Rogers, was part Cherokee. His plays were heavily autobiographical. He watched his home in Indian Territory become a part of the new state, and he used the Indian-White conflicts and the isolation of Oklahoma farms for plots. His own mother died young and his father married a woman whom Lynn learned to hate. He fled to an aunt whose speech, mannerisms, and humor appear in Aunt Eller, and while he never married, he was close to his sister, who ultimately inherited and then ran the family farm alone. She is repeatedly characterized in Laurey. *Green Grow the Lilacs* was his twelfth play out of thirty-one copyrighted tries. Only four made it to Broadway, and these for sadly short runs.

A strange background for a multi-million-dollar success. Can we find the link from the carbon-copy manuscript to the modern classic? Let's go to Broadway.

We find that in 1931 the Theatre Guild came across the *Lilacs* manuscript and decided to stage it. Franchot Tone was cast in the lead role of Curly, and Lee Strasberg played the peddler. The play ran sixty-four performances in New York, went on a nine-week "national tour," and closed. It was put back in the cabinet.

So we turn to the Library's newspaper collection. Can we learn anything from how the critics reacted? While most libraries have their local papers and something from New York and Washington, the Library of Congress keeps 1,648 current papers from all over the world—487 U.S. and 1,161 from abroad. (Oddly enough, with the high mortality of newspapers, the numbers on its shelves that are "closed entries" far exceed those which are alive; the Library has over 10,000 completed newspaper titles in its stacks.) As we follow *Green Grow the Lilacs* around the country, there is little that would explain the nation's later love affair with the *Lilacs* characters. Several reviewers comment favorably on the language. To our present taste, Riggs had a heavy hand with dialect. (In the opening lines, Laurey comes in having "Heared a voice a-talkin' rumbly." Curly tries to inveigle her to the box supper describing "A bran' new surry with fringe on the top four inches long—and *yeller!* And two white horses a-rarin' and faunchin'. . . ," with Laurey soon expressing her love of the farm by saying, "If we ever had to leave this here place, Aunt Eller, I'd shore miss it. I like it. I like the thicket down by the branch whur the 'possums live, don't you? And the way we set around in the evenings in thrashin' time, a-eatin' mushmelons and singin'. . . .") Today this would be considered slightly embarrassing. In 1931, it drew about the only praise the reviewers could bestow. We are beginning to see the play and the characters as continuing entities, but still nothing to explain its potential immortality.

It is time to turn to the manuscripts. Here the Library of Congress is like few places on earth. The political and creative great have deposited with the Library their personal papers—correspondence, working drafts, rejected ideas, incomplete projects—which give an insight into the minds and personalities of the figures like no other research source. It is quite inappropriate in our demonstration here to go into the papers with any depth or analysis, but you may get some feel of the material if we simply limit ourselves to a few anecdotes that suggest the style of the participants in this example. In the particular case of *Oklahoma!* we are dealing with some incredibly talented people who are themselves remarkably attractive. The more of their papers you read, the more you admire them personally. A singularly appealing group of artists.

Mid-1942 caught all of the contributors to the musical at a difficult time in their personal lives. The idea to make a musical comedy out of Lynn Riggs' play came from the two directors of the Theatre Guild, Lawrence Langer and Theresa

The pencilled original score of Oklahoma! *contains all the familiar songs we now associate with the show, as well as one love song which satisfied neither Rodgers nor Hammerstein: "Boys and Girls." This was ultimately discarded in favor of "People Will Say We're in Love." Also in the score folder are scraps of scribbled notes showing rough quick themes and sketches.*

Helburn. The Guild was nearly bankrupt at this point, having made money on only two of its last sixteen productions. It could not afford another failure.

The Guild took their idea to Jerome Kern (who had written *Show Boat*, a similar kind of Americana), and he rejected outright the offer to do the music. He said the plot was weak and the second act hopeless.

They turned next to the team of Rodgers and Hart. Lorenz Hart, the word man, had begun to lose control over a longtime drinking problem, and as the months passed could do less and less work, refused medical help, kept disappearing, and ultimately died soon after the opening of the show. On the other hand, Richard Rodgers, the music man, was a brilliant, innovative composer, marvelously organized and productive but emotionally tied to Hart, with whom he had worked for twenty years. When given the opportunity to do the show, he was eager to accept the challenge, but feared that if he turned to another lyricist, it would

hasten Hart's deterioration. After marking time for months, he decided to approach Oscar Hammerstein with an offer of collaboration.

Hammerstein was forty-six at the time, with his last two movies and last four plays being total, embarrassing failures. He was going through a period of self-doubt, frightened that he had written himself out, and fearful of taking another chance with his own reputation as well as threatening Rodgers'. He was seriously considering leaving theater completely.

Agnes De Mille, the choreographer, was professionally so desperate that when she heard of the Guild's plans she wrote and pleaded for a chance to show what she could do. She had been dancing, designing dances, and running a small dance troupe for twelve years without a single triumph. She offered to design the dances for a minor cash fee and accept no royalties.

With such strengths as these, they began to work. The papers of the participants reveal the following minor details and fill out a picture of some interest:

Hammerstein wrote the words first. He would spend days developing a lyric, testing it on his tongue, thinking it over and over again until it was finally what he wanted, and then he would hand it to Rodgers (they worked at their homes in Pennsylvania and Connecticut, respectively, and would meet once a week). Rodgers would read the lyric, think about it, and, in some cases, literally within a day write the complete melody.

Until *Oklahoma!* came along, musicals opened with loud, cheerful numbers and with the chorus (preferably showing a great deal of leg) coming on quickly. Hammerstein decided to start *Oklahoma!* in the same way Riggs had, with a single woman quietly churning butter on a porch and the voice of a cowboy coming in from a distance off stage. Hammerstein, in fact, tried to hold as much of Riggs as he could. He had to cut at least forty minutes from the original play to make room for musical numbers but the reduction of Riggs' 160 pages to Hammerstein's 77 tightened the dialogue and permitted the lyrics and ballet to advance the plot by themselves. The latter device went on to become *Oklahoma!*'s major contribution to the American stage.

Hammerstein built *Oklahoma!* a layer at a time, writing sequentially and developing each scene in detail as he progressed. On the first pass through he did only one song: the first one to set the mood.

It came from Riggs' initial stage direction opening *Green Grow the Lilacs*:

It is a radiant summer morning several years ago, the kind of morning which, enveloping the shapes of earth—men, cattle in the meadow, blades of the young corn, streams—makes them seem to exist now for the first time, their images giving off a visible golden emanation that is partly true and partly a trick of imagination, focusing to keep alive a loveliness that may pass away.

Hammerstein took three weeks to write the lyrics on this single song but from them came "There's a bright, golden haze on the meadow . . . Oh, what a beautiful mornin', Oh, what a beautiful day." He notes that he spent two days worrying about the "Oh": was it needed? (Recall, with the music as we know it it was essential, but the music did not exist when he did the words. Without the "Oh," Rodgers would have written a different song.) When Hammerstein finished the opening lyric he brought it to Rodgers, who read it and in ten minutes wrote the melody which we now feel was sublimely appropriate. How else could *Oklahoma!* open except with . . . ?

Hammerstein then completed all the spoken

Opposite: *In addition to the original* Oklahoma! *score, Oscar Hammerstein gave the Library of Congress three albums of clippings and memorabilia related to the show, which he dedicated to his wife, Dorothy. One volume is open to the cover of* Coronet *for June 1944, in which appeared a major article on* Oklahoma!

Above: *Two pictures from the* Coronet *article show scenes from the Agnes De Mille ballet. The story in dance within the story in words was one of many innovations by the Rodgers and Hammerstein team.*

parts and wrote the play straight through to the end, spending no more time on songs beyond setting rough titles in the middle of the script pages with a short statement of purpose or content beneath.

When he completed the first draft he had one song, the majority of the words, and he needed a script that could be seen outside the Rodgers and Hammerstein team. He had a clean copy typed and sent it to the Library to get copyright protection. It is the first of sixty-nine copyrighted script versions and songs that flowed through the Copyright Office—and from which we can watch the show develop, trying this, discarding that.

Where are the great songs? Not in the first draft. You do have "Oh, What a Beautiful Morning," but this is followed by Aunt Eller singing "She Likes You Quite a Lot," Jud's "All That I Want," the peddler singing "Peddler's Pack," and the first act finale: "How Would It Be?" If you can't quite recall how these went, don't be concerned. None of them survived in their original form. The second act has only one song in it, a single sentence describing "The Farmer and the Cowboy Must Be Friends," and no sign of the ultimate "All Er Nothin'" or "Oklahoma!" at all.

And if you wonder what kind of a Hammerstein lyric could possibly end up in a wastebasket, the first one went like this (designed to let the audience know that Laurey and Curly have a thing about each other and that Laurey is baiting him by acting as if she is interested in the hired hand). She sings:

> *You're shy and you got no confidence.*
> *You hide in a hole like a crawfish.*
> *Folks cain't account for the way you act.*
> *And they say you act stand-offish.*
> *I understand how you feel.*
> *Onct I was jist like you.*
> *Nen love come along and cured me*
>   *[She looks off as if she means Jud]*
> *And 'at's what'll cure you, too.*

> *Someone will teach you and clearly explain*
> *Why you are the cream of the crowd.*
> *Someone will teach you to walk down a lane*
> *As if you were ridin' a cloud.*
> *Someone will kiss you and tell you you're*
>   *wonderful,*
> *You'll think you're wonderful, too.*
> *Fer somehow the right one can make you believe*
> *They's no one on earth like you.*

(Curly answers: *"But jist don't take the first feller that comes . . . Mebbe some day you'll do better."*)

On further reflection, Hammerstein discarded every word of this song except for the single rhyme: crawfish and stand-offish. This he rather liked and he loaded it back into Ado Annie's second act pledge of relative fidelity.

Hammerstein had originally intended to explain Jud Fry's introverted problems through a dialogue between two of the parallel characters (you note Jeeter has become "Jud"; *Tobacco Road* had preempted the former), but he says he abandoned the discussion idea since he could not believe that any of the participants was sufficiently sophisticated to analyze Jud's psyche. He then put Jud's problems in Jud's own mouth in "Lonely Room" and in his neighbor's perception in "Pore Jud Is Dead"—two fine examples of letting the music advance the play.

In some of their letters, Rodgers admits that there was one melody written before the words: "People Will Say We're in Love." Hammerstein reports that he has always had trouble writing love songs since there are so few ways you can say the same thing without either copying someone else or making the case in just the way everyone would expect you to. Hammerstein took pride in the fact that his lyrics never generalized but used specific words which symbolized the theme he was expressing, and he wanted every line he wrote to be without precedent. Given these boundaries, love songs made him tongue-tied. In the early drafts the love lyric was called "Boys and Girls" and went like this:

LAUREY: *Boys and girls like you and me*
> *Walk beneath the skies.*
> *They love just as we love*
> *With the same dream in their eyes.*
> *Songs and kings and many things*
> *Have their day and are gone,*
> *But boys and girls like you and me,*
> *We go on and on.*
> *We walk—*
CURLY: *On ev'ry city street*
LAUREY: *We walk—*
CURLY: *In lanes where branches meet*
LAUREY
AND CURLY: *and Stars send down their blessing from*
> *the blue.*
CURLY: *We go—*
LAUREY: *Through storms of doubt and fear,*
CURLY: *And so*

Elaborations on a theme: the simple melody line of the score as originally conceived by Richard Rodgers, through more elaborate harmonies, to the full-blown arrangement used by the pit orchestra as developed by Robert Russell Bennett.

LAUREY: *We walk from year to year,*

LAUREY
AND CURLY: *Believing in each other, as we do,*
Bravely marching forward, two by two—

CURLY: *Boys and girls like you and me*
Walk beneath the skies.
They love just as we love,
With the same dream in their eyes.

This failed to satisfy Rodgers (and Hammerstein wasn't too pleased with it either) so, after some time had slipped away, Rodgers said he had written a melody which might break the log jam. He then presented Hammerstein with the only notes written without words, and the lyricist soon handed back the lines: "Don't throw bouquets at me, don't please my folks too much . . . People will say we're in love."

Hugh Fordin recalls an incident from Agnes De Mille's first day at work. She was anxious to appear crisply professional and very experienced so she announced firmly at the outset that there must be no one in the dance line that she had not personally approved. Hammerstein replied with a perfectly straight face, "Oh, pshaw!" He then said that he

was sorry she felt this way since there was his "regular girl friend" and the head of the Theatre Guild had two, and Rodgers always "counted on some." De Mille finally figured out she was being teased and laid that concern to rest.

The play was finally written and the music passed to Robert Russell Bennett to elaborate the simple songs into full orchestrations (the Library has thick packs of penciled drafts followed by ink sketches which ultimately resulted in the handwritten scores used in the pit through rehearsals).

The producers became desperate for money. Backers were brought to rehearsals and left shaking their heads, and parties were held in wealthy potential donors' apartments but no one wanted a piece of the show. The Guild's folly became a joke in Manhattan and the word was "no gags, no girls, no chance." The Guild barely got enough money together to get the show to New Haven, and much of what they had had come in pieces of $1,500, each drawn from the personal friends of the participants.

The papers tell anguished stories of the tryouts. It opened at the Shubert Theatre in New Haven on March 11, 1943, under the title of *Away, We Go!* It had little advance publicity, so the audience had no idea what to expect. They enjoyed it immensely, but the New Yorkers who had come up to see what Rodgers was doing returned reporting it wasn't much. Max Gordon, the famous producer, said the girls should be brought on sooner in the first act.

De Mille remembers the move to Boston as a nightmare; only Hammerstein kept matters sane, "quietly giving off intelligence like a stove." De Mille got German measles which spread to the ballet company, who covered their spots with grease paint. Hammerstein's wife had a high fever and was in Peter Bent Brigham Hospital, and the Theatre Guild producers all had the flu. Two scenes were dropped. "Boys and Girls Like You and Me" (which had lasted this far) was abandoned, and they decided to take a duet from the lovers and make it into a crashing finish with the whole company singing "Oklahoma!" to bring down the curtain. At the last minute they changed the name of the play.

They moved it all back to New York and a few hours before opening Hammerstein was walking with his wife and said, "I don't know what to do if they don't like this. I don't know what to do because this is the only kind of show I can write."

It opened to a partially empty theater, but the night ended with wild applause. It proceeded to

Above: *Photographs of production numbers from the Broadway run of* Oklahoma! *are included in the albums which Oscar Hammerstein eventually gave to the Library of Congress.*

Opposite: *The songs from* Oklahoma! *captivated the public from the start. Musical arrangements for all kinds of vocal groups, as well as for concert, brass and reed, and even accordion bands are numerous and are still popular today, some fifty years after the show opened on Broadway.*

run for five years playing 2,243 performances on Broadway and grossing $7,000,000 (breaking all previous theatrical records). A national company traveled for ten years, performed in some 250 cities, and played before 10,000,000 people—while grossing another $20,000,000. The New York company then took to the road and toured 71 cities during which time companies were formed to do the play in Europe, South Africa, Scandinavia, and Australia. When the smoke had cleared on the initial staging, it had made a profit of over $5,000,000 on its initial investment of $83,000. The few people who had been willing to help some old friends had gotten a return of more than $50,000 for every $1,500 contributed.

Four years after the New York opening they mounted a London show. A fat part of the *Oklahoma!* files are the resulting reviews from all over the British Isles. The Liverpool *Daily Post* notes: "As it has an all-American cast, only regular filmgoers can understand all the dialogue." The Birmingham *Post* sighs, "The production brings home the jaded condition of the people of these islands after seven years of austerity and deprivation, when contrasted with the freshness of the Americans and their abounding vitality." The *London Daily Express* reports:

Well, down came the final curtain at ten minutes before ten o'clock—and after 14 calls for this sparklingly brilliant cast you might have

Mayor Fiorello LaGuardia of New York joined Richard Rodgers and the cast of Oklahoma! *to celebrate the show's first birthday on March 31, 1944. (Hammerstein can be seen at the far right.)*

thought the folks would have been reaching for their hats.

But no one in the theatre left. They sat there, clapping away and shouting and whistling, increasingly clamant for more.

So they got more. The girls hitched up their pretty frocks, the men slapped their thighs, and off we went on "Oh, What A Beautiful Morning" again. And after that came more songs, and more shouting for them.

When I left the theatre, 20 minutes after the official finale, you could hear the singing around the empty crates in Covent Garden—and for all I know, it will still be going on when the porters come to work...

The show broke all records in the three-hundred-year history of the Drury Lane Theatre.

Thus, we have found original and unique materials of the play in the Library's Copyright Office, the Music Division, the Recorded Sound Division, the Serial Divison, the stacks. Let's take a quick run to the Motion Picture Section where we come on eighteen reels of 35mm film in metal canisters, the result of their copyright deposit of October 13, 1955.

Rodgers and Hammerstein had postponed any motion picture treatment until all the stage companies had had a chance to complete their runs. By then the play was recognized as being a genuine piece of Americana, and everyone concerned wanted to be certain that the movie was "done right." To avoid any chance of Hollywood improving it out of all recognition, the authors held the complete production in their own hands.

They wanted it shot in Oklahoma but gave this up in frustration when they were unable to find a location without the anachronisms of concrete, telephone wires, steel fences, or contour plowing. A search of Kansas failed equally, but a cameraman finally saw a cover picture on a copy of *Arizona Highways* that looked so right they bought the land—which turned out to be forty miles northeast of Nogales.

They built a farm on it using weathered boards and a used mining hut for the smokehouse. The corn was planted in January, hand-watered through the summer, and it reached sixteen feet by August. Hammerstein said, "It looks as high as the eye of an elephant who is standing on another elephant." Some of the stalks were put in boxes so the rows could be moved aside to let the cameras follow

Decca Records sold over a million copies of the original-cast album of Oklahoma!, *the first commercial recording made of an entire musical show, and the Library's collections grow as successive generations of performers cut their versions of the score.*

Eighteen reels of 35mm film were deposited with the Copyright Office to protect the rights to the film Oklahoma! *in October 1955. Like all the Library's motion-picture and television film and tapes, they are available for viewing by any scholar with a serious purpose.*

Top: *Theresa Helburn, director of the Theatre Guild, was escorted to the Oklahoma City gala performance in appropriate style.* Above: Oklahoma *governor Robert S. Kerr met the* Oklahoma! *cast at the train station with a coach when Broadway came to Oklahoma City in 1946.*

Curly. (The peach orchard did not grow peaches as well as the corn grew corn so some two thousand wax peaches were hung by hand before shooting.)

The two hired Fred Zinnemann of *High Noon* and *Member of the Wedding* to direct the show, and they started casting with the players firmly fixed in their minds. They held conferences and/or screen tests with Richard Burton to do Jud, Joanne Woodward as Laurey; James Dean and Paul Newman were equal candidates for Curly. Burton was tied up with other commitments, so they moved on to Eli Wallach and Rod Steiger and became enthusiastic about the latter. Steiger not only got the job but

he danced the Jud role in the ballet as well as doing the speaking part. They found Newman too stiff, and James Dean lacked "the necessary romantic quality," according to Zinnemann. By the time they started shooting, Rodgers and Hammerstein had completely reversed themselves (they had intended to have dramatic actors do the parts and dub the singing voices), and they cast Gordon MacRae as Curly with Shirley Jones as Laurey. These performers both sang and spoke.

When it was all over, the movie had cost nearly $7,000,000 to film and like everything else about the play was a massive success. The team went on to write *Carousel, South Pacific, The King and I, Flower Drum Song,* and *The Sound of Music,* in spite of Samuel Goldwyn's famous advice. Goldwyn had seen *Oklahoma!* at a matinee and called Rodgers to meet him at the theater. Rodgers rushed over from his office to find Goldwyn bubbling. He kissed Rodgers on the cheek and said, "This is such a wonderful show! I just had to see you to give you some advice. You know what you should do next?"

"What?"

"Shoot yourself." He was convinced they could never create another show as good as *Oklahoma!*

So what is my point? Well, my point is that I want to try to give you a sense of how all these treasures are nested in reinforcement. Presumably our main "treasure" here is the holograph score of Richard Rodgers' pencilled notations on simple music staffs...or is it Hammerstein's pencilled memories of the thousandth performance...or maybe Robert Russell Bennett's complex orchestrations as he takes the music from Rodgers' three-note chords up to full symphonic development and then back down to high-school choral arrangements and marching band transcriptions. But whatever the "treasure" is, the supporting paper is what I hope you'll remember: the thank-you notes in Hammerstein's hand revealing the contributions of specific individuals for elements that made the show a success. Sheaves of weekly income and out-go records showing all the tiny details of where the money goes to keep a great hit moving with vigor for five years. (Terre Haute, Dec. 18: Salaries, royalties, publicity, road expenses....) Dialogues with translators on how to characterize Americanisms for Swedish audiences and ultimately the Swedish script itself for Swedish actresses to do Laurey and Ado Annie in Stockholm. (Å, for ein strålande morgon....) The awesome stream of script after script, each one changed, distilled, and sharpened

Nine different versions of the scripts of Oklahoma! *show its development from the original Lynn Riggs play,* Green Grow the Lilacs, *published in 1931, through the various scripts for the stage show to the screenplay used in the 1954 movie based on the Broadway play. A British edition of the libretto and a script for the play in Swedish are also shown.*

from Riggs in Oklahoma to Riggs on Broadway to Hammerstein in Doylesville to Hammerstein in New Haven, Boston, New York, Hollywood, and Nogales—every one different and fascinatingly revealing of how the principals' perception of the play changed with time. And then the vast book, magazine, newspaper, and microform collections of the Library to draw upon.

What we saw with *Oklahoma!* could be done with the Library's holdings of *Porgy and Bess, Show Boat, West Side Story* (the costume sketches for *Show Boat* complete with fabric swatches are fascinating). It has equivalent blocks of original treasure/research material for the Victor Herbert musicals, Copland ballets, Gershwin motion pictures, Gian Carlo Menotti operas. Every piece of paper or film reinforces something else and gives it more meaning. The treasure is simply the pivot point.

CHAPTER IV

Where in the World Are We?

Maps. Fascinating things. Some of us can look at a mass of lines on a service station map and paint mental pictures of waves crashing on Mount Desert or see saguaro cacti in the Sonora. Others of us can't understand a five-block diagram to get us to the shopping center. But maps have been with us as far back as the mind of man remembreth not. The Library of Congress has four million of them, the largest map collection in the world.

To the map curators, maps are to be *used*, not worshipped or breathed hard over. If you were to walk through the reading room of the Library's Geography and Map Division today you would see people looking at oceanographic charts of the sea bottom, mosaic maps of the back of the moon, the distribution of black-owned businesses in New York City, but you would not find readers using the maps we are going to see here. These are six of the rarest treasures of the Library, carefully preserved in acid-free envelopes of cold Mylar and Plexiglas, yet capturing acts of human effort and intelligence that fire the mind. They are thrilling, awesome—and most of them reveal a whole series of errors which were either committed at the time or were fed to us in school five hundred years later.

The first map is the oldest portolan chart in America. Portolanos were a common working tool of sailors. They were invented during Greek and Roman times, and for hundreds of years they were simply sailing instructions passed from one boat to another or from father to son. They told which side of the black rock to stay on when you left the harbor, which way the wind blew off Sicily during different seasons of the year, how deep the canals were in Venice. Up until about 1300, portolanos were simply handwritten books, but about this time, maps were added to the books.

The portolano on page 93 was drawn sometime between 1320 and 1350. The last Crusade had just ended, Kublai Khan had just died, the battles of Crécy and Poitiers were about to be fought. You might assume that the maps of the time would be pretty primitive, and we've been told the sailors never dared sail out of sight of land for fear of circling endlessly in the open sea, or falling off the edge of the flat earth. Utter, outrageous nonsense.

Our map shows that the sailors had an astonishing knowledge of where they were. They knew how their world looked, how the Black Sea sat in relation to Gibraltar, how to get from one place to another. This portolano follows the conventions that appear on the thirty-odd examples drawn before 1350 that are still scattered around the world. All are oriented with north at the top of the chart; all show ports written at right angles to the shoreline (and no drawing inland, for the sailors were only interested in ports and harbors). Shoals are shown by dots, and rocks by crosses. Although fourteenth-century sailors had what to us appear to be ridiculously clumsy instruments, they used them with great skill. That brings us to two important questions: How did sailors know where they were and how did they know how to get somewhere else?

Sailors had known how far they were north and south of anything since the sixth century B.C. The early Greeks had invented the gnomon, a simple

Four examples from the almost four million maps in the Library's collections. Above left is a Japanese military map of Kikaiga Shima molded in rubber. In a rainbow of colors the legend shows among other things rifle pits, trenches, cave bastions, and rocket racks. Above right is an Eskimo map given by Adm. R.E. Byrd. Islands, ice shelf, channels are shown by patches of fur and driftwood and stitched to a sealskin base. At left is a Fiberglas relief model of the moon crater Copernicus. This four-foot model was designed to be viewed through closed-circuit television from a moon landing module mock-up. The purpose of the exercise was to help the astronauts become familiar with the appearance of the crater and its nearby terrain and thus aid them in choosing the optimum landing point for touchdown. At left bottom is a Micronesian stick map. The sticks represent the time required to sail an outrigged canoe from one island (represented by shells) to another: the chevrons show wave patterns and direction of currents. The large shell in the center is Kwajalein in the Marshall Islands.

Opposite: *This map is thought to be the oldest map in the Western Hemisphere. It is a working portolan drawn on vellum between 1320 and 1350. It shows the Mediterranean and Black Seas from the coast of Israel to the east coast of Spain and, since it was a sailing chart, it shows only ports. Nothing is represented inland. Of an age when maps are thought to be primitive, the precision of the Italian shoreline, for example, is astonishing.*

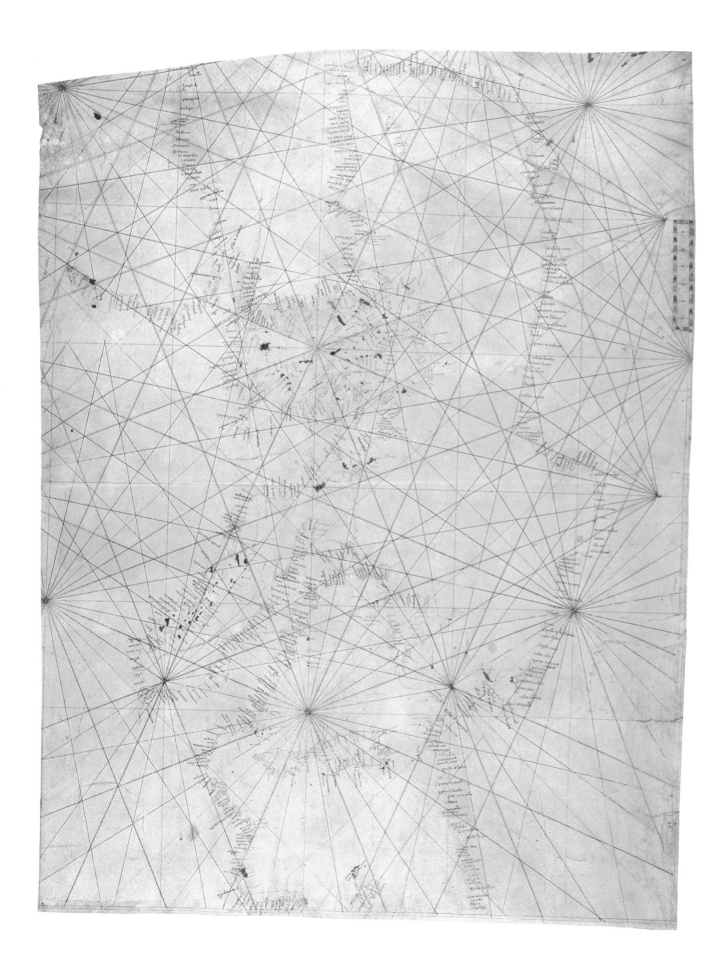

Caspar Vopell's manuscript globe of the earth was made in 1543. The bands encircling it trace the paths of the planets according to the old Ptolemaic conception. Ironically, the globe was made in the very year that Copernicus destroyed the idea of an earth-centered universe.

device which amounted to the placing of a straight stick in the ground and measuring the length and angle of the shadow it threw. They knew that the sun went around the circular earth in twenty-four hours; they divided the circle into halves and then fourths and then eighths and ultimately set on 360 parts which gave them what we now call degrees. Simple measurements of the shadow and its angle revealed that it took an hour to go fifteen degrees, and with this knowledge they could tell how far apart towns and countries were anywhere the sun shone.

For example (indeed a stunning experiment), a Greek by the name of Eratosthenes decided that Aswan in Egypt must lie on the edge of the summer swing of the sun since at noon on the summer solstice the sun was directly overhead and a straight stick stuck in the sand cast no shadow at all. On the same day in Alexandria (which he figured to be just about five hundred miles to the north of Aswan from the length of time it took to walk it beside a straight Nile) a stick cast a shadow "that could be measured as the 50th part of a circle." He was

therefore convinced that the earth must be fifty times the distance between Aswan and Alexandria, or 25,000 miles in circumference. The astonishing thing is that we now know (thanks to complicated modern electronic measurements) the actual distance to be 24,860 miles. He was only off by 140 miles out of 25,000 using a protractor and a stick in the ground!

The Greeks thus could go north and south with great accuracy by measuring the North Star above the horizon at night and the tilt of the sun by day. Eratosthenes' calculations held up for nearly three hundred years. They became commonly accepted —until a revisionist appeared and caused enormous damage. One Posidonius, working about 50 B.C., decided to recheck Eratosthenes' measurements and concluded he was wrong. He came up with a new set of figures that "proved" that the proper circumference of the earth was 18,000 miles around instead of 25,000. The 18,000 mile figure got into Strabo's *Geographia*; it was picked up by Ptolemy for his atlas and went unchallenged for 1,600 years! Massive fallout: 1) Columbus thought Spain wasn't too far away from China (he was working with a smaller earth) and 2) when he did strike the New World (given an 18,000 mile circumference) the Caribbean islands were almost precisely where Japan and the Spice Islands should have been. On his second voyage he landed in Cuba and made his men swear they had gone ashore on the Malay peninsula.

Note two things here. One, that the error in circumference only caused trouble going east and west (the gnomon and its sisters the quadrant and the cross staff still gave reasonably accurate readings north and south), and two, you will note that everyone understood the earth was round. Sailors, any kind of scholar—indeed any educated person through the centuries—conceived of the earth as round. The great myth of the flat earth may have been started by textbook writers in the nineteenth century to make the Columbus story sound more exciting. Globes of the spherical earth were being made and sold commonly through the Middle Ages and in the Renaissance long before Columbus' time, and the phenomenon of a curved horizon and ships disappearing down the far side was universally understood by people living near the sea. Indeed, as Aristotle had pointed out, you can see the round shadow of the earth crossing the moon in every eclipse.

Thus from well back in Western history we have

had a firm grip in north and south distances (latitude), but how did they know where they were east and west during all this time? (The *directions* of east and west were defined by the rising and setting sun, but *distances*?)

The answer is by dead reckoning.

Dead reckoning was clumsier than measuring the height of the sun or Polaris, but easier to understand. It was simply a matter of keeping track of how far you'd gone from the last place you knew the position of—usually home port. Large distances were kept track of in terms of a day's sail. Smaller distances were deduced by speed. You could time the passage of a block of wood dropped at the bow until it passed the stern of the ship. You knew how long the ship was and therefore how far you were going during every hour or whatever time period was chosen. On the larger ships they threw a triangular board over the stern and paid it out on a line from a reel. The amount of line that ran out in a given time showed the speed and, later, knots were tied in the line and the time they took going over the rail was counted by the sailor's pulse or a sand glass. (And from this, of course, came the term knot, meaning one nautical mile per hour.)

With these two approaches you could get from one place to another in the Mediterranean with ease, and sailors from Acre seeking tin in England could make it there and back out of sight of land most of the way. They knew their latitude at home port and the latitude of Gibraltar. They would simply sail on straight lines east or west to reach a point, make right angle turns stairstepping up to avoid the bulge of Africa and back down to pass out to the Atlantic off Spain; once there they sailed toward the North Star, stairstepping to the east as needed to make the landfall they wanted. Much less of a problem than it appeared to be *so long as you were sailing from a known place to a known place.* Portolan charts were strictly limited to the Mediterranean and the western coast of Europe. The Great Unknown Out There was another thing entirely.

The second of the rare treasures we are considering is the 1482 edition of Claudius Ptolemy's (page 98) atlas showing the edges of Terra Incognita being pushed back for the first time in well over a thousand years. Ptolemy's atlas is an unlikely volume. Ptolemy was a Greek who lived in Alexandria during the times of Hadrian and Antoninus, and he wrote a *Geographia* in eight volumes which drew together everything known about the world as of the second century A.D. Seven of the

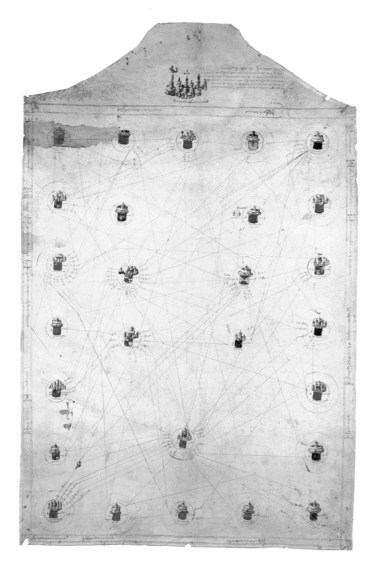

A 1484 guide to weights and measures by Arnaldo Domenech. Until as recently as 1973 this was thought to show distances between the principal mercantile towns of Europe and the Levant. It is now recognized as a vellum wall chart showing the number of pounds or rottoli per hundredweight units at each of the 27 towns listed; the equivalent weights for converting from one municipal system to another; and standard measures used in the cloth trade of named towns. Each town is represented by a miniature of its most characteristic building.

books contained place names: eight thousand cities, islands, mountains, river mouths, each with their location, all drawn from travellers, sailors, and military commanders he interviewed. There is no evidence he ever went anywhere himself.

But the eighth volume was an atlas of twenty-six regional maps and one large world map. Ptolemy described the earth as a stationary sphere around which the heavens spun, and (here is the strange part) his atlas was first dispersed throughout the Roman world and then continued to be used almost unchanged for 1,300 years! Ancient manuscript copies of it have been found on Mount Athos, in the Vatican Library, and in Arab and Byzantine libraries.

The oldest drawings, regardless of where they have been found, are almost identical, and therefore the cartographic scholars believe that they are very close to the way they looked in Roman times. We thus have an astonishing insight into the Roman knowledge of the world. It has surprising breadth—and amusing errors.

The great rivers—the Nile, Rhine, Danube, Indus, Ganges, Tigris, and Euphrates—are in their proper places, and both the European and western Asian mountains are properly located and drawn.

As noted above, Ptolemy's latitudes are quite accurate. His east-west lines march properly across Europe and down to an equator that the Romans could only have heard about. The Mediterranean is properly related to Europe and northern Africa—but badly out of line east and west. In spite of how well they would have known their own sea, their ability to measure longitudinal distances was so flawed that the atlas shows the Mediterranean greatly lengthened east and west making it over 65 degrees from Gibraltar to Syria instead of the less than 45 degrees it really is. The farthest coast of China is 110 degrees from Europe on toward the east instead of the true distance of 85 degrees. (Though it is something of a miracle that Ptolemy had even heard of the east coast of China! No European would describe it until Marco Polo's book 1,100 years later.) The northern limit of the world is Ultima Thule beyond which nothing is known (although it is shown at 63 degrees or the level of Iceland), and as you can see from the Africa page we have illustrated, Ptolemy held out little hope of getting around the Dark Continent. Ethiopia ran solidly to the south pole.

But that brings us to the changes in the maps. Once the great age of exploration began, "Ptolemy" was changed and changed—almost yearly to keep abreast of new edges.

Our illustration is from the Library's 1482 edition. This is the fourth edition that appeared after the invention of printing, and it is a woodblock that was tinted after it came off the hand press. It represents the edges of Africa as they were known in 1482, for in 1400 the Portuguese had turned left out of Lisbon, gone firmly past the Pillars of Her-

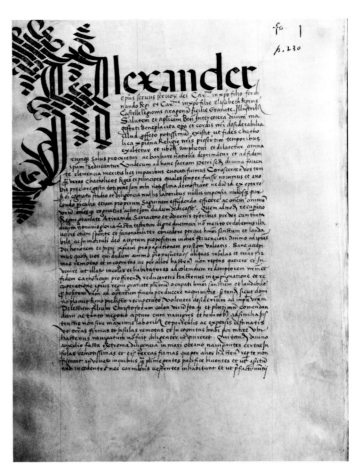

Columbus Codex (Book of Privileges), 1502. The Spanish monarchs had promised to make Columbus a don, admiral, viceroy, and governor of any lands he could discover. Fearful that they would forget, Columbus had four copies made of the listed privileges and placed them in monasteries for safe keeping. The Library's, one of the original four, is the only one that includes the Papal Bull of 1493 concerning the New World.

cules, and year after year pressed farther south. By the 1480s they had gotten this far down the west coast. The maps still said there was a great mass ahead of them, but it kept receding over the horizon. By the time of this chart, Europeans had accompanied Arab ships down the Red Sea, and the chart is growing accurately. They know where the Nile comes out and have heard of where it starts—in two rivers draining two lakes at the foot of the Mountains of the Moon; it will take another four hundred years for the Victorians to get there and verify this rumor.

By 1488, Bartolomeu Dias has finally made it to the Cape of Good Hope, found Africa to be an "island," come around the end and looked toward the spice ports of India that the Portuguese had known via overland caravans. The mapmakers revised their plates and the world was set for Columbus' great try into the westward unknown. (It is intriguing to note that when every bay around the African continent had been logged, the coastlines were marvellously accurate—north and south. A Portuguese world map of 1502 shows the southern tip of South Africa to be 32° South—satellite readings now put it at 34° 50', only 3° off—but the width of the continent was very inaccurate. The run from the Gambia to the Niger is hundreds of miles too long, and the Sahara nearly a thousand miles too wide. Longitude calculations are worse than ever.)

When I was a college freshman, one of the most sophisticated jokes on campus ran: Columbus was the perfect example of the educated man—when he left home he didn't know where he was going, when he got there he didn't know where he was, and when he got home he had no idea of where he'd been. There is just enough truth in the epigram to give it life.

When the Admiral of the Ocean Sea died, fifteen years and three more voyages to the New World past 1492, he still insisted he had made it to Asia. After his last trip he told the Crown that he was only nineteen days' sail from the mouth of the Ganges, and only the condition of his ships and his crew prevented him from going the distance. He

genuinely believed it, and the mapmakers of Europe agreed with him for ten more years until the world's knowledge of itself exploded and data came rushing back by the bale. Each ship charted another snippet of the shoreline and when it was added to the ones before, the edges of the New World grew with astonishing speed.

The first map we still have with us of the great discovery was drawn by Juan de la Cosa, who sailed with Columbus in 1492-94. Almost at once, Columbus' enemies complained about how he was administering Hispaniola, so Ferdinand and Isabella dispatched a royal commission to survey the situation in 1497. Its leader was an able bureaucrat, one Amerigo Vespucci, an Italian. Vespucci made several mapping voyages while he was on the scene and on his return wrote them up with such precision that when Martin Waldseemüller cumulated everything that had been learned about the New World up to 1507, he thought it must have been discovered by Vespucci himself and named it "America" in his honor. (Waldseemüller detected his error quite promptly and tried to undo the mistake for the rest of his life; there is no evidence that Vespucci had anything to do with it before or after the fact.) When Vespucci got back to Spain he was put in charge of the royal chart office and given the task of adding each returning captain's reports to

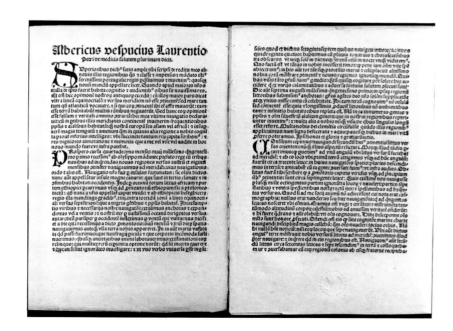

Amerigo Vespucci was sent to the New World in 1497 to investigate the complaints against Columbus' administration of the Caribbean colonies. While there, Vespucci made four voyages of exploration. His descriptive letters home were best sellers in Europe; this is a Latin edition printed in Strasbourg in 1504.

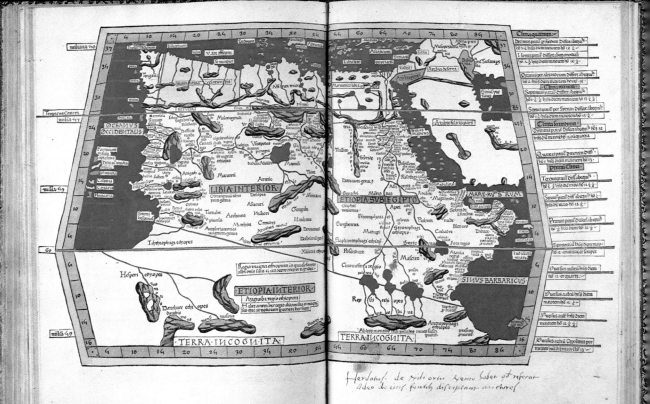

the official map. It was no mean feat. The passage to the New World was getting clogged with ships: in 1508 sixty-six galleons went out to the Caribbean; by 1520 over a hundred ships a year were going out and back.

The colonists in the Caribbean were mapping the islands. Balboa was landing more settlers in Central America from 1510 on; he himself thrashed through the underbrush in 1513 and came on to the Pacific Ocean. (He came on it from an east-west bluff in Darien and, since he saw it stretching in both directions at his feet, named it the South Sea; it was so carried until 1521 when Magellan's captain returned home and clarified everyone's thinking.)

In 1497, barely four years after Columbus returned, a Venetian spice merchant named Giovanni Caboto thought he would go around the new lands via a northwest passage, but he could raise no support in Italy, Spain, or Portugal so he changed his name to John Cabot and went to England. One would have thought his accent might have drawn attention, but Henry VII declared him an Englishman and backed him for an expedition straight west out of Britain. Cabot sailed for fifty-two days and hit Cape Breton Island, where he saw schools of cod so great that they "sumtymes stayed his shippes."

Our third treasure is Battista Agnese's atlas of 1544. Note how much has been learned in the fifty years since Columbus came ashore in the Bahamas. The Caribbean is mapped in reasonable detail and the eastern coasts of North and South America are recognizable north and south but badly distorted east and west (the longitude problem again). There is a strange island off the Carolinas which perpetuates an error of Giovanni da Verrazano. Verrazano had seen the sandspit at Hatteras in 1524 and, looking into Pamlico Sound, reported an island or an isthmus like Panama. The resultant landmass appeared on maps for half a century. Agnese's atlas shows that the narrow spine of Central America is understood and lower California is properly in place, but the great news is the two lines Agnese has drawn on his world map: the dotted line from Spain to Panama, across and down to Peru for the gold of the Incas; and the world-encircling route of Ferdinand Magellan.

The dotted line was the route of the treasure ships, and the galleons went out and came back heavily laden (and heavily armed). Their presence drew the English privateers and pirates in general, and the dots became a battle line for two hundred

years. As late as the reign of King George II, England was seizing galleons. In 1744 the British captured so much silver in that one year that they completely re-monetized their currency, calling in all coins in circulation and reissuing new coins struck from the "Lima treasure."

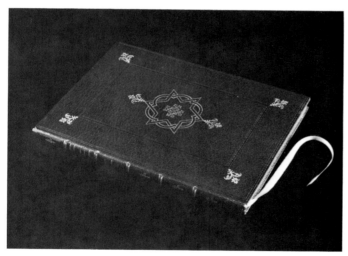

Above: *Martin Waldseemüller's* Introduction to Cosmography *was issued in 1507 and through a misunderstanding he credited the discovery of the New World to Amerigo Vespucci. Out of respect he therefore named the continent "America" and the first time the word ever appeared in print is seen on the left page above.*

Opposite: Cosmographia, *Claudius Ptolemy's atlas, 1482 edition with handcolored woodblocks. This was the basic atlas in use at the time that Columbus was considering the feasibility of going to China by sailing west. Note* (opposite above) *that the Indian Ocean was perceived as a closed sea like the Mediterranean. Below, the Portuguese had started down the two coasts of Africa, but the possibility of sailing from one side to the other was not believed likely. (The figures on the right side show the number of sun hours on the longest day of the year at that latitude.)*

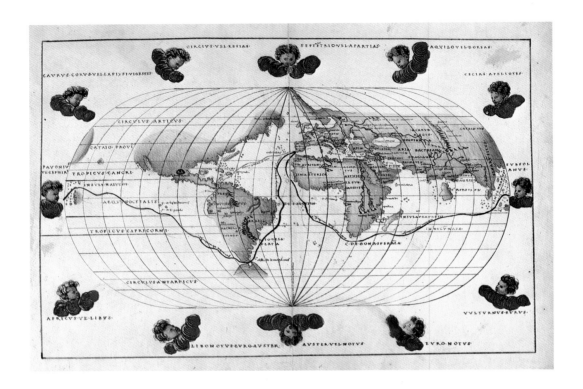

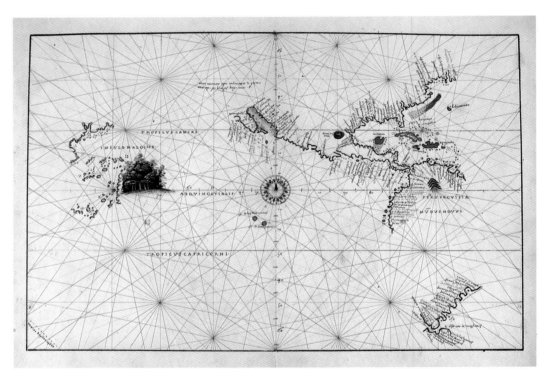

Battista Agnese's Portolan Atlas, Venice, 1544. Hand-drawn and painted on vellum, the ten double-page maps were prepared for the Abbot of St. Vaast at Arras. The one at top shows the route taken by Magellan in circumnavigating the globe, 1519-21, and the still limited knowledge of the New World. The lower map is a good example of the way news of exploration was brought back to Europe and shows little edges of land, fairly accurately determined north and south, but essentially "estimated" east and west.

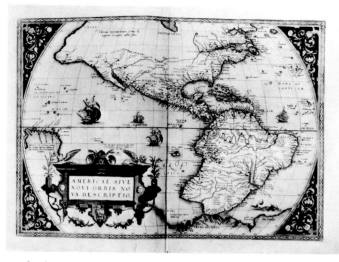

Abraham Ortelius' Theatrum orbis terrarum, *1571, was the first atlas in the modern sense. It had seventy different maps and became a best seller, going through forty editions in two generations. By 1571 the Caribbean was well mapped, and the eastern seaboards were improving.*

The solid line represents the awesome voyage of Magellan, in many respects as astonishing as Columbus' own. Recall that once he and his crew had left the hump of Brazil they were sailing into the unknown. Magellan went south and south and the weather grew colder and colder. When he was finally in an area of continual storms, ice, and snow he found an indentation in the coast and pushed in. He struggled for thirty-eight days in unrelenting gales and finally came out the other side into such a calm, flat, peaceful body of water he named it the Pacific—and then fell victim to the small earth error left over from Posidonius in 50 B.C. Magellan took his readings and calculated he was so close to Japan that he could slant off in the proper angle and reach food and land in a week or two. In fact he sailed for ninety-eight days before he sighted anything but salt water, his crew ultimately living on sawdust, leather, and rats—but with his arrival in the Philippines, Europeans had finally circled the globe and come on a place where they had been before. The size of the earth was immediately corrected to where it had been in Eratosthenes' time.

The lines on the charts now take on precision and detail. The huge map of Diego Gutiérrez (1562) is a wide step beyond Agnese and has South America correct. It is the first map to use the name "California" (the Library's is one of only two known copies). Ortelius' best-selling atlas of 1570 has the

Diego Gutierrez' map of 1562 (one of two known copies) was the first to use the word "California." Its great detail with few facts recalls Swift:

> *So Geographers in* Afric-*maps*
> *With Savage-Pictures fill their Gaps;*
> *And o'er unhabitable Downs*
> *Place Elephants for want of Towns.*

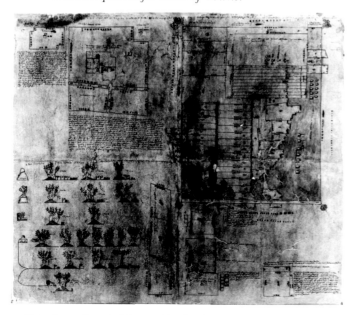

Oztoticpac Lands Map, c. 1540. The manuscript shows the property of the nobility of Texcoco, Mexico, and was prepared for a lawsuit to recover the land of Don Carlos Chichimecatecotl, whose property had been seized on his conviction for "heretical dogmatizing." Lower left on map is an inventory of his orchards also showing how he had grafted Spanish trees on to native roots. The drawings identify pear, quince, apple, and peach trees.

Caribbean as accurately as we know it today, but the New England coast is clumsy and the California coast only a raw guess. By 1600 Gabriel Tatton has absorbed more information, but California is in little better shape and is about to suffer one of the biggest mistakes in map-making.

In 1533 Hernando Cortes had sent a fleet out from Mexico to see what was up north and discovered California. In 1540 he had gone up the Gulf of California and identified the lower reaches of the Colorado. In June and July of 1579, Sir Francis Drake sailed up the entire coast of California, cleaned his ships north of San Francisco Bay, and headed west to reach England in 1580. Everyone knew where California was and what it looked like—but suddenly in 1625 an English map labels it "sometymes supposed to be a part of ye western continent, but scince by a Spanish charte…it is found to be a goodly Islande." Then all the maps and atlases shifted to carry it as a huge island right

through the seventeenth century. The beautifully drawn Dutch map of 1639 seems to show everything but the San Diego Zoo—quite wrongly.

How could this happen? Because so few of the people who drew the maps had actually been there, and so many of the lines for so long were based on a single report or the reading of a single crew. In many respects even in "modern" times the maps were like the medieval manuscripts: once an error was in place, it was passed along dutifully and unchallenged while other explorers searched for different unknowns. So we turn to the individuals who cleaned up the mistakes by going out to see for themselves. In the Library of Congress' collections, the highly personalized maps of Samuel de Champlain and Captain John Smith are splendid examples of on-site corrections.

The Champlain map is the absolute real thing; it is *it*—the actual piece of vellum on which Champlain drew as he worked his way south from

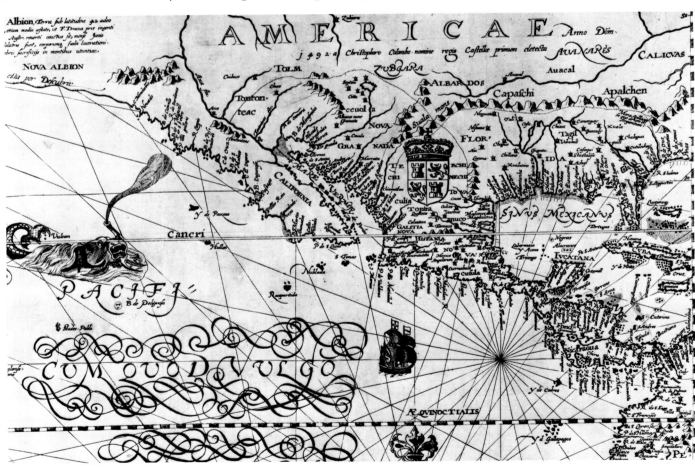

Gabriel Tatton's map of the Pacific Ocean, 1600. This is a detail from the portion showing the central Spanish colonies. Although Tatton was an Englishman working in London and Amsterdam, he had collected enough data about the Spanish possessions that, when it was all assembled on a single map, he got a fairly accurate picture of the coastlines.

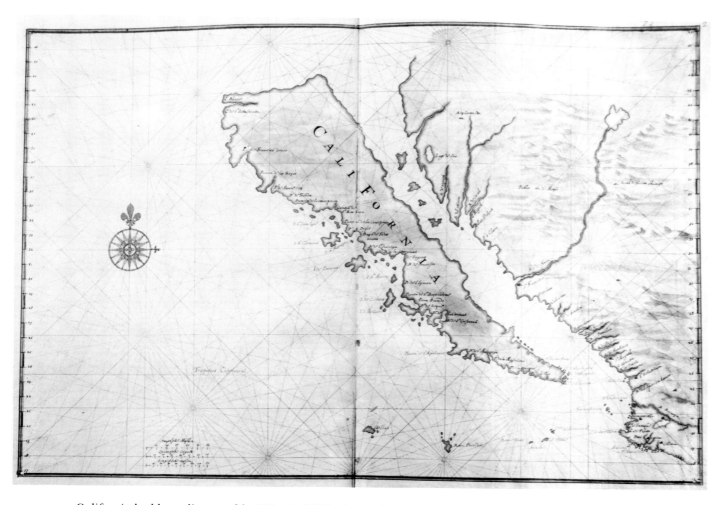

California had been discovered by Ulloa in 1539, Coronado had explored the Colorado River and the Gulf of California in 1540-42, Drake spent June and July 1579 on the beach north of San Francisco—the explorers knew California well until 1600 when the word circulated among French, British, and Dutch mapmakers that it really was an island. Thereafter it is shown as such on new maps right up to the 1700s. This is Joan Vingboons' watercolor map of 1639.

Lahave, Nova Scotia, to Martha's Vineyard in the winter of 1606–7. The shorelines he drew are those he could see from the rail of a fairly large ship taken from his home port of Port Royal. The extent of the river mouths that he drew was determined by the depth of the water available to support the ship's broad bottom. He drew what he saw and left it there; no guessing of what must be up the river or over the mountain.

Shoals are marked in the same way as in the fourteenth-century portolano: tiny dots. The anchors are where Champlain himself anchored (sometimes quite dangerously), and the clusters of buildings represent native settlements he could see from his ship. The one exception is Port Royal, which has a turreted structure to identify a European village. The dotted line coming out of Port Royal shows the

best route to take to avoid the many clam flats and buried rocks along the shore (and the route he recommends for ships to and from France).

This is the first reasonably accurate map drawn of the New England coast, and those who know Massachusetts and Maine will recognize po aux coquilles (Campobello Island), Quenibegui (the Kennebec River), cap aux Isles (Cape Ann), baye des Isles (Massachusetts Bay), po St louis (Plymouth Harbor), and la douteuse Isle (Martha's Vineyard).

Champlain was getting closer—much closer than his predecessors—but there is still trouble. He set his prime meridian on his home port, Port Royal, but it is 9° too far east and the resultant error is unfortunate. Because of this (and because the details of this very map were incorporated in the French maps when Champlain returned home),

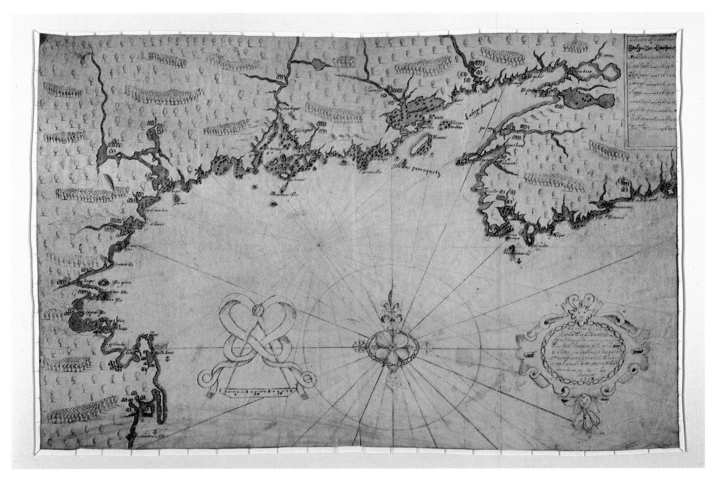

Samuel de Champlain's vellum manuscript map of Northeastern America. Drawn in the winter of 1606-7, it shows his personal surveys of shoals and anchorages. His location of the Indian villages have been proved archeologically accurate.

Opposite: The huge map at the top was engraved by Vincenzo Coronelli in 1688 and was designed to be pasted on a ball to become a cartographic globe. (California is still shown as an island.) The modern globe in the foreground was one of four made at Franklin D. Roosevelt's instruction. He gave copies to Winston Churchill and to the heads of the U.S. House and Senate so he could talk to any of them by phone or radio and know that everyone was working from a single frame of geographic reference. It stands over four feet high.

the entire Atlantic coast was drawn too close to the St. Lawrence for many more years.

Captain John Smith came even closer on his try—in exactly the same year, 1607. Smith was an exuberant twenty-seven-year-old traveler who accompanied the three small ships landing in Jamestown, Virginia, May 14 of that year. Smith had so irritated his shipmates on the passage over that he was excluded from the governing body at the outset, but his good sense and vigorous leadership raised him to Council President in 1608 and 1609 (when he returned to England).

The group practically landed running. They had been sent out by the London Company as a cold-blooded commercial venture and one of their major requirements was to look for a water passage to the Orient. Everyone was still hoping that the North American shoreline would be like the Central American, where a short trip over the mountains put you on the Pacific, from which you could either go to China or Spanish gold depending on your taste. The Jamestown settlers were directed: "You must observe if you can whether the river on which you plant doth spring out of mountains or out of lakes. If it be out of any lake, the passage to the other sea will be more easy." One week after the ships tied up to the shore the commander took off with twenty-four men and worked his way to the head of the James River (the site of present-day Richmond). When they got back, Smith took a boat

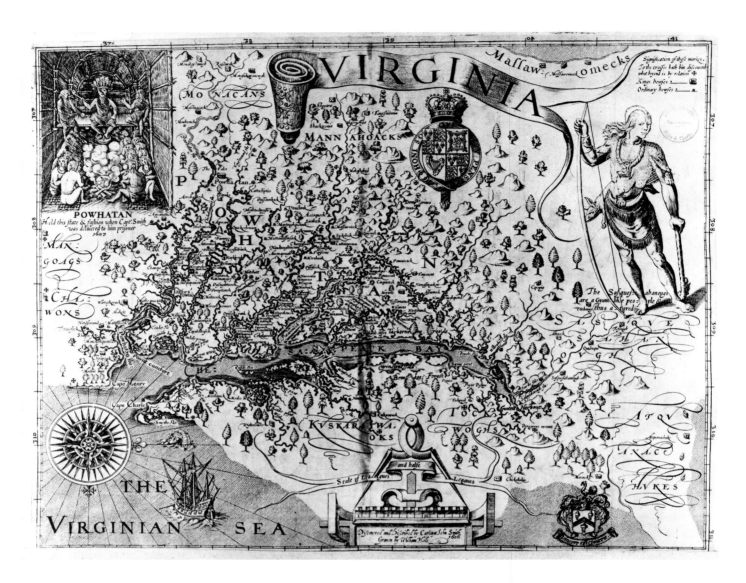

Captain John Smith was twenty-eight years old when he took a barge and twelve men and rowed 3,000 miles to the head of Chesapeake Bay and the fall lines of the Potomac, the Rappahannock, and the Susquehanna. This is an engraving of his hand-drawn map of 1608, published 1612.

and went up the heads of all the neighboring creeks and streams looking for food for the hungry colonists.

The next spring Captain Smith set out to do it right, and with a large barge and twelve men to row it explored the Potomac and Chesapeake Bay in detail. He went up the "Toppahanock" (we call it the Rappahannock) to the present site of Fredericksburg, and up the Chesapeake to the mouth of Sasqusahanough (the Susquehanna). He was away from Jamestown for three months and traveled over three thousand miles by pulled oar.

What he got for his time and effort is revealed in his map (taken back to England and ultimately printed in 1612). It is an astonishing product in view of Smith's amateur status as a mapmaker. He took a reading at Cape Henry and set its latitude at 36°56′. Our present-day satellites call it 37°02′— only a tenth of a degree difference. The longitude which was so difficult and which Champlain missed by nine full degrees, Smith managed to get within one eighth of a single degree as read by our electronic devices. His readings throughout his map are equally accurate. To get the feel of the map today, it must be rotated so north is at the top, and then the present configuration of Norfolk, Williamsburg, the Bay Country leaps out at you.

His smallest "squiggles" prove to be precisely accurate representations of bays, bars, and creek mouths. He put small crosses up each stream to show how far he actually went himself, but then questioned the nearest Indians about what lay beyond. He includes this too, having shown where his own observations stop and hearsay begins. It is astonishing to find that the names we know for the area are already in place within a year of the first settlers: Appamatuck (Appomattox of Civil War memory), Poynte Comfort (Old Point Comfort), and Cape Charles.

There are over two hundred names on the chart: the thought of Smith working his way from smoky wigwam to brush hut making notes of where he was told he was is stirring. Simply converting the spoken name to English orthography must have been as much a challenge as finding the daily latitude. He reports the following tribes and villages: Acquintanacsuck, Muttanmussinsack, Martoughquaimk, Vitamussamacoma, Namoraughquend, Anrcuapeugh, Nandtanghtacund, and a hundred and fifty more.

In short, the first try at Chesapeake Bay country gave us a map more detailed than many parts of the Atlantic seaboard received for a century and a half.

Smith's map was incorporated in all of the major European atlases (Blaeu, Mercator, Jansson) and influenced maps of America up to the War of 1812.

And with John Smith's map we leave the drawings of "the greate unknown outte there." From this point on, the maps become a record of individual colonies in general and specific landholdings in particular. In Chapter IX we will find Augustine Herrman's map *Virginia and Maryland As It Is Planted and Inhabited This Present Year 1670*, Joan Vingboons' *Manatus* (Manhattan Island), 1639, and Spanish manuscript maps of California and the Rio Grande.

The astonishing thing about map-making is that it seems never to be finished. Indeed it seems never to slow down; the same surfaces either change or can be recorded with perpetually greater precision. In the last decade, the Library has received four million new sheet maps of the surface of the Earth —approximately 50,000 a year without even noting the new charts of astronomical bodies that are being produced from the space exploration data coming in. If "of making many books there is no end," consider maps. The unbroken stream of maps from Ptolemy to NASA increases endlessly and (of course) geometrically.

CHAPTER V

A Fine Line

Here's another anomaly. Fine prints in a library. Not just some, but well over 100,000 from the rarest Rembrandts to the most extensive collection of marginalia of any major institution in the world. The Library's collection of the great masters is splendid; its collection of modern printmakers in some areas is without peer anywhere. How did this happen? What are these prints? How are they kept and how are they used?

When I first discovered this major area of the Library's holdings, the above questions were my own. Having one of the world's great collections of fine prints and drawings seemed like a major distraction of purpose. Prints should be found in art museums, not libraries. I made the mistake of expressing this thought aloud and the appropriate curators clarified my thinking with vigor. Their case:

● Art museums are really rather recent inventions. The great names—New York's Metropolitan, the fine art museums of Boston, Philadelphia, even the Louvre—didn't really take on substance until the late 1800s. Picture collections, "print cabinets," were in the great European *libraries* all the way back to the 1600s. The national libraries of Austria, Spain, Scandinavia all had complete departments, or "halls," of fine prints from the days of Louis XIV.

● Until Napoleon's time, fine prints were stored (indeed drawn with the intent to be seen) in large albums...books. For the first three hundred years of printmaking people pictured them in books and books in libraries, so our predecessors would not have understood our confusion. (Also, the artists assumed that their prints would be looked at in volumes and therefore created them with the expectation that the viewer would be at arm's length; no farther.)

● It was fine prints that created copyright laws as we know them. The first general copyright law was passed by the British Parliament in 1735 on petition of the artist William Hogarth and his friends to protect their engravings from plagiarism. Thereafter, all the famous series of Hogarth prints, like "The Rake's Progress," bear the line "Published according to Act of Parliament." The point is that wherever copyright holdings were collected (as in the British Museum), there the nation's most complete print collection accumulated. Equally with the Library of Congress. It automatically absorbed the most complete evidence of American taste and artistic skill simply by receiving the copyright deposits.

● Having the accumulated holdings, the Main Building was designed with galleries to display the prints nearly half a century before the National Gallery of Art was even conceived, and thus has established a tradition of showing, loaning, purchasing, and publicizing American printmakers for nearly a hundred years.

● Such a tradition attracted private collections as legacies, gifts. Leading print collectors (some of whom actually started their collections after having seen prints for the first time in the Library's halls) bestowed their own holdings on the Library, knowing that there was a tradition of attention and display here and that their own collections would be appreciated and used. The ultimate result was that a rich collection got richer.

● Acquiring holdings by automatic deposit and gift

gives a much broader, more realistic, more democratic collection than the usual art museum approach. An art museum must seek out the finest example, usually the peak expression of a technique or a style. The copyright/gift approach accumulates the whole spectrum; trends and changes in taste and technique are absorbed along the way to give a truer picture of a nation's work than the delicate choice of gems as perceived by individual museum procurement officers.

And that's their case; but let's move on to just what the collection is and how it is kept and used. Most of us have had the different printing techniques explained at some point (the difference between an etching, an engraving, and a lithograph), but the information tends to blur a bit with time. A short explanation might be useful to get the feel of what the gems really are.

The invention of printmaking ties very closely to the invention of printing. Indeed, it is possible that the search for fast, duplicable pictures may have been the source of the idea of the printing process in the first place. The earliest woodblock we know of is the Brussels Madonna, dated 1418. Gutenberg didn't get his technique developed until 1450. (The Chinese and Japanese were using woodblocks five hundred years earlier, but there is no evidence that the West ever saw one of them.)

A woodblock, of course, looks and works like our present-day rubber stamps where the printing face stands up from the block, carries ink, and is pressed against the paper. In the earliest fifteenth-century versions the artist's line was drawn on a piece of pear or apple board—literally the face of a wooden plank—and the white part of the picture was cut away, leaving a thin ridge where the lines were wanted. Ink was smeared on the ridges with a leather ball or pad, paper was laid on *top* of the wood and was either pressed down with the palm of the hand or with the back of a kitchen spoon rubbed around on the block. The paper was then lifted off, and you had a crisp black-and-white picture, cheaply, and of reasonably uniform quality. The idea worked very well right from the start: even after they invented the press to get a hard, even pressure down on the block, the thin wooden ridges could print as many as eight to ten thousand impressions before the lines would splinter or mash down. Indeed the original woodblocks worked so effectively in the early days of printing that when they were incorporated in a text as book illustrations, the printers would run off their usual two or three hundred copies of the typical edition of the time, and then they would pull the cuts out and send them off to the next town, where they would be used in the books those local printers were printing. The early pictures thus keep turning up all over Central Europe, deceptively identical, leaving us with the same pictures but with different type in different books.

The early woodblocks became very sophisticated very quickly. The idea, of course, was to make the picture look as much like the original ink drawing as possible. The artist would have drawn with a quill pen, so the two sides of the ridge would be cut in as closely as possible to leave the standing ridge as narrow as the ink line. Who were the first printmakers? In the smaller towns almost invariably the local armorer; in the larger cities they were the goldsmiths. Both of these types of craftsmen were used to cutting lines in metal, so cutting wood was not only logical but actually easier than their usual trade.

Interestingly, at the outset the commonest use of the woodblock was to print playing cards. This was a major business, but it quickly moved into cards sold to pilgrims at shrines, then larger religious scenes, and ultimately illustrations in books. The first innovation was color—first painted on by hand and then printed from multiple blocks of different tones or colors to duplicate the more dramatic paintings of the time. These original tints are almost unbelievably brilliant today. When you open a medieval block book or atlas, the color is so intense it is hard to believe it is even dry, much less five hundred years old.

The woodblock as a medium for pictures lasted for about a hundred years and reached its peak at the beginning of the 1500s. Its limitation was the grain of the wood. The line could never be carved as finely as the artists wanted, and it tended to produce a picture with harsh outlines rather than soft shadings. They solved the problem with the *engraving*.

In a woodcut the line to be printed stands up and you put ink on it. In engraving it is cut down into the surface of the plate and ink is pressed into the crack. The plate is wiped clean of ink on the surface, but the ink stays in the base of the crevice, where it is held clean, thin, and sharp-edged. Paper is then laid on the plate and a very strong press mashes the paper into the cracks, where it soaks up the ink. The result is a thinner line drawn with greater control.

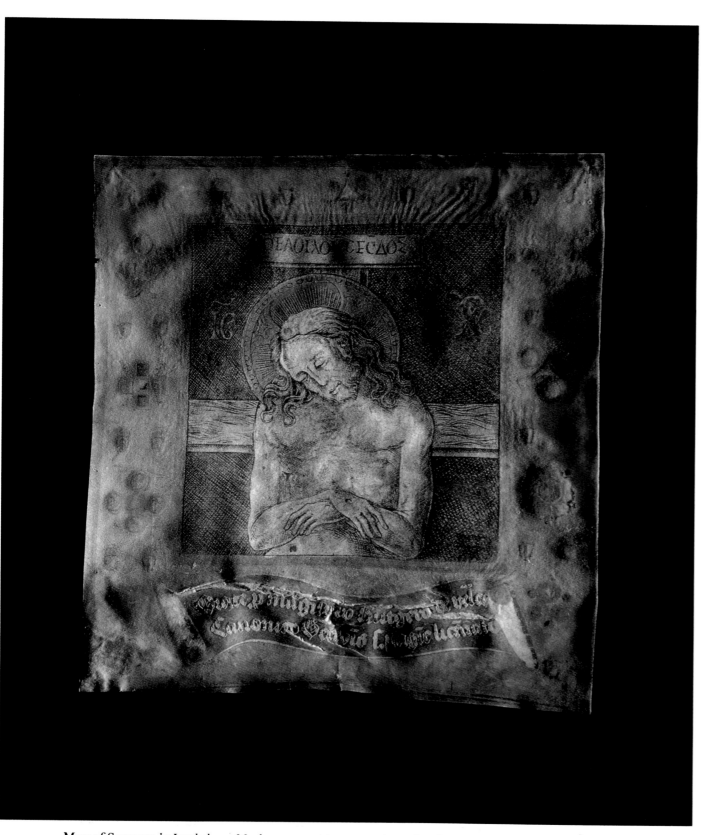

Man of Sorrows *by Israhel van Meckenem, a copper engraving printed on parchment, c. 1495. Hand-tinted, the composition is a traditional one frequently seen in illuminated manuscripts of the thirteenth and fourteenth centuries.*

Above: **River Gods** *by Domenico Beccafumi, a six-teenth-century chiaroscuro woodcut. This technique was the Renaissance equivalent of our museum reproductions. The colored tones were built up by separate printings from multiple blocks.*

Right: St. Catherine on the Wheel, *woodblock by Albrecht Dürer. St. Catherine was an early Christian martyr tortured on a spiked wheel by Emperor Maxentius for defending her faith at a pagan feast.*

Apocalypsis Sancti Johannis *or "Revelation of St. John" is one of the great monuments of block-book printing. Essentially picture books with lessons, block books were so heavily used by their owners that they rarely survive in such splendid condition. The colors were applied by hand, not printed.*

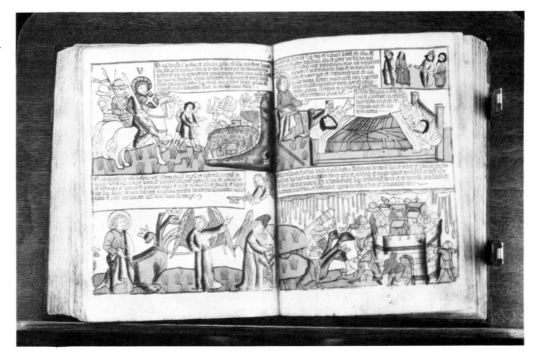

September *by Elias Holl the Younger, 1638. One of twelve etchings from a calendar, each showing a typical activity of the month.*

The product was excellent, but making engravings was hard work. Wood was out of the question for the printing field—the grain interfered with the lines and it splintered, so the plate had to be some kind of metal. The early printmakers used steel, iron, and copper, and although the latter were relatively softer, the steel cutting instrument still had to be pushed into the metal, creating a furrow which would hold the ink. Obviously the deeper you cut, the wider the furrow and the bolder the line. But it was slow, tiring work, so the next innovation was a faster, easier shortcut which ultimately had benefits beyond the labor-saving purpose at the first. The advance was the *etching*.

The artists still wanted a line in the metal but they didn't want to work so hard. They got their line by coating the plate with black asphalt and then drawing with a steel needle. They sketched directly into the asphalt and now they could see how their picture was developing as they worked—and the smooth, waxy surface gave them a graceful, fluid line with very little effort. Once the drawing was complete they would lower the whole plate into a weak acid bath and let the acid "bite" the lines down into the plate. The artist controlled the depth and width of the line by how long he let the acid eat the metal. Delicate edges of clouds could be put in and taken out at once, the acid washed off and that part of the picture painted over with varnish so it was shielded from further acid. The plate was then put back into the pot and the biting began again, cut and cover, in and out, until the picture went from light to dark and the blackest lines were eaten deep and wide. The plate was finally scrubbed clean; ink was smeared across with a "dabber" and the plate was wiped clean with a cloth; paper was laid on and pressed down to the ink in the bottom of the lines and again you had a picture, this time much softer, much more delicate and controlled than you could get with a woodblock. Even the ink had improved. Woodblocks had been printed with lampblack mixed in linseed oil. By the time they invented etching, they had learned to mix burnt umber in with the lampblack and they got a velvety brown/black tone that was much more pleasant than the harsh black on white of the woodblock and lasted just as well. You could get five hundred excellent prints from a copper etching, and another five hundred of usable quality.

It is odd how small, incremental progress seems to come from the day-to-day practitioners of a skill, but the quantum jumps—the major breakthroughs—seem to come from single innovative minds. The towering practitioner of the skills we've been talking about here—the man who took the innovations so far ahead it was nearly a hundred years before anything more really new was developed—was the German, Albrecht Dürer. As an artist, he had an endless curiosity and an incredible eye for detail. Erasmus said that no artist using colors could express himself as well as Dürer did using only black lines "even if it were a question of representing fire, storm, light or the soul of man himself." Martin Luther knew him and called him an enlightened, God-fearing man, "the best." The great humanist Willibald Pirkheimer was a friend for thirty years, and on Dürer's death in 1528 was as devastated as if he had lost a member of his own family: "I have lost in Albrecht my best friend, and nothing grieves me more than his death, which, by God's will, can have been directly caused by none other than his wife, who tormented him so that his death was hastened. Day and night she urged him to work so that he might earn money which she would inherit on his death. She behaved and still behaves as if she were near bankruptcy, and yet

Albrecht has left her a fortune of about six thousand florins." For whatever reason, Dürer was breathtakingly prolific, completing several thousand prints that we know of, and perhaps many more that are now lost.

Like all true innovators he created styles and modes that were so frequently copied they became models for generations of successors: he drew animals and plants with microscopic detail; he drew fantasies of destruction and creation that anticipated William Blake and Paul Gustave Doré by centuries; he designed religious iconography in the most chaste and traditional manner and then restated the same themes in warm, sensitive, loving images. Rembrandt credited him with "everything he knew."

Indeed Rembrandt represents the next development in printmaking. He followed Dürer by a hundred years and is the towering figure in printmaking that Beethoven is in music. Dürer drew everything he saw with great precision, capturing reality; Rembrandt was primarily interested in mood, emotions. His prints play with shadows, beams of sunlight opening gloomy landscapes, chiaroscuro portraits with barely suggested edges. And ironically, his favorite medium was the etching, the technique which had been praised for its precision and cleanness of line.

Among the cognoscenti of printmaking, Rembrandt's *Three Crosses* is considered the finest plate ever drawn—a unanimity of taste that is unusual in such a volatile field. So many artists have risen and fallen from favor (Vermeer went from the master status to having his work hang in taverns in the nineteenth century and Dürer, who was worshipped from the 1500s through the 1700s, fell to being a historical oddity in Victorian times), but Rembrandt's reputation has never wavered. Enormously respected in his own day, there has never been a time in history when he was not considered

Two engravings by Albrecht Dürer. Above: The Coat of Arms of Death. Left: The Nativity.

Above: The Three Crosses *by Rembrandt van Rijn, etching and drypoint, c. 1660, possibly the most famous print ever made. Rembrandt reworked it through some six years, changing it, in four successive states, from a sunlit scene to a darker, brooding, dramatic tour de force of the etching technique. This one is from the fourth state.*

Opposite: Madonna *by Albrecht Dürer. An engraving restating the Mother and Child theme in a natural setting.*

among the chosen few at the top of the artistic universe. In printmaking, every successive generation has considered him the master practitioner of the art.

The etching, as the favorite print form, ruled the world of printmaking with minor modifications up to Napoleonic times. Around 1750, a Frenchman, Jean Baptiste Le Prince, was looking for a way to produce the effects of wash drawings or watercolors and came up with what is called the *aquatint*; it proved to be an ingenious solution. Here the usual metal plate is "salted" or "sanded" with granules of resin. The plate is then heated and the resin melts into little pools or pellets that become acid-resisting dots. The plate is then "bitten" in stages, eating around the dots deeper and deeper to hold

The Head of Christ *by Anthony Van Dyck. A drawing in black and red chalk, heightened with white.*

The Library's collection of prints reflects its interest in the development of its artists, their sketchbooks, trial runs, and incremental plates, as well as the final prints. Above: *A sketchbook of Thomas Stothard, c. 1790.*

an increasing amount of ink. White areas are quickly varnished over, blacks are repeatedly etched. The result is tones, washes of ink, rather than lines (although lines are frequently cut into the metal with a ruby or sapphire tool, giving a drypoint line). The end product is a delicate surface that will produce only two to three hundred prints but with subtle gradations of tone.

A variation on the resin technique was the *mezzotint*, which was invented to give the rich tones needed to reproduce colored oil paints in black and white. Here, instead of etching the holes to hold the ink, a rocker or roulette is run back and forth over the surface of the plate in the same way a roller is used to pound or soften a tough piece of steak. The rocker leaves thousands of pits which hold ink (and print pure black when the paper is pressed into them). Here the artist takes a scraper and smooths out the scarred surface, flattening and wiping out the pits to make the area lighter and lighter. The printmaker is working in tones from dark to light in this case, and ends up with an approximation of paintings. A mezzotint can produce up to three hundred prints of which the first one hundred fifty are good.

There are only two more innovations to be noted in the world of printmaking, but both have a huge field to themselves. The first is the *lithograph*. As unlikely as it seems, this is actually drawing on stone and, for the first hundred years, a special kind of limestone at that—blocks found only in Solenhofen, Germany.

The lithograph has the advantage that the artist is able to sketch, draw, shade, and create directly onto the printing surface using a simple crayon or soft pencil, thus avoiding the self-conscious unfamiliarity of cutting or carving or eating the lines away in acids.

Lithography is based on the simple fact that oily ink will not stick to wet stone. With this fundamental antipathy, the artist draws his picture with a greasy crayon and when his picture is complete he soaks the stone in water. He then rolls the ink across the face and the ink sticks to the points of crayon and ignores the rest. Paper is laid on, a press smooths it onto the surface, and you get a picture that is closer to free-hand drawing than any other form.

The granular surface of the lithograph is particularly useful for color work, and after Newton pointed out that it only took three colors to make any combination in the spectrum, the colored litho-

The Banjo Lesson *by Mary Cassatt, 1894. A drypoint and aquatint by the leading American participant in the Impressionist movement. Cassatt lived and worked in France, closely associated with Degas. Her brother was president of the Pennsylvania Railroad.*

graph became the commonest device for both "fine printing" and commercial reproduction. You can make eight hundred to one thousand good lithographs from a single drawing on a stone. We have Currier and Ives prints where over seventy thousand sheets were lifted off a single drawing.

Color leads us to the final area of printmaking, the silk screen or serigraph, which was developed in the United States as recently as the 1930s. It began as a way of making posters and placards but it has become both elaborate and flexible. It is the easiest of all forms of printmaking and something that can be done at home without complicated presses and machinery.

The general principle is that of the stencil, which originally was a cut-out design (paper or metal) laid over the paper with the color brushed where the hole had been cut. The innovators here substituted a sheet of plain silk or nylon mounted across a frame like a drumhead, and painted the whole cloth with glue. Then instead of cutting the "hole"

119

Cotton Mather, *by Peter Pelham, the first mezzotint made in America (1727). Mather was a leading Boston Puritan, an early advocate of inoculation for smallpox, and a figure in the Salem witchcraft trials.*

with scissors where the ink was to come through, they melted the glue with kerosene, leaving a permeable space in the cloth. The paper was laid on the table, the cloth (screen) was set on the paper, ink was poured on the screen, swiped with a squeegee to squirt it through, and the screen was then lifted off, revealing the printed paper If done in black ink on white paper the result was a startling, stenciled picture. If done in series with various inks, colors, tones, the picture could be subtly built up in dozens of layers to create a unique form of print.

The above processes (with many variations, of course) add up to the universe of "fine prints." Their fascination, to the practitioners, seems to be a thousand-fold but closely tied to the element of the happy accident, the "gift," the variable. In every technique there is an endless series of unknowns mainly stemming from the lack of real control the artist has over his medium. The woodblock carver (the "formschneider," splendid word) can't really tell what the wood grain will do to his picture. The

engraver can't really know how the ink will fill the lines. The etcher even more can't know what the acid is doing to his design. The lithographer is smearing greasy stuff on a stone, but he can't tell how much of the grease is sticking, how the ink will take to it, what the effect of the press will be. Repeatedly there is the matter of the happy accident.

Similarly, of course, there are as many variables in the way the print will come up on successive inkings, wipings, and pressings. One of the variations on the engraving process is something called a drypoint, where a soft metal is used and the furrow actually rises up and makes ruffled ridges on each side of the line. The first print from this is velvety and rich and the furrows hold ink actually above the face of the plate, but each successive pressing mashes down these ridges and sharpens up the picture as the edges of the lines smooth out.

The amateur collector should know that the successive changes of a plate have great impact on the price one pays for an "original" print. Only since the first of this century have prints been numbered ("8/30"—the eighth print out of a run of thirty), but there is no validity in the thought that the lower the number the better the print. The artist can become increasingly skilled in wiping and toning as he gets familiar with printing a plate, the lines can soften more attractively (and frequently the numbers are written on after a stack of prints has been assembled with the highest on the top of the pile, the last run being given the "1" of the series!).

The series—the normal "run"—incidentally, seems to get smaller and smaller each successive year. This appears to be one of the great ironies in printmaking. Originally a "fine print" was the most democratic of all forms of art. It was not the great painting for the head of state, but a picture that every citizen who had a few pennies could hang on his wall. The student and the wage earner could have the product of the greatest artists of their age for the price of a meal, and right up to the nineteenth century the great printmakers tried to get as many copies off a plate as they could. We now go to the other extreme. Rarely will a run of anything exceed fifty impressions, and runs of ten to fifteen are common. You can get a lively argument going at any exhibition between people who support the position that the limitation is to drive the price up by guaranteeing exclusivity (uniqueness?; my unique print is uniquer than yours) versus those who feel that printmakers simply become bored repeating the same one-at-a-time printing se-

Above, left: Approaches to Gatun Lock, *by Joseph Pennell, lithograph, 1912. Pennell was a popular print-maker who gave his complete collection of over 1,500 of his own works to the Library as well as a large endowment with which the Library has continued to buy new, current works.*

Above: Blast Furnaces, South Chicago, *by Joseph Pennell, lithograph, 1916. Pennell's wife said he reacted to the American industrial scene as traditional artists did to French cathedral towns.*

Left: Self-portrait *by Josef Albers, lithograph, 1916–18. An early drawing by the artist of the famous Homage to the Square.*

Opposite, left: The Letter *by Mary Cassatt, aquatint, 1894. This print shows the influence of the Japanese woodblock style, which had a major impact on the Impressionist movement.*

Opposite, right: *Joseph Pennell was a neighbor to James M. Whistler in London and when Whistler died Pennell inherited Whistler's artistic files. Among the materials were many Oriental prints of which this is a typical example. Subsequently, Pennell transferred all his Whistleriana to the Library.*

Left: The Engraver Joseph Tourney, *by Edgar Degas, etching, 1857. Degas was twenty-one when he made this print of the man who taught him etching. The two sketches of clerics' heads at the bottom of the picture were effaced when "serious" prints were later struck from the plate.*

Bottom: Self-portrait *by Chuck Close, etching, 1970. Four successive details of this work which measures 90 x 133 cm. overall.*

The Evening Wind *by Edward Hopper, etching, 1921.*

quence after a few dozen sheets and want to get on to the next creative challenge.

That is a few thousand words on what the one hundred thousand prints are all about. Question: What is different about the Library of Congress' collection, and how is it used?

Thanks to the copyright deposit the Library would have ended up with a staggering print collection if it had done nothing but open its mail (Ainsworth Spofford had counted 54,236 prints when he was preparing for the move to the new building, and they were increasing at the rate of over 11,000 a year). But two individuals made the Library's fine print collection into one of the world's finest cabinets. The first was the widow of Gardiner Greene Hubbard.

Gardiner Greene Hubbard was a pretty unlikely figure himself. In any book but this one, we would be exploring his roles as the first president of the National Geographic Society, the man who conceived the idea of renting telephones instead of selling them, and as the developer of the first interurban streetcar line.

Here, we're only interested in the fact that his hobby was collecting master prints. He had the time, taste, and money to do it right and he thus accumulated one of the nation's great private collections, including Dürers, Mantegnas, Callots, and Rembrandts in impressive numbers. He died in 1897, just as the new Library was opening, and his widow conceived the idea of memorializing him with a special gallery in the new building. The new Librarian agreed to her stipulation that it be run by a print specialist as superintendent, and he in turn repaid the gift by publishing a "Catalogue of the Gardiner Greene Hubbard Collection of Engravings" in 1905. The catalogue revealed nearly three thousand rarities from the first three centuries of the art. Mrs. Hubbard then put the Library in her own will and when she died in 1909 the Library acquired a substantial sum of money "to yield an annual income for the purchase of prints."-Thus by World War I the Library had quantity through the copyright deposit, high quality through the Hubbard collection, new European prints coming in steadily with the purchase money, and a gallery complete with overseer to stage fairly dramatic, changing exhibitions. The latter brought in the second gift.

In the first quarter of this century one of the leading American printmakers was Joseph Pennell. Dramatic and swaggering, Pennell was a dynamic

Icarus *by Leonard Baskin, color woodcut. 1960 s version of the Renaissance chiaroscuro print. The artist called this figure his archangel.*

figure and so were his pictures; they were strong works of blast furnaces, skyscraper construction, the building of the Panama Canal. His wife used to say that Pittsburgh and Gary affected Pennell like Rheims and the Sainte Chapelle did most artists. He was very popular. He produced some six hundred lithographs and over nine hundred etchings and mezzotints, and made an excellent living at it, well recognized in his own time. Up until World War I he lived in London as a neighbor to his great friend James M. Whistler, but with the war he returned to America to discover the Library's deep involvement in fine prints. He was particularly impressed with the program of loans and exhibitions the Library was sponsoring, and when he died in 1926 the Library was pleasantly astonished to find it had been given his entire personal collection (essentially two or more of everything he'd ever done)

Limoges by John Taylor Arms, etching, 1932. From Arms' series of French churches. The picture is a single plate, demonstrating the range of tone possible from deepening the successive acid cuts.

Two pages from a watercolor sketchbook of Joseph Pennell; these are part of a series of evening scenes painted on lower Manhattan Island: skyscrapers and the Brooklyn Bridge.

Left: Self-portrait *by James Abbott McNeill Whistler, 1880. A rare pen-and-ink drawing given to the Library as a part of the Gardiner Greene Hubbard Collection. Mrs. Hubbard, wife of the financial founder of the Bell Telephone System, gave nearly 3,000 early prints and drawings to augment the tens of thousands acquired through the copyright deposit.*

Below: Explosion *by Miroslav Sutej, 1967. A serigraph by this Yugoslavian artist who is known for his studies of "bulges in space." A typical example of current purchase from the Pennell Fund.*

Nocturne by James Abbott McNeill Whistler, 1880. This etching was a part of a series on Venice and employs the technique of retroussage, *which is wiping the ink off the plate with a rag, rather than engraving or cutting lines to make shadows. While it gives great flexibility, and creates a mood, it means that no two prints in the series are identical.*

plus a complete collection of Whistler papers, memorabilia, and hundreds of works by his French and English contemporaries. His wife, in turn, gave a substantial amount of money for acquisitions in 1936 that has subsequently been used to stage competitions, sponsor touring print shows, and buy contemporary prints to keep the collection current and comprehensive.

All this activity reinforced itself, strength drawing strength. The George Lothrop Bradley Collection was received in 1919, the Charles L. Freer Collection followed, the very fine collection of Oliver Wendell Holmes, Supreme Court justice, was acquired in 1953 (including a very professional etching drawn by his own hand). In addition there has been a continuing series of gifts and legacies from American printmakers themselves—almost

complete runs of the prints of George Bellows, John Sloan, Childe Hassam, and nearly eight hundred different plates from John Taylor Arms.

How do you keep one hundred thousand prints and how are they used? Each one is matted and gives the appearance of having just been removed from a frame. The mat board is of rag, acid-free stock (as is the back board), and the print is hinged behind the window with gummed linen tape, never the "sticky" kind. The prints are arranged by century and stored flat in Solander boxes (not in cradles as is usual in print shops). A user can request a whole boxful in the same way a book is called for.

Who uses them? Art editors selecting plates for books and magazines; museum curators putting shows together. At any time as much as twenty percent of the master collection is out on loan to mu-

The Gargoyle and His Quarry by *John Taylor Arms,
1920. One of a series of his etchings on the Notre Dame
Cathedral, Paris.*

The Sarah Jane by *John Taylor Arms, 1920. Another
example of different styles of this artist, who gave the
Library one or more copies of his entire lifetime's production of nearly 800 works.*

seums in the United States and abroad. Some of the
most intriguing applications are those pursued by
historians, costume and set designers, furniture
makers and architects. Look at the questions our
own selections will answer: How was a wheelbarrow
held together in 1640 before nails and screws were
available? What does a seventeenth-century
farmer's shoe look like? What was the sequence of
plates in fifteenth-century horse armor? Did the
Puritans tolerate wigs?

That's as much time and space as we dare spend
on the world of fine prints. We must now move on

to the next development in the capture of the visual
image.

The prints, of course, are works of imagination,
created with the artist's selective eye. Given a particular scene or concept, the image that is passed on
to us is controlled by which elements the artist de-
cides to share with us, which piece of his mental
picture he will lift out to trace and leave behind.

We now turn to the opposite extreme—the photographic eye, which sees everything and discards
nothing. We move to another form of memory
which produces its own form of treasures.

CHAPTER VI

Master Photographers

We are about to see a whole chapter of visual "first-times"—the first time these scenes were seen or these effects were tried or this image was captured just this way. Each of the pictures that follow comes directly from the original print or negative; they are not pictures of pictures of pictures. The Library of Congress' print is the one that was the beginning of the line, and the odds are high that you have seen the majority of them before.

They bear looking at again, however, because they are both the prototypes of photography as we know it and our reminder of the very real people who stand behind the prints. These are the minds who were the very first to perceive a Dust Bowl mother, early morning dew on a spider web, a high-fashion gown blown by seawind on a wet beach, in just this way. Since then we have all been copying their ideas.

These master photographers are the ones who set the genre, and the pictures represent but a thin sample of the 3,500 original images in the Library's Master Photographer Collection. But before we look at what these innovators really did, they deserve a moment from us to note what they thought they were trying to do. Their great creative leaps were essentially a mixture of technology and taste; skill seems to have had very little to do with it.

It all started in 1839 with the invention of a chemical to keep brown silver salts from fading. It was not the light-sensitive halides that were the breakthrough—the potter Thomas Wedgwood had solved that problem in 1802. It was not the inven-

tion of the camera itself that made the difference, either. The camera had been around literally for centuries. Did you realize that those near-photographic paintings of Venice by the Canaletto family were in fact done with a camera? All the cabinets-ful of tinted engravings of country houses in England and the geometric gardens and facade drawings of Versailles were laboriously drawn on a camera obscura that no good landscape artist would have been without. (Leonardo da Vinci, as always, explained how he used his to get his perspective right—with illustrations, as always.)

A camera obscura is based on a phenomenon we read about in medieval writings: if you can find a closet opposite a window, go inside and shut the door, punch a pinhole in the door and, quite like magic, a picture of the scene outside the window will appear on the opposite wall of the closet (upside down and in color at that!). The phenomenon was absolutely inexplicable at the time but the effect was good for much diversion on clear days and once lenses got to be common in the 1600s, people found first that they could make the picture much larger on the wall and then, ultimately, that the whole phenomenon could be duplicated in a box—the camera obscura. The Canalettos simply projected a scene directly onto a canvas and drew the pictures in place; the landscape artists slanted a mirror inside the box and projected the scene onto a piece of tissue paper lying on the glass top. (Vermeer found if he aimed his through a doorway, he could get a whole interior wall in the frame.) By

This is the earliest known photographic image of the Capitol—a daguerreotype attributed to John Plumbe, Jr., showing the Charles Bulfinch dome as it looked in 1846. The plate was discovered in an old trunk in San Francisco in 1972.

Opposite: *One of the earliest known pictures of Abraham Lincoln and his bride of four years, Mary Todd Lincoln. These daguerreotypes were taken by N.H. Shepherd in Springfield, Illinois, 1846, and are preserved in their original case, typical of the velvet lined boxes in which the delicate daguerreotypes were preserved.*

Victorian times, no upper-class household was without one, and it was the fast way for daughter to copy a rose which she then painted on the family china. In short, in 1839 the camera was in no way new.

Keeping the image it saw was. Louis Daguerre made the breakthrough. Daguerre was a stage designer in Paris who had made a name for himself with his scenic effects. He used magic lanterns to project fires and storms on translucent screens so that his whole stage seemed to be surrounded by catastrophe, and he was therefore well supplied with lenses and projectors. In the course of experimenting with various ways to make his lantern slides he developed the daguerreotype which was almost certainly the least transparent picture ever created.

Daguerre got his technique worked out in 1839 and promptly told the world about how he did it so everyone could share his delight. The optical trade scooped it up and within weeks anyone who had a camera obscura (and later a daguerreotype camera) could produce a picture. The steps were these: from your local eyeglass-maker you bought a copper plate which had been silvered on one side and polished to look like a mirror. Just before you took a picture, you fumed the plate with iodine and placed it in the camera. You opened the lens for

from twenty to thirty minutes, re-capped the lens, and removed the plate. The plate was then fumed over a pan of hot mercury to bring out the picture. What you saw was what you got. One picture, no way to make additional copies, no enlargements, and the plate was preserved in frames or cases. It sounds despairingly clumsy, but at the time "everybody" did it. In 1853, there were over 10,000 practicing daguerreotypists in America who took three million plates in that one year! Thanks to their pinhole apertures, the pictures were marvelously sharp and the tones and gradations are very accurately reproduced. The earliest known photograph of the Capitol is a daguerreotype, made in 1846. The lines of the front steps and cast-iron palings in the fence could not be sharper if they had been taken with a modern, computer-designed lens.

At about the same time the daguerreotypes were evolving, William Henry Fox Talbot, an English aristocrat, invented the calotype. His technique proved to be the way photography would ultimately go and today's simple camera traces back directly to his solution. Talbot soaked tissue paper in silver nitrate, put the tissue in his camera obscura until the light parts turned dark and then while the paper "negative" was still wet put the tissue paper on heavier, pre-soaked final paper to burn in the final

picture. The ultimate print was, understandably, a bit soft but only slightly. The pictures were as sharp as drugstore prints are today, but the tonal span from very dark to very light was quite short and the "color" was all golden sepia. Recall that the only light source available until well after the Civil War was sunlight, so if a photographer were doing portraits, he would take the picture under a diffused skylight, rush into a dark room to fuss with the chemicals, and then come back out to a window to print the picture in direct sun. It could take as long as three to four hours to burn through to the paper to print the image—yet in an astonishingly short time, people were making pictures all over Europe and America! And speaking of sepia, all of the early pictures are rich golden tones or equally rich, browned platinum. Both of these have an antique feel that seems wholly appropriate for their subjects, but the color is neither age nor design. Sepia was simply the color the chemicals produced at the time. Black-and-white photographs come from bromide emulsions and were seventy-five years into the future.

One of Julia Margaret Cameron's collodion process portraits—this of her next-door neighbor, Poet Laureate Alfred Lord Tennyson, 1867.

In 1851 one Frederick Scott Archer invented the glass negative and both the daguerreotype and the calotype sank slowly into oblivion. Glass negatives meant the collodion process which was hailed as a thrilling breakthrough for convenience and clarity at the time—a judgment that can scarcely be believed today. This is the process that Brady used to photograph the Civil War, Carleton Watkins used to capture the first shots of Yosemite—and the process Julia Margaret Cameron used when she took portraits of Tennyson, Longfellow, Browning, and Darwin. Mrs. Cameron, for example, would begin with a vat full of highly volatile collodion (which was a sort of liquid celluloid) and dissolve in one half of the required halide mixture. She then dipped a piece of glass the size of the back of her camera into the collodion, let some of it drip back into the crock until it was down to a thin film, and then, working quickly while the collodion was still tacky, she would plunge the glass into a silver nitrate solution to complete the creation of the light-sensitive halides. The wet plate was laid into a light-tight carrier, locked on to the camera, the exposure made (by now down to merely thirty seconds) and then rushed back into the darkroom for development. The photographer had only fifteen minutes to get from creation to completion or the collodion would turn hard and impervious to everything— yet this was the way it was done from the 1850s until 1880 when gelatin plates came in. (We're still using gelatin, incidentally; it's now in roll film, but it is the same material they invented a hundred years ago—in fact, except for advances in the sensitivity of the halides, there has been almost no change in the film process from 1880 to date.)

With the glass negative Mrs. Cameron was only half way through. She still had to float her printing paper in silver nitrate to sensitize the chemicals for the final print, expose it as a contact shot, develop it, and ultimately dry it in the sun. But the result was the beautiful gold-toned portraits we still have with us today, very permanent, and very handsome.

The point of the above complications for us, the inheriting posterity, is that when we look at these incunabula of photography we should be aware of three things: one, the great pictures we have here were *taken* great; the creative process was in the light and focus and composition at the front end, not in the final printing where we do so much today with dodging, cropping, multiple-textured papers, filters, and screens. Two, the famous pictures are small, and they show us literally the size of the ground glass on which they were composed; today, studio prints are blown up for convenient viewing—at the time of most of these pictures there was no practical enlarging and could not be until the invention of the electric light bulb. And three, most of these pictures now exist as paper prints only. The plates and negatives have long since gone and indeed the prints were almost unique even in their own time since duplication was so complicated. At the Library of Congress, each master print is mounted on hard cardboard and kept in flat boxes holding eight or ten of the masterworks per box. The mounted print is the original; it came from the hand of the master photographer, and all of the photographer's prints are kept in "collections." Thus, when you ask for "the Bradys" or "Toni Frissell," you will get a truck loaded with acid-free, cardboard storage boxes filled with the original creative product.

Enough. Who were these innovators who set our image of what a photograph should look like, and who make up the Master Photographer Collection of the Library of Congress?

They start with the two founders: Daguerre and Talbot. Their attitude toward the "secret" of their new inventions is ironic. Daguerre was a showman who lived by his wits, but as soon as he had figured out his new process, he gave it to the public without hesitation so everyone could try it for himself. (His little booklet on "how to" went through twenty-nine editions in four months and was translated into six languages; all profits went to the printers—he kept nothing for himself.)

Talbot, on the other hand, lived in his family's historic Lacock Abbey, but even in 1839 was so pressed to keep up the thirteenth-century building, the grounds, parks, and huge staff that he was perpetually searching for money and he saw the photographic process as a source of funds to keep the Abbey going. He draped patents over every part of the calotype process and tried—unsuccessfully—to control it as an integrated product (as George Eastman did so successfully with "Kodak" fifty years later).

Daguerre and his friends gave us the first portraits. For nearly fifty years a photographic "studio portrait" looked the way the early daguerreotypists thought a portrait should look. They arrived at the model fairly quickly, but by an interesting progression. Daguerre had solved the chemical problems by 1839, but he was still frustrated by *time*. If he opened his lens wide enough to let light rush in,

the picture got fuzzy. But if he kept it stopped down to keep the edges sharp it took over half an hour to expose the plate. The result was that the early daguerreotypes are of buildings and still lifes. But what the pioneers really cared about was people, so all their early efforts were directed toward some way to capture breathing humans before they moved or paralysis set in. Daguerre finally brought it off by getting his chemical sensitivity up so that a fifteen-to-thirty-minute exposure sufficed, and then by inventing head clamps, armrests, and carefully designed poses that looked halfway casual—although the sitters could be locked in for as much as half an hour. (Blinking was permitted. The exposures took so long the closed eyelid wouldn't register if you opened it again quickly; the secret was to keep looking at precisely the same place throughout the whole shot. The whole problem of poses was brought to a fine art in the Crimean and American Civil wars. The photographers would stage their "action shots" very carefully ahead of time and then burn them into the plates through the long, multiminute exposures.)

Daguerre and his friends thus set the norm for portraits: a portrait had chairs, fluted columns, draperies, and a painted backdrop of either a formal balustrade or a forest path. The effect was that of a painted portrait just like those that the rich commissioned—and they became fantastically popular. They were literally produced by the millions. "Stopping by the photographer's" became such a rage that when Napoleon III led the French Army off to Italy in 1859, he marched it through the center of Paris past André Adolphe Disdéri's photographic studio and went in to have a few exposures made while the troops waited in the street. The Library of Congress' collection captures the custom with over five hundred original daguerreotypes from the 1840s and 1850s including portraits of Jenny Lind, Brigham Young, John Quincy Adams, and James K. Polk.

Talbot's *paper* picture (as contrasted with the copper plate of Daguerre) came within months of Daguerre's breakthrough and had several advantages: it was trivially cheap, you could make multiple copies (if you had all day to do it), and the resulting picture could be kept in an album or sent through the mail. Indeed, the first printed book ever illustrated with photographs was Talbot's *The Pencil of Nature* (1844). It contained twenty-four pictures of the facades of cathedrals, the light and shade of trees and gardens, and English country

Daguerreotype plates give us our first photographic images of historic public figures. Earlier than is usually realized, the daguerreotype camera captured pictures of the great as "direct positives" — there was no way to make copies of the single mirrored picture. A daguerreotype also has the minor idiosyncracy of producing a reversed image — men's coats are buttoned backward, Jackson's apparent left cheek is in fact his right, and scars and facial blemishes familiar to their contemporaries shift from one side to the other. At left are six notables captured by the daguerreotype process.

Top row: left, *Horace Greeley of "Go west, young man" fame, Congressman and founder of the N.Y. Tribune;* center, *President Andrew Jackson, "Old Hickory";* right, *Cornelius Vanderbilt, railway and steamboat magnate.* Bottom row: left, *Sam Houston, frontier hero and President of Texas;* center, *Henry Clay, "The Great Pacificator";* right, *author Washington Irving, U.S. Minister to Spain and creator of Ichabod Crane.*

scenes. There were few portraits and little that was artistic, but the pictures were crisply focused and all edges were sharp. Talbot was as fascinated with the product as the viewer was and assures us in the beginning of the book: "Notice to the Reader: The plates in the present work are impressed by the agency of light alone, without any aid whatever from the artist's pencil. They are sun pictures themselves, and not, as some persons have imagined, engravings in imitation." Talbot printed three hundred copies of the book (with all the photographs hand-tipped in place) and there are only about two dozen complete copies known to exist today. The Library's is one of these.

While the early daguerreotypists concentrated on achieving a convenient, effective means of making portraits, Talbot explored the landscape potential of the invention. He began with cathedrals and stately homes until he was satisfied with his focus and his ability to reproduce light and depth of field. He then worked on shadows until he had

The Pencil of Nature, *written and published by William Henry Fox Talbot in 1844, was the first book ever published with photographic illustrations. Three hundred copies were distributed (with the photographs pasted in by hand) and the author promised the reader that the pictures were "impressed by the agency of light alone"; they were not "engravings in imitation."*

developed the chiaroscuro effects that became the "art" shots of his successors, and finally he worked in textures: stone, shingles, and wood grain. Thus between Daguerre's portraits and Talbot's exteriors the potential applications of the medium were fairly well identified in the first decade of the technique—and the first esthetic arguments were tripped, the ones which still continue today.

What is photography's legitimate artistic role? Do good taste and valid esthetics limit it to duplicating strictly what its lens/eye sees, or is it valid to blur, tone, fog, or in general fiddle around with the image of reality? The result of the early argument was the almost immediate establishment of three fairly well-defined schools. One group held that the camera should record people and events for posterity. "Tell it like it is." Honest portraits and unromantic history. Another group concentrated on "mood," the "inner spirit" and "character" of the sitter, "impressions" of time and place and people. A third believed it should create new pictures as a painter builds from his imagination. This last group became the specialists in "theme" pictures and the titles of their works suggest their content: "Pray God, bring Father safely home," "Fading Away," "Two Ways of Life." (Incidentally, the real painters of the time became enamored of the camera as a sketchbook for their canvases; Degas took endless pictures that became his ballet scenes and portraits, Daumier used it as a basis for his caricatures, and so on.) All three schools are richly represented in the Library's collections.

The real-scene recorders are seen in the Library's holdings of Mathew Brady, Alexander Gardner, Timothy O'Sullivan, and William Henry Jackson.

Brady ran two portrait studios simultaneously, one in New York and the other in Washington, and he was enormously fashionable—if you were anybody you had your picture taken by Brady, and you weren't much until you had. The result is that he did indeed (as he intended) chronicle the "doers" of nineteenth-century America, and the Library of Congress preserves the record he captured in hundreds of portraits. Brady's own eyesight was so bad (and steadily worsening as he grew older) that he took fewer and fewer portraits himself but employed and trained dozens of photographers to "do it Brady's way." Brady's way was a solid, straightforward, right-into-the-camera shot which, without flattery or distraction, appears to tell us pretty much what his sitters looked like. In any event, they are the way we remember them. Our image of Lin-

Mathew Brady's picture of Robert E. Lee standing on his back porch in Richmond eleven days after his surrender to Grant. Lee did not wish to pose, but ultimately acceded as a courtesy to Brady, an old friend from before the war.

coln (the "five dollar bill portrait") is Brady's; the two photographs of Robert E. Lee are similarly his.

When the Civil War broke out, Brady was already nationally known as a portrait photographer, but he immediately recognized the potential of the camera as a recorder of history. He proceeded to put together teams of cameramen (he had roughly fifteen people in the field at any one time) and assigned them to the northern armies on the several campaign fronts. The photographers worked with wet plates out of light-proof wagons, and the time required to expose photographs was still so long that we have almost no pictures of actual battles. We have many pictures of the morning after— Gettysburg, Antietam, Petersburg—and the pictures do a chillingly effective job of recording the waste of war.

The Brady connection with the War had two interesting by-products beyond the actual pictures themselves. First, he deserves great credit for selecting and training the men to give a uniform

Top: *Dead of the 24th Michigan Infantry at Gettysburg. Part of the famous Iron Brigade, the 24th lost 399 of its 496 men in two days. Picture by Timothy O'Sullivan, July 1863.*

Bottom: *When Lee withdrew from Richmond, his officers set fire to all military stores which might be of use to the surrounding Union troops. The fires got out of control and the central part of the city was gutted. Here a picture, probably by Mathew Brady himself, of the Confederate Capitol across the James River, April 1865.*

Opposite: *Confederate dead lying where they fell below Marye's Heights, Fredericksburg, May 3, 1863. Picture by Capt. A. J. Russell.*

"Brady style" of clear, straightforward, honest reporting which set a long-time standard for American war photography. This differed sharply from the more romanticized European techniques used from the Crimean War to World War I. Secondly, the Brady-trained photographers went on to become the recorders of the American West in the post-war days. Alexander Gardner was the official photographer for the Union Pacific Railroad as it worked its way across the prairie. Timothy O'Sullivan (who had had two cameras shot out from under him as he was setting up pictures on Union breastworks) proceeded to be the first photographer to go down the Colorado, took the first mine photographs in the Comstock Lode (an early application of magnesium flares), and photographed his way across the Isthmus of Panama, recording what was later to be the route of the ship canal, and ultimately died while photographing Indian pueblos in the Southwest.

O'Sullivan had taken part in a government survey of the 40th parallel in 1867–69, and had been so technically successful that his methods became a routine standard and led to the hiring of William Henry Jackson, the man who showed the world the scenic West. Between 1870 and 1877, Jackson accompanied eight geological survey teams to the Continental Divide and had a canyon and a lake named after him. His pictures of Yellowstone convinced Congress it should create a new concept of wilderness protection that became our National Parks; he followed wagon trains on the western trails, and gave us pictures of pioneers and the Indians they displaced as they really were, not as the novelists of the time had portrayed them.

The practice of "going out to where nobody had been before" got to be big business right when the incredibly clumsy collodion process was at its height. The Library's "topographical description" files leave one awed. There are prints of Yucatan in Mexico, Karnak on the Nile (the photographer reported great difficulties keeping sand and flies off

Timothy O'Sullivan was one of Mathew Brady's ablest assistants during the Civil War. In 1867 he joined the "Clarence King Geological Exploration of the 40th Parallel" as official photographer. In this picture, O'Sullivan's darkroom wagon sits near Humboldt Hot Springs in the Nevada desert.

William Bell's picture of the Mouth of Kanab on the Colorado River, taken during the 1872 Expedition in the West.

the sticky wet plates). There are endless shots of the Alps and Niagara Falls, but Carleton Watkins' pictures of Yosemite were the hit of the 1867 Paris International Exhibition and deservedly so; he had lugged a camera that took glass plates a foot-and-a-half wide by two feet tall all the way up to the Valley, dragging the collodion vats behind him through the woods.

Amateur photographers will understand another problem with which the early landscape photographers had to cope. The collodion plates could be exposed for light clouds or for dark foreground, but not for both at the same time. The result is that many of the most spectacular shots of the time are really from two plates, exposed sequentially, and printed one on top of the other in the contact frame.

At this point in the history of the art, we meet the women of photography. Consistently, from now on in the development of the medium, women are innovators, among its most skilled and sensitive practitioners. Julia Margaret Cameron, Frances Benjamin Johnston, Dorothea Lange, Margaret Bourke-White, Toni Frissell leap out of the history having broken new ground and set new standards of technique.

Julia Margaret Cameron was almost a caricature of the good Victorian wife and mother. She was what her contemporaries called a "strong character." She was a daughter of one British colonial official and the wife of another. Born in India in 1815, she married a man twenty years her elder and spent ten years as a colonial wife. Then, when he retired, they came home to the Isle of Wight where

Half Dome. *Probably the first time this favorite tourist scene was ever photographed. The picture was made by Carleton E. Watkins in 1861 and was one of 27 prints done on collodion plates in a home-made camera. The negative was 18" high and 22" across. He sent the pictures of "Yo Semite" as it was then called to France where they won First Prize at the world's fair.*

Six pictures by Victorian women photographers. This page: *Frances Benjamin Johnston's portrait of Booker T. Washington* (top left) *and a group of teachers and students* (top right); *both taken at Tuskegee Institute. Gertrude Kasebier's portrait of Auguste Rodin* (bottom left) *and Julia Margaret Cameron's portrait* The Lord Bishop of Winchester. Opposite: *Cameron's* Pensive Girl in Front of Tree (top) *and Kasebier's* The Vision (bottom).

(at her insistence) they bought a house next door to Alfred Lord Tennyson so she could get to know the Poet Laureate. In 1864 when she was forty-nine, her daughters gave her a camera and a home developing kit (recall we are in the midst of wet collodion and glass plates), and she took her first picture. She processed it in the potting shed.

Before she was finished she had done all the Victorian greats and was recognized as one of the leading portraitists of her time. Poor Tennyson got trapped almost daily. He appears as his distinguished self, but he also appears wearing theatrical headgear and frayed blankets playing the various literary characters she liked to recreate. She did studies of Garibaldi, the Crown Prince of Prussia, Robert Browning, Charles Darwin, Herschel, Ellen Terry. Henry Wadsworth Longfellow recalled that in 1868 Tennyson led him through her side gate and said, "Longfellow, you will have to do whatever she tells you. I'll come back soon and see what is left of you." She said she sought "the greatness of the inner as well as the features of the outer man," and after a day of such search, Carlyle was so shattered his family reported he was not himself for a week.

On the technical side, Cameron was the first to use a solid black background and highlights on forehead and cheekbones. She replaced the full-body Daguerre/Brady portrait with dramatically modeled heads that filled her pictures; and in truth we owe to her that close up, soft, slightly blurred focus that has characterized studio portraits right up to our own time.

The creative photographers like Cameron had moved photography from mechanical reproduction to creative selectivity—and they set up the audience for Alfred Stieglitz and his generation.

Alfred Stieglitz considered himself an artist and he thought photography was an art form. It infuriated him that no one took either him or it as seriously as he thought they both deserved. He had a marvelously productive career of over sixty years and by the end he had triumphed over both of his frustrations. He tells it best himself, recalling his early irritation in the 1880s:

It gradually dawned on me that something must be wrong with the art of painting as practiced at that time. With my camera I could procure the same results as those attained by painters—in black and white for the time being, perhaps in color later on. I could ex-

The photographer as artist as shown in three platinum prints from the turn of the century. Upper left, Torso *by Clarence White (under Alfred Stieglitz' tutelage).* Upper right, Ancient Crypt Cellars *in Provins, France, and* above, Landscape, *both by Frederick Evans.*

press the same moods. Artists who saw my earlier photographs began to tell me that they envied me; that they felt my photographs were superior to their paintings, but that unfortunately, photography was not an art. I could not understand why the artists should envy me for my work, yet, in the same breath, decry it because it was machine-made—their "art" painting, because hand-made, being considered necessarily superior. Then and there I started my fight—or rather my conscious struggle for the recognition of photography as a new medium of expression, to be respected in its own right, on the same basis as any other art form.

He produced pictures, entered competitions. He opened a photographic art gallery; he established and edited the first photographic magazines. He "discovered" Edward Steichen, Georgia O'Keeffe, Ansel Adams, and was involved in staging the famous New York Armory Show that introduced "modern art" to the traditional art scene of 1913 America. In spite of his deliberate effort to link photography to creative art, he resisted every effort to make his photographs look like paintings, and he demanded that his disciples keep their pictures "pure." To sustain the purity of his own work, he gradually withdrew from taking pictures of people and concentrated instead on clouds, on dew, trees, and houses constantly pressing the edges of light and form. The result, of course, is that he is thought of as the pre-eminent pioneer of the "art picture."

He was famous for standing hours in one place waiting for that breathless moment "when everything is in balance," and this brings to mind the mysterious measurement of personal style: Why does a picture "look like a Stieglitz," a Karsh, an Avedon? How do such figures construct a picture? Can it be identified, set down, and duplicated? Apparently it is rarely deliberate. Henri Cartier-Bresson says,

You wait and wait, and then finally you press the button—and you depart with the feeling (though you don't know why) that you've really got something. Later...you'll observe that, if the shutter was released at the decisive moment, you have instinctively fixed a geometric pattern without which the photograph would have been both formless and lifeless....

Composition must be one of our constant preoccupations, but at the moment of shooting it can stem only from our intuition.

Similarly, when a friend of Edward Weston was claiming that Weston deliberately organized scenes geometrically, Weston replied, "No,...to stop and calculate would be to miss most of them." It seems to be totally mystical. The photographer's individual style can be recognized but it is extraordinarily difficult to fabricate precisely. The sense of how a particular point is expressed is especially evident in the documentary photographers.

As you might expect, the Library of Congress has the most complete collection of photographic social documentation in the nation. The work of Lewis W. Hine, Dorothea Lange, Arthur Rothstein, Russell Lee, Jack Delano, Marjorie Post-Wolcott, John Vachon, and Ben Shahn are either represented in their totality or with great richness. Two of these stand above their peers: Hine and Lange. Hine was a New York City geography teacher who, at the age of thirty-seven, wrote a book that dealt with what happened to the immigrants after they got here. It was a textual study of child labor and sweatshop working conditions at the turn of the century and he decided to illustrate it with pictures—which he found he had to take himself. The result was so effective that when the National Child Labor Committee was set up, Hine was talked into being their official photographer and did volume after volume of pictures of children working in mines and in mills of every variety. World War I broke out and, at the close of America's involvement, Hine was sent to Europe by the National Red Cross to record the before-and-after of war relief and rehabilitation. It was his style and technique of social documentation, that was accepted as the norm and set the model, but it was Dorothea Lange who took the concept one dramatic step further to the image we know today. Hine's pictures of grimy children in gloomy, bare rooms are intellectually distressing but somehow permit the viewer to remain detached—remain an observer. Lange's pictures capture the individuality of the affected person with such striking dignity and pathos that you cannot remain unmoved.

Dorothea Lange was born in 1895, studied photography under Clarence White at Columbia, and worked for Arnold Genthe who gave her the first camera she ever owned. She opened a portrait studio in San Francisco and was satisfyingly successful.

147

Top: *Symbolism of Light by Clarence White, 1907.* Above: *Portrait of the actress Ethel Barrymore, by Arnold Genthe, 1904.*

She married the artist Maynard Dixon, had children, and one summer while touring the Southwest decided that her concentration on people's faces was an esthetic error. She proceeded to spend the next three months in the mountains photographing scenery and then (she reports) in the middle of a thunderstorm "it came to me that what I had to do was to take pictures and concentrate on people, only people, all kinds of people, people who paid me and people who didn't." She proceeded to do so with a deliberate, paced intensity that riveted the attention of her viewers.

Among her audience was a professor of economics at the University of California, Paul Taylor, who had just been asked to do an economic report for the state on the problems of the migrant laborer in California. With Lange's portraits in his mind, he went to the photographer and asked her to capture the problem in images to make his study real to the reader. Lange agreed; it was 1935 and she was forty.

Her pictures were so startling and so honest that they began to be published in newspapers and magazines to symbolize the whole spectrum of social troubles bound up in the Depression and the Dust Bowl crisis. Pare Lorentz, the documentary cinematographer, said, "Her people stand straight and look you in the eye. They have the simple dignity of people who have leaned against the wind, and worked in the sun, and owned their own land." Someone else referred to "the terrible reality of her people." From her California work, she came to the attention of another economist in Washington, Roy Stryker, who asked her to come and work on a national scale. It is these pictures from her Farm Security Administration period that are best known. Here she was working with Walker Evans, Ben Shahn, and Arthur Rothstein, and the four left a record that has etched an era in the national memory so that we recall a historical period through the images from their lenses. Lange herself has given us the most precise definition of what a Lange photograph looks like: "My own approach is based upon three considerations. First—hands off. Whatever I photograph I do not molest or tamper with or arrange. Second—a sense of place. I try to picture it as part of its surroundings, as having roots. Third—a sense of time. Whatever I photograph, I try to show as having its position in the past or in the present."

And so we move on and end our glance at the image-makers with a woman of our own time: Toni Frissell. In the course of her career she has worked

Two of Lewis W. Hine's pictures of child labor conditions, 1911. Top: *Breaker boys at a Pennsylvania anthracite mine; their job was to pick out pieces of slate from the heaps of broken coal.* Bottom: *A girl in a New England textile mill.*

The work of the Farm Security Administration photographers capturing Depression America. Opposite: *Dorothea Lange's* Migrant Mother, *1936* (upper left) *and* Damaged Child (upper right). *Jack Delano's* Polish Tobacco Farmers, Windsor Locks, Connecticut, 1940 (lower left). *Arthur Rothstein's* Sharecropper's Wife and Child, *Arkansas, 1935* (lower right) *and* Prelude to Afternoon Meal (above).

in almost every photographic field and succeeded in everything she tried—but what makes her so especially appealing is the zest with which she did it.

She was introduced to cameras by her brother Varick, who was a Pathé news photographer and one of the creators of what we now know as "documentary style." Frissell, fresh out of the progressive Lincoln School, started as a photographer for *Vogue* in 1931, and very quickly introduced her personal innovation: taking the flawlessly dressed models out of carefully lit studios and photographing them instead in fields, on beaches, against stones, amid ruins. After eleven years with *Vogue*, she moved on to *Harper's Bazaar* where her startling pictures of

high society kept her among the very top of her profession right up to the outbreak of World War II. At the outset of that conflict, she got herself sent to the European Front, first to do Red Cross publicity pictures and then as the official photographer for the Women's Army Corps. Her famous pictures of bomber squadrons—and the portraits of Winston Churchill and his family—come from this period. After the War, she turned to sports photography, and her work for *Sports Illustrated* set many of the styles and treatments that are still used in that very successful magazine.

When she finally retired in the early 1970s, she gave her entire collection of photographs, the work

Four pictures by Toni Frissell. Top left: *From her Red Cross and Women's Army Corps tours,* Shock—V2 London—Parents Buried in Rubble. Bottom left: *From her fashion-photography period,* Floating Boat, Montego Bay, Jamaica, *for* Harper's Bazaar, *1946.* Top and bottom right: *From her society period,* John and Jackie Kennedy Wedding, *1953.*

Toni Frissell's Spring of the Mermaid, *Weeki Wachee Spring, Florida, for* Harper's Bazaar, *December 1947.*

of an astonishingly productive lifetime, to the Library of Congress. She noted her suspicion "that [her] work will have greater value in the next century as a record of a vanished way of life" than now. And in a commentary she wrote for an IBM retrospective show of her photographs, she gives us a statement of her art that could in fact summarize the complete photographic collection of the Library of Congress. She tells us:

...I have tried to capture a number of things I have seen around me, at work and on holidays, a child's world of discovery. My own varied fields of travel, ways of life both simple and splendid, and on my assignment in the European theater in World War II. Here also are moments of relaxation as well as of achievement. And most of all, here are faces that I have found memorable. If they are not all as happy as kings, it is because in this imperfect world and these hazardous times, the camera's eye, like the eye of a child, often sees true.

Wood engraving from an eighteenth-century French manual of machines and machinery plans.

CHAPTER VII

"Newe Science That Men Lere"

Right about now the poor visitor to the Library of Congress who has been bathed in the Library's endless statistics about more and more begins to have a rising sense of doom. Where are all these acquisitions going to end? Doesn't the Library ever say, "We've got enough books on X, let's stop, no more"? The answer to the question is, of course, no, it does not. But if every year more and more pictures are taken, more maps made, more books written and if every year the Library puts more and more into its collections, doesn't the Library ever throw anything away? The answer is still, no. Therefore let us consider for a moment gross bulk, redundancy, and obsolescence.

Once the Library of Congress gets something, processes it, and puts it on the shelf it does indeed keep it forever. What shrinkage there is comes at the beginning. The Library is very careful about what it takes. In an average year about ten million pieces of material will be received but six-and-a-half million of these will be rejected at the outset before they become a part of the collections. How can the librarians be sure they have taken the right things? They can't be. They simply must do the best they can. But, you say, since we can't know what we will need in the future, why not keep everything (since the Library gets most of it free anyway) just in case it is needed? It can't be done because *space* is incredibly expensive.

It's expensive just to build the floor that supports the books. Take a bedroom in your own home. It will have cost you many thousands of dollars to build or buy and if you fill it with books absolutely

from floor to ceiling it will hold about 7,000 volumes with aisles so narrow you can barely slip between the stacks. But the Library of Congress adds 7,000 books every working day and it stores them on thick, fireproof and load-bearing floors far more expensive than your bedroom. And this is just the beginning; the real cost comes from the fact that *there they will stay forever.* Straight ahead into the infinity of time those 7,000 books will be heated in winter and cooled in summer, they will be lighted, guarded against fire and theft, they will have the air about them humidified, the dust removed, the mold ionized...and so will tomorrow's 7,000 volumes and the next day's 7,000, and so on generation after generation just as the Library is doing with the books acquired a century ago.

How can the librarians know what to keep (or increase their odds of being right)? They do it with the help of endlessly refined "Canons of Selection" which set up rules of what to take and what to keep and which, in turn, are constantly reviewed by specialists in the subject fields. Recall that only a fourth of the books are in English; three-fourths are in one hundred twenty foreign languages (over half of which are not even in the Roman alphabet).

The thought that someone really ought to go through the collections every so often to see whether the books are holding up, are still useful, has occurred to everyone at one time or another, but this solution melts under the enormity of the task. Quite aside from determining criteria of value, if you were to limit your examination to one minute per book, eight hours a day, five days a

week, it would take sixty-four years to get from one end of the collection to the other—during which time another ninety-six million volumes would have been added behind your back. (If you posit teams instead of a lone referee, it's still a nightmare of quantity, multiple languages, and criteria for discard.)

I bring up the subject of choice and obsolescence at this point because we have come to the science collections and nowhere in the Library are these problems more poignant. It takes something of an effort to remember that there *is* science in the Library of Congress since the building so reeks of the humanities. With busts of poets and historians sitting over every window and toga-ed philosophers peering down from the frescoes, it requires deliber-

Seen here and overleaf are examples of the thirty-seven volvelles *or moveable circles in Petrus Apianus'* Astronomicum Caesareum, *1540. Some involve as many as six dials for solving astronomical problems. Petrus believed that moveable diagrams were more useful than mathematical tables for calculating orbits and relationships of moving bodies. He also described the comet of 1531, which later became known as Halley's Comet.*

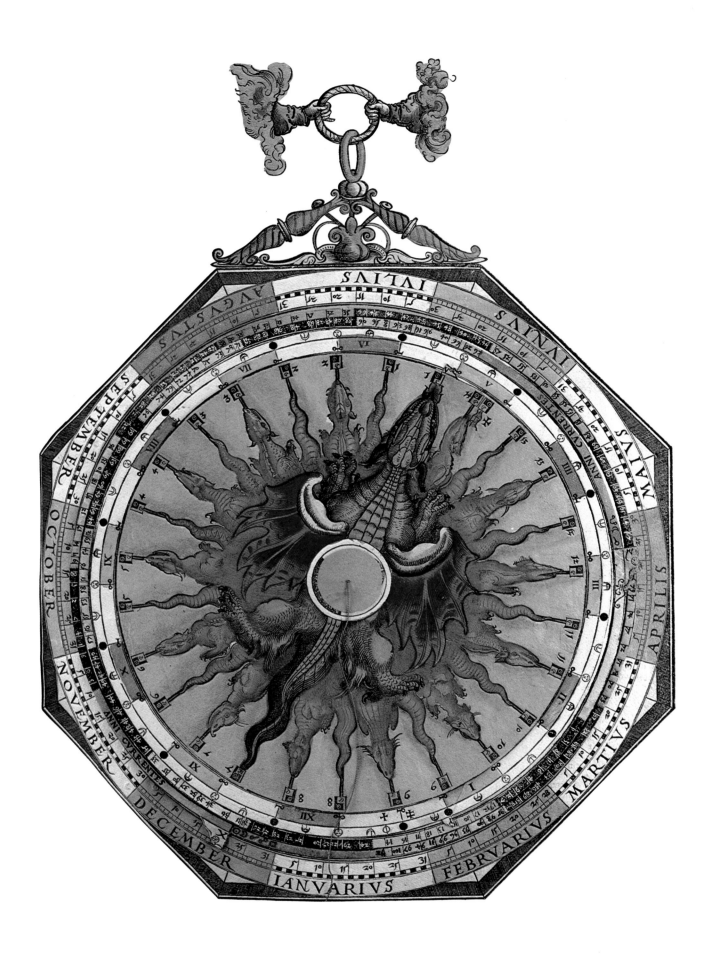

ate thought to recall that six million volumes fall into the hard sciences and applied technology classifications. A substantial number of all books requested by the daily reader/visitor comes from the science shelves.

Scientific publications are a professional pain for librarians. They require a great deal of staff time and cost a great deal of money because 1) they must be secured very quickly and processed immediately to be of real use to their audiences, 2) they usually appear in journals or thin, near-print research reports which together form the most expensive sources of information a librarian has to handle, and 3) they age with breathtaking speed.

The predicament fits a parable: When I was a teenager in Kansas, our little town of 10,000 was suddenly galvanized into life by the arrival of surveyors from the Santa Fe railroad who came to put in a cut-off between Tulsa and Kansas City. I spent the better part of a summer watching the actual laying of the track, and it was fascinating.

The prairie was absolutely flat, so no grading was necessary other than scratching a run-off ditch on either side of the right-of-way, but the black loam was so soft it could not support a train on top of the soil. The engineers solved their problem by spreading a thick, rock roadbed, putting ties on the crushed rock, and rails on the ties. The process was like laying boards ahead of you as you walk across thin ice.

The surveyors would mark the line across the empty range, a train would push a gondola of rock up to the edge of the last rails laid, and the men would shovel the gravel out ahead of the track. The train would go back for more gravel and while it was gone the men would lay ties and set the rails on the new rock. When the train came back, it would run out on the new rails, the men would shovel new gravel out ahead, and repeat the operation—so far as I could see right on to the end of the world.

The point of this small homily is that this is exactly the way science materials are used at the Library of Congress. New research is pouring in daily, it is analyzed, indexed, and the controls are loaded into the computer where the scientific community falls on it like gandy dancers. The data is shoved out ahead and new research is laid over it. What is useful is used, the rest is ignored, and in a startlingly short time the material becomes dated, superseded, redundant, and this vast block of once-burning thought is left to lie there while the edge of the scientific road rolls on away from it.

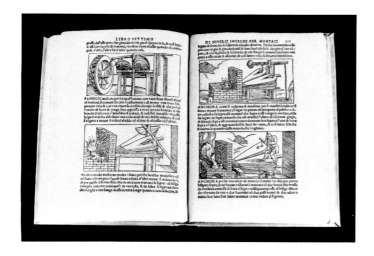

Vanoccio Biringuccio's De La Pirotechnia *gives us startling information about the 1540 formulas and techniques for making fireworks, gunpowder, and chemical-warfare agents. Printed on vellum in Venice, it was written for the practicing metallurgist, foundryman, dyer, type-founder, or glass maker.*

The chance that our present-day researchers will use 1910 data on cloth-covered airfoils, 1920 experiments on the vacuum tube, 1930 metallurgy of cast iron is extremely small. Indeed, the amount of dead data stored in an institution like the Library of Congress is enormous. But much, much later, the light of re-examination begins to flood these same materials and suddenly, simply because it *was* preserved, it becomes valuable in the extreme. From it we can find the purpose and expectations of the original research. We can find the mistakes, the point where the solution veered off to become counter-productive (indeed in the case of chemicals and biologicals, the point where a benign substance became dangerous). For the triumphs, we can find why they succeeded and try to duplicate the techniques to increase our efficiency in the future.

Let's look at three kinds of scientific materials that time has lifted above the mass of passive data and converted into the genuine treasure of the scientific fields. Let's start with a single piece from the High Renaissance that meets all our criteria for rarity, value, and significance. (Please see page 160.)

We are looking at Nicolaus Copernicus' *De revolutionibus orbium coelestium* (On the Revolution of the Celestial Spheres), a rare first edition—and another of the gifts to the Library from the largess of Lessing J. Rosenwald. This is the book that made the greatest break with the medieval past and did

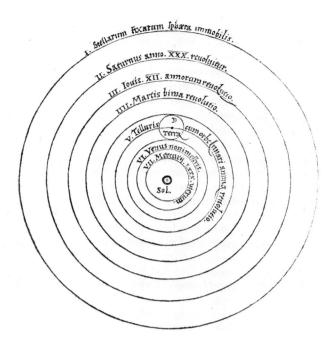

De revolutionibus orbium coelestium *(On the Revolution of the Celestial Spheres) by Nicolaus Copernicus, 1543. This is the first edition of the landmark volume, and this illustration shows us the first time the universe was pictured with the* sun, *not the earth, at the center of the circling planets.*

more than any other work to usher in the age of modern science. The book was published in 1543 in Nuremberg when the author was seventy and dying. Although he had finished the text some ten years earlier, we know that he waited until he believed he was on his deathbed to release it for print. We don't know why he waited so long. Depending on their perception of the age, some scholars believe it was to make the book the capstone of a triumphant career, the monument he would leave to his peers. Others think it was to avoid being burned at the stake.

Copernicus was born in 1473 within a couple of years of Albrecht Dürer and Michelangelo. Dante's *Divine Comedy* had just been printed for the first time, and William Caxton had just published the first book in English. When Copernicus was ten his father died and a prestigious uncle, Lucas Watzelrode, took over his care and upbringing. Watzelrode became the Bishop of Varmia (today's Prussia) and virtually ruled the country, effectively and well. The Bishop appointed Copernicus canon at his cathedral in Frauenburg, thus giving him an income for life, and then sent him off to the University of Cracow at the age of nineteen. It was 1492 and Columbus had just discovered the New World.

The result of this timing was that Copernicus' university years exactly coincided with the shock of displaced horizons that followed the first news of a whole new continent across the sea. This was succeeded by the circumnavigation of the world which confirmed the intellectual belief that the world was round and gave the idea the same reality that the astronauts' picture of the blue earth in black space has done for our own time. We are told that the global discoveries opened up all the studies in the schools of the day and made it far easier to think of the earth as an individual object quite separate from the heavens of fixed stars. But the earth was still considered to be the stationary platform on which God's favorite creation stood and around which the entire universe revolved for the benefit of man.

For the next ten years Copernicus was bathed in scholarly nutrients which resulted in an almost perfect model of the Renaissance mind. For some reason we all know about Galileo and Michelangelo; we should be using Nicolaus Copernicus as the prototype.

He studied mathematics and astronomy in Cracow. He then went to Bologna and started a decade in Italy at the very time that Cesare Borgia, Savonarola, Leonardo, and Machiavelli were flourishing. He spent four years in Bologna studying more mathematics, astronomy, and Greek but mainly being part of one of the finest universities in Europe. (Its claim to have the highest salaries and finest buildings enticed most of the leading faculty on the continent; the city spent half of all its revenues on its school.)

From Bologna Copernicus went to Rome and managed to reach the Eternal City in the Jubilee Year of Christianity, 1500, when pilgrims from all over the West flooded the monuments. He writes of his exhilaration from talking to representatives of an incredible number of disparate cultures.

In 1501 he returned to Poland to study medicine. Medicine was closely allied to astronomy in those days with close attention being given to the effect of the planets on the human body, and Copernicus became famous in Northern Europe for his use of complicated mixtures, potions, and pills. With a flourishing practice as a base, he returned to Italy to expand his medical knowledge at Padua, the most famous medical school of the time. Between studies he added to his arts and became a recog-

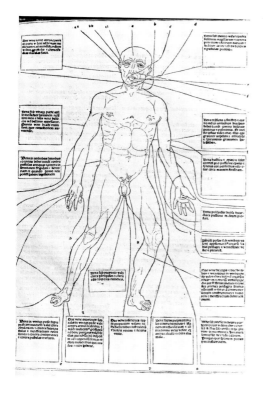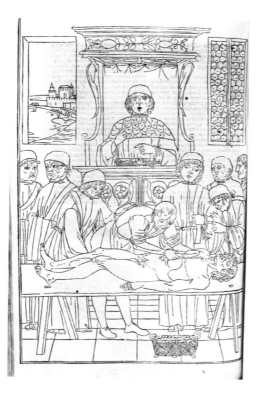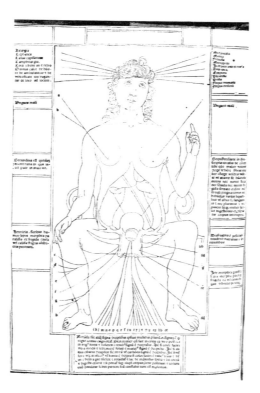

Fasciculus medicinae by Johannes de Ketham was printed in Venice in October 1495 and is the finest medical book of the incunabula. The book is a compilation of medical treatises—including this detailed explanation of the effects of the various planets on specific organs of the body. Each anatomical element was influenced by a different astrological sign. The book contains ten woodcuts which are anatomically accurate and some think were drawn by the artist Gentile Bellini.

nized portrait painter in good standing with a well-established clientele pressing to be immortalized. At the close of the four-year course he returned home; he was thirty-three, he had ten years of Italian education and a record of success at everything he'd thus far tried.

He became private secretary to the archbishop—and thus essentially free to pursue his astronomical studies. He made endless observations and calculations, and his reputation as an astronomer grew quickly. In 1514 he was called to Rome to advise on the reform of the calendar and, like a true Renaissance humanist, produced his first book—a Latin translation of a Greek literary work by a writer named Theophylactus Simocatta. Harsh reality overtook him and he was appointed governor of Allenstein Castle, which he soon had to defend against a siege by the Teutonic knights. He brought this off with his customary skill and in the course of it became concerned about the welfare and prosperity of the local peasants. He became intrigued by the effects of the flood of Spanish gold coming

into Europe from the Americas and did a series of studies on the causes of monetary inflation. He noted, in anticipation of Sir Thomas Gresham, that bad money drives out good. He declared that bad money destroyed initiative, encouraged laziness, and raised the cost of living. He was convinced that the primary causes of the decline of nations were inflation, social discord, disease, and poverty of the soil. He had surely one of the most broadly based scientific minds of his age—or possibly of any other.

Copernicus began his celestial observations as early as 1497 and continued for some thirty years taking readings and collecting data, intending to redetermine the orbits of the sun, moon, and planets. According to the then conventional wisdom, all these bodies circled around the earth with logical and predictable precision. Unfortunately, as the years went by, Copernicus' calculations never quite seemed to work out. The gap never closed between what ought to be and what was. The traditional Ptolemaic system, which was always defended as being simple and self-evident, required a disturbing number of "minor adjustments" to meet the observed facts.

Apparently it was Copernicus' reading in Greek philosophical literature that led him to test the idea that the sun, not the earth, was the center of things. He says that once he began a systematic search of the ancient literature he found references to the idea in Cicero, Plutarch, and Ecphantus, and that one Philolaus held that the earth "is moved about the element of fire in an oblique circle" while Heraclides Ponticus claimed the earth itself spun "after the manner of a wheel being carried on its own axis."

Given these assurances that the idea he was exploring might have validity, Copernicus proceeded to rework his own measurements and "found at length by much and long observation [that] if the motions of the other planets were added to the rotation of the earth and calculated for the revolution of that planet, not only the phenomena of the others followed from this, but it also bound together both the order and magnitude of all the planets and the spheres and the heaven itself, that in no single part could one thing be altered without confusion among the other parts and in the universe." Our illustration, from the first chapter of *Revolutionibus*, shows the first time the universe had been portrayed without the earth being the center of all things. The book has six sections which prove Copernicus' thesis in detail, using words and figures to meet both philosophical and mathematical challenges.

His book got prompt attention and poor reviews. Martin Luther called Copernicus a "new astrologer who wanted to prove that the earth was moving and revolving.... such are the times we live in: he who wants to be clever must invent something all his own and what he makes up he naturally thinks is the best thing ever! This fool wants to turn the whole of astronomy upside down." Melanchthon, the Protestant philosopher, was so irritated by the volume that he wrote "wise rulers should tame the unrestraint of men's minds." Rome either missed the point or it takes a bureaucracy longer to react; the volume and the idea were not declared to be heresy by the Church for nearly fifty years.

The idea that the sun might be the center of the universe was as severe a shock to new Renaissance man as it was to those still following medieval tradition. The Renaissance humanist was even more certain that mankind was the focus of all things and

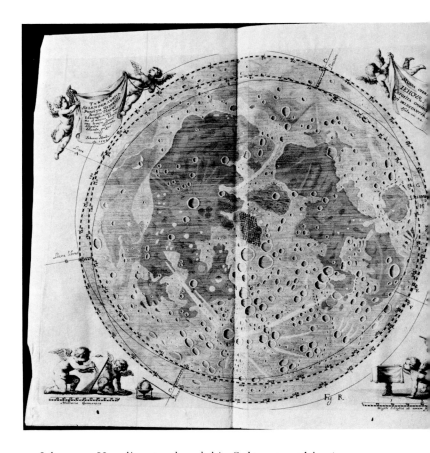

Johannes Hevelius produced his Selenographia *(a 563-page atlas of the moon, 1647) after building an observatory in his house and laboriously observing by night and drawing during the day. He is considered the founder of lunar topography. His careful chartings have held up well in light of our present explorations. In addition to the moon work, he catalogued 1,564 stars, described sunspots, and discovered four comets.*

that everything that mattered circled around him and the platform on which he stood. When Copernicus casually moved him and the earth off to the side and simply added him to the other items circling the source of light, it was a rude shock indeed at the very time that the new philosophy was holding that the individual *was* the most important thing in the system. And for the learned, the sense of *scale* was badly jarred. The ancients' planets and stars circled a stationary earth not very far away. Copernicus pushed everything back a great distance in order to give all his circles room to work in.

Oddly enough, the concept had the effect of pushing the sciences apart as well. Medicine and astrology had been closely linked—the effects of the planets on the flesh. Now, with the heavens at great distance and operating around something other than man on earth, their interaction appeared less likely and medicine opened up to new paths of inquiry. Within a short time, this had the effect of separating biology from physics.

When *man* was the center of all purpose and all things, inquiry looked out *from* him. Once Copernicus reduced him to something on a whirling globe among many globes, man himself was reduced in scale and significance—inexorably leading to the study of man as an entity, the social studies, and anthropology itself.

The invention of the printed book so closely coincides with the chain reaction of new scientific perceptions that almost all the scientific historians have been struck by the linkage of printing and the explosion of science. The very year that our first edition Copernicus appeared Andreas Vesalius produced the first modern anatomy. A year earlier (1542) Leonhard Fuchs had printed his classic botany and at almost the same time Georgius Agricola brought out the first text on mineralogy and physical geology.

Printing seems to have accomplished at least three things with a rush: it permitted the circulation of observations and measurements so each man could start where his predecessor had left off rather than having to reinvent the total wheel of his special interest; it democratized knowledge so new concepts were quickly sown throughout the read-

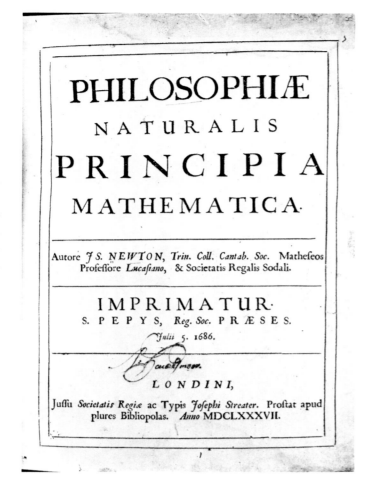

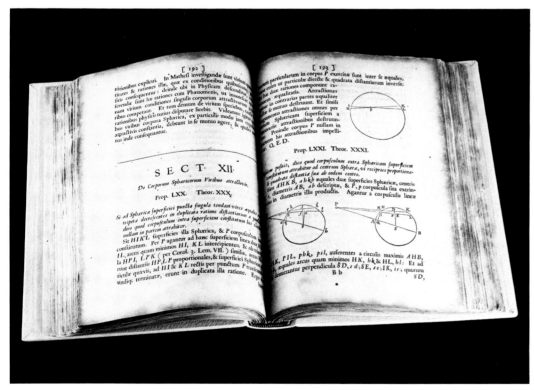

Sir Isaac Newton's Philosophiae Naturalis Principia Mathematica, *1687. The Library's many editions of this printed work (probably the most important on exact science ever published) start with the first issue of the first edition illustrated here. The S. Pepys on the title page is the famous diarist, who was President of the Royal Society, 1685–86.*

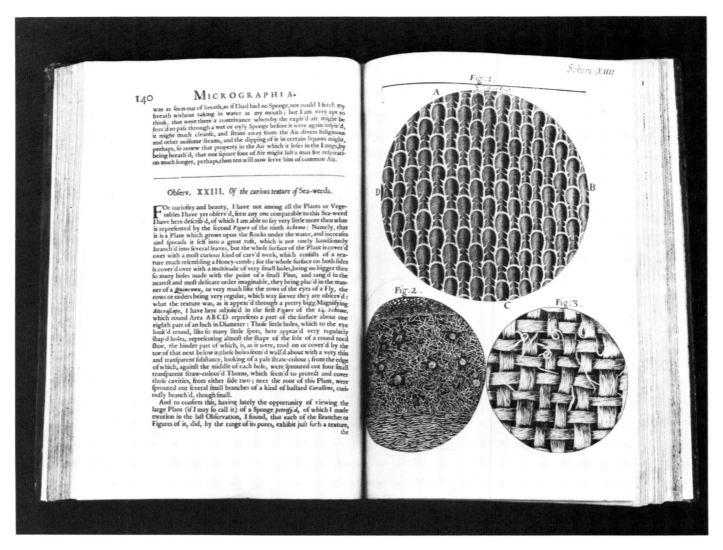

Robert Hooke's Micrographia: or Some physiological descriptions of minute bodies made by magnifying glasses, *1665. In 1665, Hooke discovered that a bottle cork cut from the bark of a cork tree was made up of tiny compartments. He described these holes as "cells" like the little rooms or cells in a monastery. It is the first time "cell" is used in a book in the biological sense, and the first time one was illustrated. He proceeded to look at all kinds of objects and with the help of Sir Christopher Wren (acting as draftsman) produced this splendid volume, which was also the first to be published by the Royal Society of England.*

ing public; and it stimulated new thoughts in geometric progression rather than in straight line, serial sequence. But probably most important of all, printing "saved" the thoughts of the innovators. The "unthinkable" ideas of Copernicus and Galileo, once printed and distributed, once out of the bottle, could not be put back or obliterated. They ultimately won out on the strength of their own rightness and they were preserved during the fight—in much ink on many pages in many places.

Let's move on to the modern, working collections—the dull, gritty record of experiments (usually more failures than successes) and the long runs

of data—the tiny changes of one degree of heat, one gram of weight, one second of time. We're looking for the unique and the important in this book, so we should not get sidetracked here into looking at the riches of the open stacks, but we must not forget either that they are there or that they, in their comprehensiveness, are a national treasure without equal in the Americas.

The Library of Congress owes its vast scientific collections to the Smithsonian Institution. You will recall that in the course of Librarian Spofford's great accumulations, he worked out an agreement with the Secretary of the Smithsonian, physicist

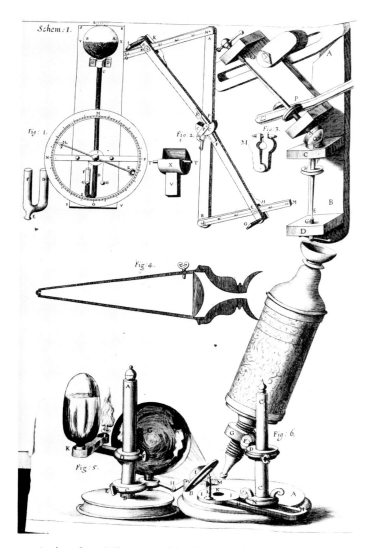

A plate from Micrographia *showing the instrument that Hooke and the artist used to gather the data that he and Wren had observed and described.*

the Institution has not only the free use of its own books, but those of the Library of Congress. On the other hand the collection of books owned by the Library of Congress would not be worthy of the name of the National Library were it not for the Smithsonian Deposit."

One can never think of the Smithsonian without being awed at what an enormous contribution it has made to the nation—and how easily it could have turned out differently. The very risks of its acquisition are chilling in view of the vagaries of routine government. James Smithson made his will in 1826 and he died three years later. Another six years passed before the American Legation in London was even told about it (the money had grown to 100,000 pounds between 1829 and 1835). The question of whether the nation should accept the gift was then passed to the Congress and they debated it for *ten years* before they grudgingly passed an act in 1846 to take the money. The Smithsonian's growth as the great *scientific* institution in the nation was equally fortuitous. The original assignment simply read: "to increase knowledge by original investigations and study in science and literature; and...to diffuse knowledge not only throughout the United States but everywhere, especially by providing an interchange of thought among those prominent in learning in all nations." Had it not been for Professor Henry's own personal interest in hard science—and his strength of character—the institution could just as well have centered on literature, politics, or indeed have been made into a national university dealing in higher education in general.

But to return to the unique, the national treasures of the Library of Congress. We have let a first edition Copernicus represent the dozens of first editions from the Enlightenment which are the original revelations of intellectual breakthroughs. The Library, of course, has essentially all of the original printings from all the recognized scientists—Newton, Darwin, Freud, Einstein—as well as more nationalistic figures better known in their own countries and their own languages. Together they add up to the complete roster of innovative understandings.

The six million scientific monographs in the regular stacks represent the second form of treasure in the Library.

The third form of treasure is the personal papers of these scientific giants. It is always a shock to the reader who comes on these riches for the first time

Joseph Henry. According to the bargain struck in 1866, the Library of Congress would take over the then Smithsonian library plus all subsequent publications that would come in through the Smithsonian's broad exchange programs. This great and growing bloc of works was augmented through the years with the Library of Congress' own copyright receipts and its international exchange materials. The result is an end product without peer.

Professor Henry's comment at the time still sums up the situation most gracefully: "The Smithson fund is relieved by this arrangement from maintenance of a separate library, while at the same time

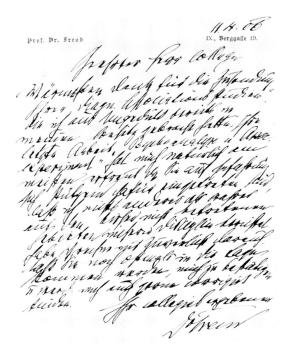

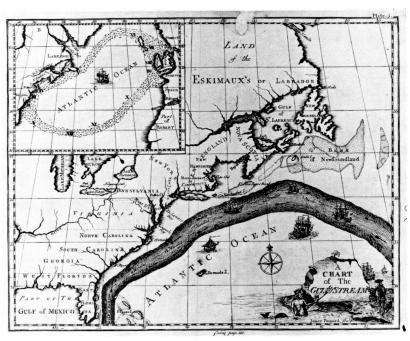

Top left: *The first of 152 letters owned by the Library of correspondence between Sigmund Freud and Carl Jung, 1906–13. Jung had sent Freud a copy of his* Diagnostische Assoziationstudien *and this is Freud's comment on it. The two did not actually meet until the following year.*

Top right: *Benjamin Franklin's Third Chart of the Gulf Stream, 1786. The chart carries the caption: "Remarks Upon the Navigation from Newfoundland to New-York In order to avoid the Gulph Stream. On one hand, and on the other the Shoals that lie to the Southward of Nantucket and of St. George's Banks."*

Above: *Samuel F.B. Morse's telegraphic tape, May 24,1844. "What hath God wrought?" was sent on the wire from the Supreme Court room in the Capitol to the railroad depot in Baltimore. The phrase had been chosen for this initial demonstration of the invention of the telegraph by his "much loved friend" Annie Ellsworth, the daughter of the U.S. Commissioner of Patents.*

to find that these treasures still exist. The Library actually has 175,000 pieces from Freud's personal files; it has Benjamin Franklin's scientific musings and observations covering fifty years of his life. It has sixty-three volumes of papers of Samuel F.B. Morse, famous for his telegraph. What are these "papers"? They are the letters to and, frequently more important, the letters *from* the notable scientists in America and abroad with whom these figures corresponded. They are their diaries, their subject files, their published and unpublished manuscripts, their notebooks, and their work papers.

Whose? Well, what subject are you interested in? Television? The Library has twenty-four volumes of Lee de Forest's diaries from 1891 through 1949,

41,000 items from Allen DuMont. Electricity? Weather control and cloud-seeding? The Library has Irving Langmuir's laboratory notebooks complete from 1902 through his career at General Electric up to 1954, plus his personal letters from the 1880s to 1957. Flight? The Library owns the Wright Brothers' papers, Charles A. Lindbergh's, Robert Goddard's, John Glenn's. Theoretical physics? The Library has 74,000 pieces from the papers of J. Robert Oppenheimer, 145,000 of Merle Tuve. Government and science? The Library has the Vannevar Bush papers, the papers of almost all of the Surgeons General and the heads of the Geological Survey, the papers of Clara Barton and the American Red Cross.

Let's take a quick look at two of the collections to

get a sense of the human aspect of the individuals, albeit superficially.

The Alexander Graham Bell papers form an exceptionally visual example of personal papers since they involve a blizzard of family photographs. Not only did every parent and child have his own camera, but they all seemed equally at home in the darkroom. The pictures dramatize the startling variety of the inventor's interests.

Most of us remember Bell for his invention of the telephone, yet he considered himself primarily a teacher of the deaf and an inventor only as a by-product of his real vocation.

Bell was born in Scotland, one of three children. His mother was almost totally deaf and Alexander acted as her interpreter during his years at home. His father had been an actor in his youth and was an elocution and speech teacher in his mature life. The family had a warm and secure time together until 1867 when Bell's brother died of tuberculosis at the age of eighteen, and then his sister passed away with the same disease three years later when she was twenty-four. When Alexander began to show the same symptoms, the parents fled the damp Scotch climate and moved to Canada. Alexander became a teacher of the deaf in Boston, and he soon developed a national reputation (his future wife, the daughter of Gardiner Greene Hubbard, learned of Bell from hearing specialists while she was being treated in Vienna). Bell's interest in lip-reading and the vibration of air to create voice sounds by those who could not hear themselves speak led him to explore the conversion of the vibrations to electrical impulses which in turn could be moved along a wire—either between immediately conversing individuals or for long distances. As he got closer to solving the problem, his future father-in-law became interested, first underwrote the cost and then helped him take out the patents which in the end made Bell exceedingly rich.

All of the above can of course be found in any encyclopedia. What is news is what appears in the mass of letters, notes, photographs, and family papers given to the Library by Bell's grandson.

These papers tell the story of the invention of the telephone as perceived by Bell himself but in equally great detail as seen by Mabel Hubbard, his wife. The two were inseparable both inside and outside the laboratory. Family snapshots show them together clocking Bell's hydrofoil models, or with his wife holding the wire of his many kite designs

or taking notes about his vacuum jacket (the fore-runner of the iron lung).

With the royalties coming in from the telephone patents, Bell had the time and resources he needed to follow the widely disparate paths where his imagination took him. He designed fishing boats and his wife piloted them. He theorized that sheep born with multiple nipples had a greater likelihood of bearing multiple lambs and he built a carefully observed and recorded flock to test his hypothesis. (Verification perpetually eluded him on this gambit, and at intervals he would sell the flock in disgust only to find that his wife had hired a front man to bid in at auction, and the sheep were still in the family.) After twenty-four years the sheep idea was finally abandoned; no correlation ever developed.

Bell invented a successful device to produce drinking water from breath condensation to help dory fishermen who became separated from their mother ships. He invented an "induction balance"

Portrait of Alexander Graham Bell, 1913. The photographer, I.D. Boyce, reports he found him "working comfortably late into the night in his dressing gown and slippers."

to find metal (gun pellets and needles) in the human body. He was enamored of the tetrahedron, a triangular pyramid providing unusual strength for its weight, and Bell built endless models to demonstrate its potential applications. He used it in pylons and an observation tower was built in Quebec according to his plans. He used it in kites and gliders and ultimately in airplane designs; Glenn H. Curtiss made his first gasoline motor to power one of Bell's tetrahedral biplanes; and Bell's high-speed power boats were based on the tetrahedral unit.

In spite of his preoccupation with scientific experiments, Bell continued to keep up his contacts with schools of the deaf. Helen Keller's father brought her to Bell for instruction when she was six years old and Bell introduced them to Annie Sullivan, thus beginning the famous story of the Miracle Worker.

The Bells continued to work together throughout forty-five years of marriage, and the papers record a close alliance to the very end. Alexander finally died in August of 1922 and Mabel passed away five months later.

How does the Library come by such materials as these? It is frequently not easy. Let's look at the papers of Wilbur and Orville Wright.

The great flight near Kitty Hawk, North Carolina, occurred on December 17, 1903. Wilbur Wright died very suddenly on May 30, 1912, leaving his entire estate to his brother Orville, and thus the "Wright Brothers' materials" became effectively those of the younger brother alone.

The first Wright manuscripts came to the Library in 1931 imbedded in a huge collection of early aeronautica put together by Gaston Tissandier. Along with 1,800 other items were many rare letters from the Montgolfier brothers, pioneers of early balloons (1782–1800), and J.A.C. Charles' correspondence relating to his use of hydrogen in balloons (1783). The Wright materials in this bloc were few and dealt with fairly trivial matters.

The next year, however, Octave Chanute's daughters gave the Library a magnificent hoard of over 3,000 items, the bulk of their father's correspondence with all of the pioneers in aeronautics from the late 1800s to his death in 1910. Chanute was an intriguing figure, frequently referred to as the patriarch of American aviation. He started as a civil engineer and that Kansas town I grew up in was named after him, in honor of his having laid the original Santa Fe railroad track down its main

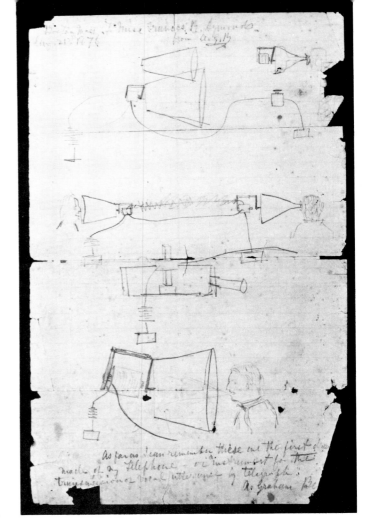

Opposite, top: *As Alexander Graham Bell notes on his sketch, "As far as I can remember these are the first drawings made of my telephone—or instrument for the transmission of vocal utterance by telegraph."*

Above: *Bell experimented in dozens of areas: boats, metal detectors, sheep breeding, flying objects. For this last, he designed numerous kites trying to discover which configuration would fly highest with least weight and greatest stability.*

Bell's wife, Mabel Hubbard, worked closely with him in all his experiments. Opposite, left: She is seen holding a kite cable. Below: Bell's daughter, Daisy, is transporting one of his tetrahedral shapes.

Wilbur Wright (on left) and Dan Tate launching Orville Wright in a glider, October 10, 1902. They chose the North Carolina dunes as a testing site because, of those recommended by the Weather Service for suitable winds, it was the closest to their hometown of Dayton, Ohio.

street (long before the cut-off of which I spoke). The roundhouse and back shops near Santa Fe Lake were designed and built by Chanute, and I was later startled to learn that the rest of the world remembered him for having taught the Wright Brothers most of what they knew about air frames.

After spending a lifetime laying out railroads and building bridges, Chanute began to read about the gliding experiments they were conducting in Europe, and he became fascinated. Although by then he was in his sixties, he built a gliding camp on the sand dunes near Lake Michigan and proceeded to make over two thousand accident-free flights in gliders that he designed and his young friends built. He was eagerly generous with everything he learned and carried on correspondence with people on both continents encouraging everyone to "try it yourself."

He was particularly intrigued with the problem of controlling and stabilizing his gliders and kept passing his data on to the Wrights as they experimented at the turn of the century. He visited the brothers on several occasions in 1901–02 when they were trying out their versions of his gliders at Kitty Hawk and thus the Chanute papers were loaded with Wright Brothers materials.

Given this lead, the head of the Library's Aeronautics Division wrote to Orville Wright in 1932 and invited him to visit the Library to see the research facilities and to talk to him about granting permission for some of his letters to be included in a book the Chanute daughters were planning.

Instead of getting the warm agreement hoped for, the initial invitation tripped a barrage of letters from Wright that 1) asked for the return of a letter that he knew Wilbur had written Octave appraising the aeronautical work of S.P. Langley, head of the Smithsonian Institution, 2) showed great reluctance to release anything he or Wilbur had written for any new publication other than in what he, Orville, might write, and that 3) ostentatiously ignored the hint that the Library would be pleased to have the Wright Brothers' papers as well. To add to the confusion, the Library found no sign of the Langley letter and therefore could not return it, which raised Wright's suspicions even further. More letters, more distress, and rising tension. (Much later the letter did turn up; Chanute had inadvertently mis-dated it which meant it had been automatically mis-filed and placed hundreds of pieces and many boxes away from where everyone was searching.)

As to where the brothers' papers would go, Orville apparently postponed that decision by drafting a will in 1937 instructing his executors "to give my aeronautical library and my files of correspondence and all other papers now contained in my laboratory...to whatever institution or institutions [they] in their best judgment may deem proper." The Institute of the Aeronautical Sciences in New

York and the Smithsonian Institution in Washington were as interested in the collection as was the Library of Congress.

But time passed. World War II came and went, and Wright became a national hero as the result of the explosive importance of air power. In 1947, fifteen years after the beginning of the conversation, a new Librarian of Congress wrote to Wright and asked if he, the Librarian, could send his new head of the aeronautics division out to talk with him. Wright promptly replied he would do better than that—he would come back to visit the Library himself. On May 21, 1947, he came to lunch and a splendid time was had by all. On September 19, 1947, all the participants visited Wright in his own office in Dayton, and arrangements were going forward smoothly for an exchange of papers when Orville suddenly died on January 30, 1948.

For the Library, a shock, but not a complete return to the beginning. Fortunately, Wright's personal secretary had been aware of the negotiations and Wright's intentions. Thus the executors listened sympathetically to the Librarian's pleas and on May 27, 1949, the 30,000 pieces of manuscripts (22 cubic feet in 68 boxes, dating from 1881 to 1948) arrived at the Library.

What was in them? Well, first, the pictures—the most famous of which appears on this page. There were 303 glass-plate negatives, mostly taken between 1898 and 1911 for the purpose of document-

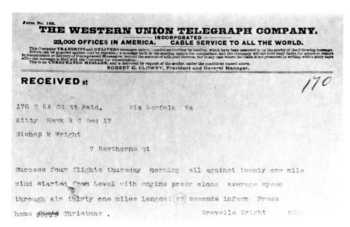

Top: *The historic photograph of the first successful powered flight near Kitty Hawk, 1903. Orville Wright is piloting in a prone position and his brother is running alongside to keep the wing from dipping into the sand. The bench on which the wing had been supported is in the foreground.*

Above: *The telegram the brothers sent to their father in Dayton, Ohio, reporting their success.*

ing success and failures with the new flying machines. Like everything else in the course of the Wright Brothers' invention, the pictures are done with great precision. (Because their work is traditionally described as taking place in their bicycle shop, they are too frequently perceived as two young tinkerers. Totally wrong. Their deliberate, methodical approach through hypothesis, research, design, model-making, wind-tunnel and full-scale experimentation could scarcely be improved on today. The only difference was that they had to invent much of their own test instrumentation as they went along. Successors merely elaborated on *their* work.)

Their pictures all tie to their notebooks which give time of exposure, stop setting, date, place, type of plate used, and subject matter for each shot. The pictures show their laboratory, their engines, the models, the runways, the flights—and the accidents. The shots of gliders, for example, cover the years from 1901 to 1903. The powered flights shown are from Kitty Hawk in 1903 and Huffman Prairie in 1904 and 1905.

The famous "first flight" shot was taken on December 17, 1903. The two brothers had gone to the dunes alone, so there was no obvious third person to witness the attempt. On the morning of the flight, Orville set up a camera on a tripod and aimed it at the point at which he hoped the plane would be airborne once it started its roll. A group from the nearby Kill Devil Life-Saving Station came over as preparations reached countdown and John T. Daniels was talked into manning the camera shutter (when and if the plane reached the end of the take-off rail).

When the great moment came the plane did indeed get to the end of the boards—by which time it was two feet in the air. Daniels pushed the shutter lever. The plane continued on for twelve more seconds (one hundred twenty feet) and rose to a height of eight to ten feet. There were three more successful flights that day and then, while the brothers talked to a group of spectators who had gathered, a gust of wind flipped the plane over and wrecked it. The Wrights took the camera home, developed the plate themselves, and we have the famous shot. (All 303 plates, incidentally, were soaked in muddy water for several days in the 1913 Dayton flood but, amazingly, only two were damaged in portions where an object was pictured. All the other bubbles and tears dutifully fell among peripheral clouds or sand dunes.)

Boxes 1 through 22 of the papers contain outgoing correspondence and have such material as a thirty-year dialogue with General H. H. Arnold, arrangements for a private demonstration flight for Kaiser Wilhelm in 1909, Admiral Richard E. Byrd's consultations regarding his Antarctic flight, and frequent letters about the "Kitty Hawk plane" itself (it was sent to England in 1928 for display in the Science Museum in Kensington where it hung until 1948; it is now in the Smithsonian's National Air and Space Museum in Washington, D.C.).

There are seven boxes of "received" correspondence which, apparently, the brothers perceived as "one-time-only" letters. Here is the letter from the Weather Bureau man at Kitty Hawk explaining about winds over the sand, a letter from Langley of the Smithsonian inquiring about the gliding experiments, and questions from Louis Blériot, who later flew the English Channel.

There are thirteen boxes of letters marked "subject" relating mostly to the media—interviews, articles, and negotiations for books. Rather unexpectedly, all of the correspondence dealing with the Dayton Art Institute, of which Orville was a founder, and the Edison Institute at Dearborn, where the bicycle shop and Wright home were moved, are here.

There are seven boxes regarding the sale of Wright planes to the military—not only to American military but to Flugmaschine Wright, their German company (1909–14) and to Thierry Brothers for the rest of Europe (1909–12).

And finally there are the twenty-nine volumes of notebooks which contain, as the Library's descriptive contents say, "formulas for the thrust of the airscrew, throw-down of air, propeller slip (air and water), centrifugal force, properties of spheres, weights, normal pressure per square foot, travel center pressure, head resistance, and lift/drag coefficients."

Documentation of the pure sciences is not news. Careful reporting, indeed publication, is a routine part of research. But not so in *technology*; here written records are rare. In earlier times the craftsmen who came up with the new solutions either could not write, or simply did not think to do so. The craft tradition was oral. Techniques were passed on by word of mouth. In more modern times, applied technology stayed out of print and therefore out of written memory because of competition. Know-how was closely guarded to give your own product an edge.

Because of these characteristics, the Library's holdings of the personal papers, the diaries, the company records of American industrialists and industries are the purest treasure. Is your interest in printing? The Library has the Hoe family papers (1830–1900) giving the story of the R. Hoe and Company's development of the rotary press. Steamboats? The Library has the diaries and papers of Robert Fulton, John Fitch, James Rumsey. Flying boats and helicopters? The Igor I. Sikorsky papers. Firearms? Edward Maynard and Rear Admiral John Adolph Dahlgren. And the Library's broad collection of Cooper-Hewitt papers, 1840–1900, not only tells us about Peter Cooper's ironworks at Ringwood, New Jersey, but the family glue factory as well.

And for you literature fans, that title at the beginning of this chapter is from Chaucer (in case you'd forgotten): "And out of olde bokes, in good feyth, cometh al this newe science that men lere."

The Library has many hundreds of collections of private papers that describe the growth of the nation's industries. Here the first computer punch card from the Hermann Hollerith papers, one of many collections recording the development of automation in the past one hundred years.

CHAPTER VIII

Orientalia

The Oriental divisions of the Library live in a world apart. Their materials come in scrolls, in folded paper books, on fascinating silks and textured papers. Their printed characters are dramatic—and everything I have just said is the source of endless frustration for them! It drives them to plead in meetings and memos, "Please don't consider us exotic!" And their point, of course, is absolutely valid. Just because most of us can't read their languages doesn't make their languages different. We're the ones who are different. And, as they point out, what is in these rather dramatic languages is exactly the same thing that is in all the rest of the library: literature, public health statistics, agricultural techniques for semi-arid clay soils, information on offshore oil production. And it is not antique; it is current and daily.

When I visited the Indic unit I found that they were receiving 2,095 magazines and journals on almost precisely the same topics as the ones we are getting from Switzerland and France. The only difference is that they come in languages I cannot even picture (indeed barely spell): 43 in Kannada, 34 in Telugu, 120 in Gujarati, 34 in Oriya, 70 in Marathi. This ignores the 225 Bengali periodicals, 516 Hindi, 240 Nepalese, and 300 in Urdu for which I have some faint feel of understanding.

When we turn to Chinese and Japanese materials, we are back in the superlatives again. The Library has more Chinese publications than any institution in the world outside of China itself. Its Japanese collection is not only the largest in the world outside of Japan but there are relatively few institutions *inside* Japan with as many Japanese titles as are here.

But say what they will, the material *is* exotic to Western eyes. Even the commonest novel or illustrated how-to manual has a thin-lined beauty that is absolutely riveting. Look at the volumes on pages 194 to 196. It is almost impossible to relate to them as "just books like everything else in the Library."

Where should we begin? Let's try to look at five things: first, let's consider the simple question of "the book" in the Orient and note its parallels and differences with the West's experience with the same invention. Next let's examine one of the languages to see what the unfamiliar swirls mean—we will look at Arabic for this. Then we will ask the question, How did a U.S. bureaucracy such as the Congressional library even get into the business of collecting Chinese and Japanese materials when, for its first full century of acquisition, not a *single* person on the staff could read those languages well enough to line up the volumes on the shelves (much less understand the contents). We will close with a quick look at how the 50,000 pieces of Asian and Mideastern materials the Library currently receives each year are found and brought to this country.

The "book" in the Orient began in much the same way as in the Greek and Roman tradition but then veered off in a different direction. The earliest forms of written material in the Far East are found, astonishingly, on oracle bones. Archeologists have found tens of thousands of tortoise shells and shoulder blades of cattle, each bearing long rows of both written characters and pictographs. What this early writing is about is at the least unusual. The upper surface of each bone is the record of a single question about a coming event which the bone's owner had asked the gods or some long-dead ancestor. Some of the queries relate to tactics to be used in an anticipated battle, others are asking for recommended treatment for a current illness, and similar matters. In their day the procedures were: the writings were cut into the bone with a metal stylus, and the piece was placed in an oven or covered with glowing coals and baked until it cracked. It was then carried to the wise men of the community for interpretation of the cracks. The effect, from our point of view, was similar to the study and analysis of chicken entrails in the Roman society but the Chinese approach had the advantage of far greater permanence so we can share the event some three thousand years later. Each oracle bone is inscribed with the year, month, and date of the query, and in the mass adds up to fascinating evidence of what concerned a Chinese citizen between 1400 and 1100 B.C. His fears centered on the ageless unknowns of health, politics, war, and economic distress. While we have these first written questions very clearly set down, regrettably we do not have the answers. We do not know what the elders perceived from the cracks in the bones they saw and which we now hold in our hands.

The first evidence of the creation of a "book"

A clay bulla with a cylinder seal impress depicting a worshipper along with a deity and a king. It dates from the Third Dynasty of Ur, Ancient Sumeria (present-day Iraq), about the twenty-first century B.C.

made to be published—distributed to pass on information among other readers—appears about a thousand years before Christ when bamboo strips and wooden boards emerge. Large, living bamboo stalks were cut into one- and two-foot sections and split into narrow strips. Since the convention of making characters in vertical columns had already been established, the narrow bamboo strips were ideal for the vertical rows of words. The longer strips were used for classical literature, while biographies and essays were written on the one-foot ones. All the slats were laced together at the bottom with silk cords or leather thongs to make individual bundles. Each bundle contained a complete essay or chapter called a *pien*. The classical literature is filled with such titles as *The Seven Pien of Mencius*, referring to the traditional number of bundles required for that particular work. Confucius is supposed to have been so taken by the *Book of Changes* that he went through—wore out—three sets of leather thongs holding the slats together.

Texts requiring more than a hundred characters were written on the bamboo strips as noted; texts requiring fewer than a hundred went on wooden boards cut thin like shingles and made into squares roughly the size of our twelve-inch foot. The square boards were saved for short essays, governmental directives, and personal correspondence. Astonishingly, thousands of these bundles of bamboo and packets of boards still exist and range from inventories of weapons to land contracts and letters home to parents. Many of the book bundles are found in their own individual bags, apparently to preserve the sequence of the strips should the cord break or rot.

About the fourth century B.C., the common bamboo and board books were joined by volumes of silk. Bamboo and boards were heavy, clumsy, and hard to transport, so the scribes began writing directly on panels of cloth. The silk began to be woven specifically for the purpose of being written on and different colors of thread were worked in to represent the traditional wooden "pages." Ultimately the whole affair became a seamless scroll, the panels running sequentially from beginning to end, right to left, in an unbroken series. The conventions were very colorful: the pages were white, the column lines were red, paragraph headings were written in red ink, and the text drawn in black.

In 221 B.C. (about the time Hannibal was crossing the Alps) China's formative, provincial years

The world's oldest extant sample of printing, Japanese dating from A.D. 770, consists of four dharani, *passages from a Buddhist sutra used as prayer charms. Empress Shotoku, grateful for the end of an eight-year civil war, ordered that the* dharani *be printed and placed in "one million" tiny wooden pagodas as a memorial to the dead. The pagodas were distributed to ten temples throughout Japan. The three original charms owned by the Library are now encased in Plexiglas for preservation purposes. The pagoda is in the center of the picture.*

came to an end and a strong figure from the Ch'in dynasty unified the area into an empire. All the books that could be found were seized and burned (to obliterate any memory of previous rulers and loyalties) and the only titles permitted to exist were those dealing with medicine, pharmacy, divination, and agriculture. Over four hundred scholars were buried alive to dramatize the edict. The result was wholesale destruction and the loss of many classical titles which are now known only by reference in other works. But with the destruction came the salutary effect of showing the value of the written word. Thousands of volumes were promptly hidden in walls, secreted in caves, and buried in the ground so that when the Emperor Han Wu Ti appeared sixty years later, one of his first acts was to

create the first governmental libraries in East Asia. A vigorous program was pursued to recover the lost volumes, make additional copies to distribute among the various branches, and create a national bibliography. Regrettably this pattern seems to have been repeated regularly throughout the next thousand years of Imperial China. Gathering the books into a single library improved control and record keeping, but made the institutions prime targets for prompt burning at each change of dynasty.

But we are now at the first major leap forward: the invention of paper. Unquestionably achieved by the Chinese, traditionally supposed to have happened in A.D. 105, the idea is credited to a eunuch in the Imperial Household of the Eastern Han dynasty, one Tsai Lun. Tsai is supposed to have experimented with tree bark to reduce molds, hemp for toughness, rags for flexibility, and old fishing nets because they were cheap. All of these worked very well (and still do), and regardless of how we may be guessing at the original date and inventor, there is no question that the use of paper simply exploded about this time and it appears everywhere throughout the Orient. From China it worked its way in every direction like waves in a pool touching Korea, Japan, and Indochina at once, and Persia, Egypt, Morocco, and Europe (via Spain) in slower, but easily identifiable progression.

Paper permitted the rapid multiplication of the books, and the wood and bamboo formats promptly disappeared. For centuries at the beginning, paper was made in sheets about one-foot square. The commonest technique was to take silk waste and bark, beat it into pulp, pour it out onto a woven bamboo screen, and when it was dry you had a very high-grade sheet of paper. These sheets were pasted side by side into scrolls as the silk books had

been. It is intriguing to note that a scroll usually carried the same number of "pages" as a bundle of bamboo strips had equalled, and thus when long works were copied, a number of scrolls was required. If a book had traditionally used five bamboo pien, it took five scrolls in silk or paper. All of these would be tagged and kept together in a cloth sack. To protect the scroll, a piece of heavy cloth was pasted to the last few sheets, and a cord was stitched on so the scroll could be tied and kept from unrolling.

The scrolls were hand-copied from each other (as the medieval vellum manuscripts had been) and both the nobility and the scholars built huge private libraries copied at their own expense with contract labor. The day of the scroll ran from about the year A.D. 420 to A.D. 1000, and during this period we read of Emperor Yang Ti ordering 89,000 scrolls copied, Emperor Tang Wen Tsung buying 56,000 scrolls, and many individual merchants owning 10,000 to 30,000 scrolls in their private libraries. What was written on the scrolls? First, like the

Above: *This is a Chinese version of the* Saddharma Pundarika Sutra *printed on a scroll 68 feet long and 6½ inches wide. The second oldest Chinese imprint in the Library of Congress, it was printed from blocks in Hang-chow, China, about A.D. 1050.*

Opposite: *Compiled by Wei Shou in the Northern Ch'i Dynasty of China (A.D. 550–577), this is probably the oldest and most accurate extant copy of the official history of the Wei Dynasty. It was printed in A.D. 1144.*

序紀第一　　魏書一

昔黃帝有子二十五人或內列諸華或外分荒
服昌意少子受封北土國有大鮮卑山因以爲
號其後世爲君長統幽都之北廣漠之野畜牧
遷徙射獵爲業淳樸爲俗簡易爲化不爲文字
刻木紀契而已世事遠近人相傳授如史官之
紀録焉黃帝以土德王北俗謂土爲托謂后爲
跋故以爲氏其裔始均入仕堯世逐女魃於弱
水之北民賴其勤帝舜嘉之命爲田祖爰歷三

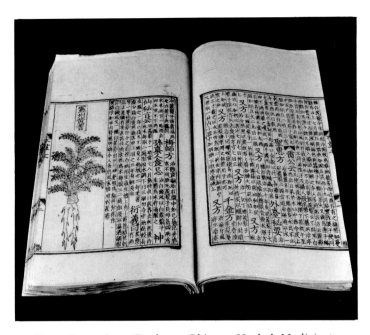

From Pen ts'ao *(Book on Chinese Herbal Medicine), compiled by T'ang Shen-wei of the Sung Dynasty and printed in Ping-yang, Shansi, in* A.D. *1249. These volumes are probably the only ones that remain of the Ch'in Dynasty printing of this book.*

Christian texts of Western medieval writings, the writings of Buddhist and Taoist scriptures and the Confucian classics were common. There were also dictionaries of the Chinese characters, medical books, geographies, novels, and poetry. The material kept remarkably well and what wasn't burned or destroyed in the interminable wars of revolution and revolt has lasted in good shape to our own time—the paper flexible and the ink unfaded. There are tens of thousands of these scrolls in existence, and with the accelerated digging going on in modern China, more are appearing with every archeological project.

About the year 1000, the scroll began to yield to folded panels, in much the way the vellum rolls became the codex in the West. In China, the frustration of rolling long scrolls back and forth to find a single passage drove the users to what was called a "sutra binding" from its common use for Buddhist texts. In this form, the long scrolls were folded back and forth on themselves to create stacks of rectangular pages which could then be easily accessed. This was further refined by pasting the first and last pages onto a single, folded sheet of paper which would keep the whole thing from springing apart like an exploding accordion.

And this is the first point of divergence between Eastern and Western bookmaking. In the West, the folded scroll became the codex, the folded page became a single sheet with writing on front and back, and the sheets became a book sewn at the spine. In the East, because the brush-written characters were so flooded with black ink that they immediately soaked through to the back of the page, the fold had to be retained. Thus the Chinese book continued as a simple series of folded pages right up to modern times. Every "page" in a traditional Oriental volume is written on one side, with either nothing or smudges on the other. This results in a perpetual confusion for Western librarians, which we will get to in a moment.

But we must first note the invention of printing, because even more important than paper, Chinese printing anticipated European by 600 years. Here again the two paths diverged. Chinese printing—and note that this is not simply a few archeological relics; printed books were as common in China in 1000 as they were in Europe in 1600—is the story of *block* printing which in modern times added some moveable type elaborations. In Europe, printing is *moveable type* with some block printing added at the edges, mostly for illustrations. The different approaches were to be expected and came about from the following steps.

In China, as in Europe, the original texts were precise pieces of religious writings, classics of literature, governmental edicts and chronologies. They were copied and passed on by fallible hands, generation after generation. Errors continued to creep in. The Chinese decided to stop the deterioration by having the basic texts cut into stone slabs and the slabs set up in the governmental centers. Scholars then came to the stones, did rubbings, and took the approved texts away with them as white writing (from the recessed characters) on black sheets.

When paper was invented, it became easy and profitable to make copies of the classical texts in large quantities. In the tradition of the official stone slabs, the printers would have a careful writing of the text they wished to publish inscribed on a piece of rice paper cut to the size of the page they intended to use. The ink on the paper promptly soaked through to the back, the ink was let dry, and the paper was pasted face down on a smooth board. The block cutter would then cut away all of the white paper, leaving the black characters standing up as a single block full of all the words for the entire page. The printing face was thus automatically reversed, ready to receive ink. A hundred-page book would thus have one hundred blocks, easy to put in the press and easy to store for future editions.

In Europe it was simpler to keep 26 letters plus a few punctuation marks and ligatures in a one-drawer font and make up words as they were needed; the moveable type would be set, printed, dispersed, and used again. But this would not work for the Chinese, of course. Because of the nature of their written words, it required at least one or two characters for every word and even as early as 1300 the printer had to stock over 30,000 different characters to cope with even a basic, fairly primitive vocabulary. (Incidentally, instead of keeping the type in a single tray frame as was done in the West, the Eastern printer had two huge lazy susans which spun on a central axis three feet off the ground. Fifteen thousand different characters were stored in tiny bamboo compartments arranged in series of their rhymed sounds and one printer would call out the sound and the specific character, while another would spin the table to select the piece to be set in the form.)

The result of all these complexities was that for centuries beyond the time the Europeans were setting type, the Chinese and the Japanese were still cutting single-page wood blocks—but the reverse was that for centuries before the Europeans began to print books at all, printed books were common throughout the Orient.

And this gets us back to the basic form of the Eastern book. Even as the brush-written book so soaked the page that it could be used on only one side, so did the block book in a simple press. Further, the continuous sheet of paper that had come from the scroll (though now accordion folded) was far too clumsy to be slid a page at a time through the press, so the solution was to continue with a basic folded book but to paste the printed sheets in place, two at a time, on top of the folded paper. At first, for a few centuries, the printed sheets were folded in the middle and the crease put in the center where our "gutter" falls on a double-page spread, but it was found that steady use split open the folded outer edges revealing the blank inner faces. Therefore, for the next few centuries the printed sheets were folded backward and slid over the outer edges of the support page. Ultimately they printed them directly as a double spread, folded them backward, and sewed them down the side (over-sewn, we would say) to make a paper spine. The final product was used right up to our

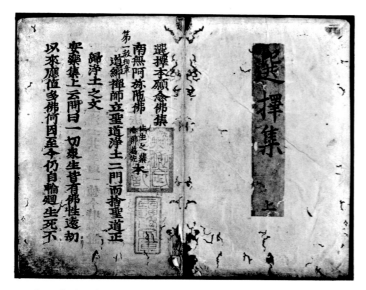

Senchaku hongan nembutsushū, *by Hōnen, a block print from early seventeenth-century Japan. This is the beginning of the basic scripture of the Jodo sect of Buddhism, which explains that* nembutsu (homage to Amida Buddha) *is the most appropriate teaching in the age of degeneration.*

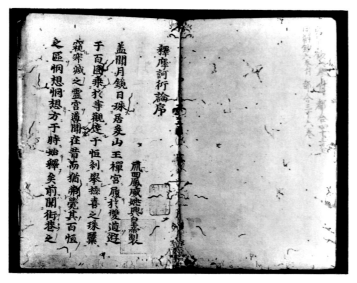

Shaku makaen ron, *a commentary on* Daijō kishin ron, *which is a summation of the central thought of Mahayana Buddhism. This is a Chinese translation, presumed to have been written by Nāgarjuna (A.D. 150–250), although the original has never been discovered. This book was block printed c. 1550 at Kōyasa and classified as Kōyasa-ban (a generic term for any book printed by the Shingon monks of the Mt. Kōya complex in Japan).*

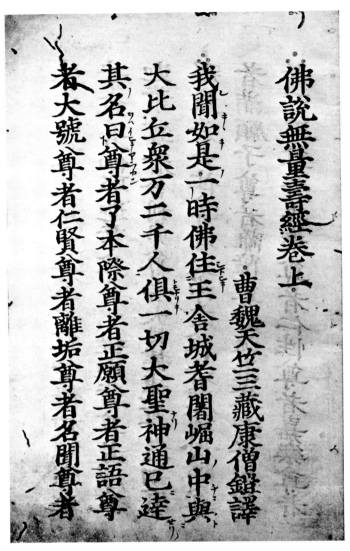

Muryōjukyō, a block-printed volume containing one of the three basic scriptures of the Pure Land school of Buddhism. Japanese scholars at the Library believe it dates from the fourteenth century.

own time: it was a paper book of folded sheets, thread sewn along the back side and unable to stand by itself. The basic Chinese book became a stack of paper-backed pamphlets, loose, limp, and requiring flat shelf storage, where they were laid stacked on their sides. This is the reason for the wild variations we get in piece counts. It is confusing in encyclopedia articles and drives librarians to frustration.

We are told that the famous Yung Lo Encyclopedia of 1407 comprised 11,915 volumes and we get an image of a whole library full of books. But these volumes were really "signatures," loose, fifty-to-one-hundred-page packets of sheets. The Library of Congress' collection of Chinese materials was reported as 3,750 volumes in 1900—but this amounted to only 370 individual titles or books. It might appear that with all these loose parts stacked around, portions would get separated or lost and the integrity of the complete books would suffer. That is exactly what happens and apparently people have been complaining about it for nearly a thousand years now.

Let's consider the scripts in some of these Eastern volumes. The accompanying illustrations in this chapter show a very limited sample of the various calligraphies that can be found on the Library's shelves. The Chinese and Japanese are fairly familiar, and surprisingly (considering how very foreign they are to Western experience) the story of their development from pictographs and miniature drawings to the formal symbols is reasonably well known. The Arabic script, however, is just as foreign and just as common, but its antecedents and characteristics are much less familiar. A few words might make the examples more meaningful.

The Arabic script is to the Arab world as the Roman letters are to the West. The Roman letters were invented to record Latin, but the English, the French, the Spanish have used the Roman alphabet to record their own spoken languages. Similarly, the Arabic letters were invented to record the language of northern Arabia (and their alphabet is somewhat *newer* than the Roman, having been developed in the early centuries after the birth of Christ), but here a strange dichotomy appears. In *written* Arabic, no matter what country it is written and read in across the whole Muslim crescent, the words are mostly the same. Newspapermen in Casablanca and Baghdad write the same words and express themselves with the same vocabularies. They do not write Algerian or Egyptian or Iraqi;

KUFI

EASTERN KUFI or QARMAṬI

TAWQI'

SUNBULI

Above: *At left is the letter* alif, *the basic letter in the Arabic alphabet. It provides the dimensions for the other twenty-seven. At center is the base shape for the second, third, and fourth letters made by adding dots above or below. At right, the sixth letter of the alphabet which again becomes two more by placing a dot over the bar or in the center of the circle.*

Left: *The verse from the Koran, "We have created you male and female," as it appears when written in four different Arabic scripts. In each case, of course, all the letters are the same, they are simply expressed in different styles.*

they write Arabic. But when they speak, there are wide differences. One Arabic scholar has said that the spoken languages vary from one Arabic country to another as the vocabularies of American sports announcers differ from the English of Chaucer.

Arabic has seventeen "graphic shapes" which become 28 letters by adding dots over, under, and within some of the figures. Arabic is written from right to left, and as a rule most of the vowels are left out. In like manner (presumably to save space in the early days of vellum and paper), there are no gaps between words and the superficial appearance is that the entire text runs together in a single line. In fact, letters are linked by touching ink, and tiny separations show the reader where one word ends and the next begins. Thus, if the Muslim creed "There is no God but Allah, and Muhammad is His Prophet" were written in English as it would be in Arabic, it would look like (reading from the right):

thprP shsi dmmhMdna ,hllA tb dGonsi rhT

Calligraphy is a fully developed art in the Muslim world, and is respected as an end in itself, not sim-

ply as an embellishment of other crafts as in the West. The source of this respect, this standing, comes from the unusual importance of the Koran in the Muslim religion. In the Judeo-Christian faith the Bible is a series of revealed histories, poems, stories told and events described by a series of individual authors. Muhammad taught that the words in the Koran are the direct and precise words of God speaking and therefore are to be treated as a sacred object in themselves. Thus, writing out the Koran (which contains 72,430 words—approximately the number in the New Testament) is a common act of piety in the Muslim world, and the beauty of the script that is used is an element of major importance and devotion in itself.

The Arabic script as we know it was specifically designed to be used to copy the Koran and was perfected in Kufa, a city in Iraq, in the early 600s. The thus "approved" script became known as Kufic and was the form of written Arabic used for all purposes for the first three hundred years after the death of Muhammad. An example of Kufic appears on page 184.

As the years passed, the religious of the time found the design difficult to read because of its

Opposite top: *A diploma certifying that Ali Ra'if has achieved competency in Arabic calligraphy,* A.D. *1791. The two panels in green are testimony (in Ijazah script) of two different masters declaring their satisfaction with his skill.*

Opposite bottom: *A Koranic verse in Kufic script saying, "By the morning when it draws breath. Truly, this is the speech of a noble messenger, powerful and secure with the Lord of the Throne."*

Left: *A sheet carrying five verses from the Koran. Each verse is separated from the next with gold "petals," and the Arabic is surrounded by "clouds" and random ornaments. The script is in Rayhani style.*

With its fine calligraphic text highlighted with gold leaf, this is a fourteenth-century manuscript copy of the Koran. The binding is of light tan morocco elaborately tooled in blind with stamps of intricate design.

severe angularity, and the scribes found the straight lines hard to draw with proper grace, so about 900 the vizier of the caliphs of Baghdad, Ibn Muqlah, invented six additional styles to be used for different applications—casual copying for study, monumental inscriptions for architecture, compact versions for portable versions of the Koran, et cetera. Of the six styles, one of them was a smooth, cursive form called Naskh and this became the commonest choice; it is the one most frequently used today for books and newspaper printing.

Ibn Muqlah set the rules for Arabic calligraphy (and his six styles, by the way, have been elaborated into dozens of modern alphabets with far more variety than is available in Western script writing). The vizier declared that the first letter of the alphabet—*alif*, essentially a vertical straight line—would determine the proportions of all the succeeding letters. It is to be used as the diameter of an imaginary circle which will hold all the subsequent forms. These in turn have their own basic shapes (as seen on page 183) and the position of the dots changes the letters from one sound to another.

The various examples of the art illustrated in this chapter speak for themselves. As a rule, each is a carefully drawn, delicately embellished single verse drawn from the Koran. They are selected from hundreds of Korans in the Library's collection, and to the layman coming on them for the first time, one of the most startling aspects of the calligraphic tradition is that it is a progression only to the historian. The various styles were developed through many centuries, but once chosen and fixed, they have become a part of the calligraphers' working palette and they appear side by side in their work through the years. A modern calligrapher is as comfortable writing with medieval forms as he is with some of the harshly modern alphabets designed in the past half century, and he will use both on successive days, a dozen in a month, depending on the purpose and the "feel" of the pieces he is inscribing. Thus as you remove a volume from the Library's shelves, scripts separated by hundreds of years sit side by side separated only by the shelf-lister's accession number; publication dates mean little here.

How did the Library get all these Oriental volumes, all quite unreadable to the average taxpaying American? It seems like a superficial question, but it touches on a number of anomalies about the Library of Congress.

First, how does the Library get most of its mate-

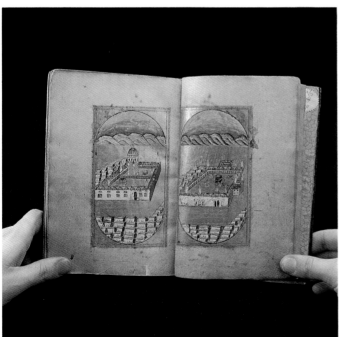

Above: *This rare Arab saddle book consisting of separate leaves of the Koran is protected by four leather cases, each fitting inside another. The leather thongs allowed the rider to hang the case on his saddle horn or around his neck.*

Left: *This 1780 Arabic manuscript copy of* The Guide for the Good *is unusual in its illustrations of the Holy Cities of Islam, Medina, and Mecca. It is a collection of prayers and recitations in praise of God and the Prophet Muhammad.*

Washington Haggadah, *Germany or North Italy, 1478. An illuminated Hebrew manuscript executed by Joel ben Simeon. The Haggadah is the book containing the Exodus narration and the order of service used at the Passover Seder.*

rials? They are overwhelmingly *given* to it. This, the world's largest library, receives the majority of its materials quite passively. It establishes the paths of receipt and then waits quietly to see what will come through its doors. In English-language materials, this means copyright deposits first, exchange relationships next (these mostly either governmental or cultural), and gifts last. The gifts are usually the most unusual and possibly the most valuable.

While these devices won't work for European materials, the receipt is still passive. Almost nothing comes in by copyright, some arrives from governments and educational institutions by exchange, but most European—and Latin American—receipt is by contract with booksellers or national bibliographic centers. The majority of these private

contractors have supplied the Library with materials for decades; they know what the Library of Congress wants, they forward it at their own initiative, and the Library pays them at the end of the month.

But in the Asian and African countries, few of these devices work at all. There is certainly no copyright deposit, there frequently are no central institutions to "exchange" anything with, and "major booksellers" are non-existent. Most publishing is done ad hoc, in small runs, prepared for a specific elite or an interest group, and it disappears as quickly as sudden rain on dry sand.

Before we note how the Library gets around these obstacles, however, we should ask, Why *does* the Library want "everything from everywhere

Below: Samgang Haengsilto (*The Three Fundamental Duties*), printed from wooden blocks in Seoul, Korea, in 1514. The text, in the Korean vernacular, describes the necesssity for filial duty and the pictures illustrate the same theme.

Above: *Two examples of fine eighteenth-century Persian calligraphy in the Nastaliq style from the Minassian collection. Acquired by the Library in the 1920s and 30s from Kirkor Minassian, an authority on Near Eastern manuscripts, the collection of over 200 items demonstrates the development of the book arts in the Middle East. The two samples shown here were copied from the fourteenth-century poet Hafiz.*

Above and opposite: Shizuka, *a book form version of Kōwakamai (ballad drama), is a manuscript with seventeen colored illustrations dating from early seventeenth-century Japan. It is a tragic tale of Shizuka, the mistress of Yoshitsume, the hero of the Minamoto family. It was based on historical fact and composed during the Muromachi period (1392–1490).*

about everything" anyway? And that is not so easy to answer. The obvious responses don't really hold up to reality. Let's try a few:

"As the national library, the Library of Congress has the obvious obligation to be the nation's central acquisition and storage point of foreign literature and culture; that's what national libraries do." Not really. There are one hundred national libraries operating around the world today and only four even make a gesture at having any quantity of materials beyond the works of their own countrymen. National libraries concentrate on national publishing; foreign publishing is sought by colleges, universities, and scholarly institutes.

Second possible explanation: "Because we are a nation of nationalities, we should know about our antecedents." A better reply. This is true of many

of our cultural and literary traditions and products, but how do we explain the fact that almost half of all the books in the Library of Congress are in languages that almost none of the readers who come through its doors can read? The Library's really astonishing holdings in Tibetan (probably the largest in the world) surely don't reflect the Tibetan voting constituency in the United States.

Third possibility: "Because the federal government must know about the nations with whom it deals diplomatically, and must live with, the central governmental library should be comprehensive in its holdings on all cultures." Better yet. Every night's news demonstrates the fact that on this shrinking globe there seems to be no nation so small nor tribe so obscure that it does not have the power to affect our lives in some way. We can never know too much

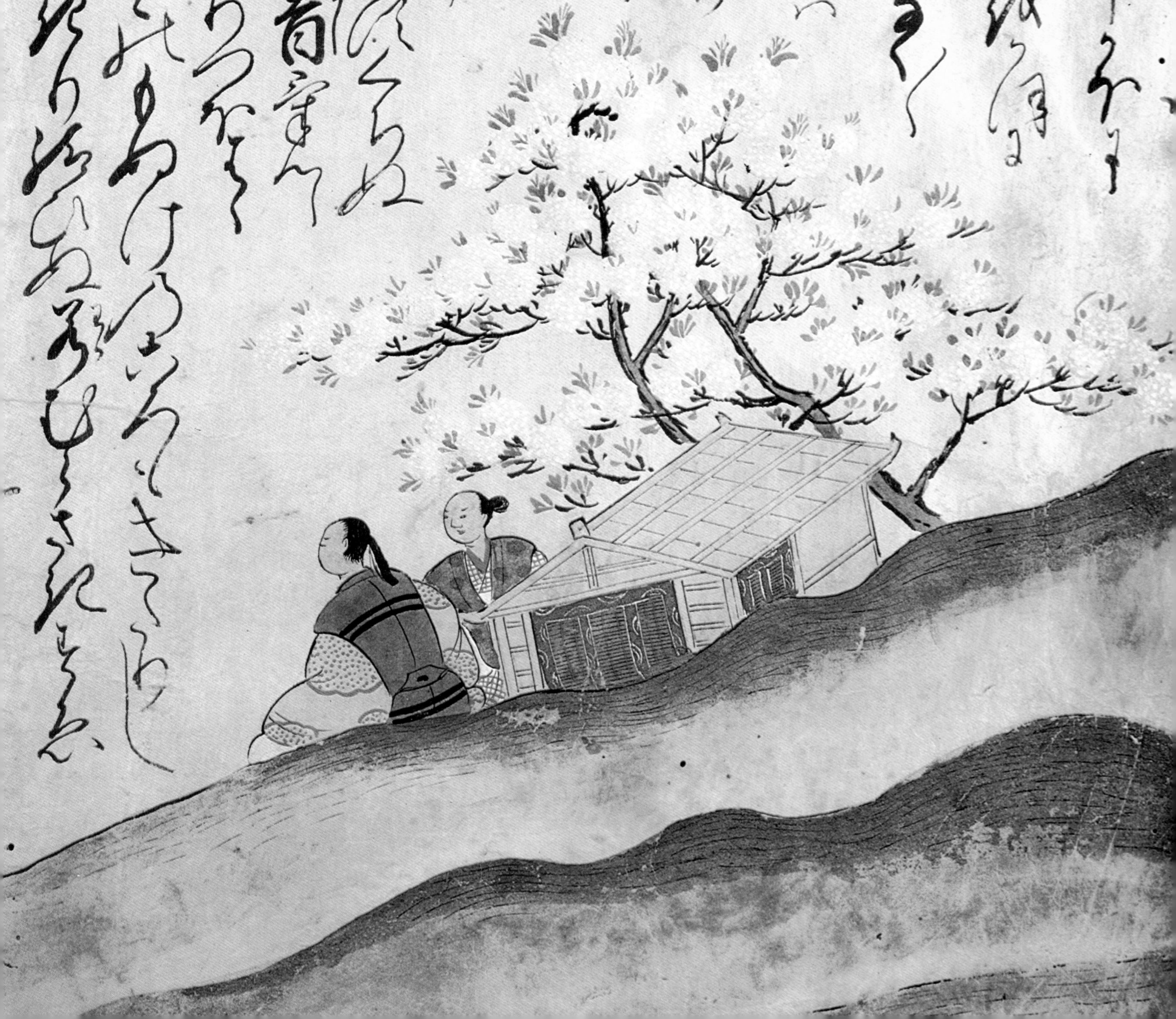

This early block-printed edition of Genji monogatari *(The Tale of Genji) provides an excellent illustration of the binding of printed books in the Orient. It consists of 60 separate volumes with soft covers, 54 of them text and illustration, with 6 supplemental volumes. It was published in Kyoto, Japan, in 1654. The author of the work, Murasaki Shikibu, was descended from a prominent literary family, and probably wrote the novel when she was in her mid-twenties. Written almost a thousand years ago,* Genji monogatari *is the world's earliest novel and one of the longest. It ranks as the undisputed masterpiece of all Japanese literature and is the subject of comment and study even today.*

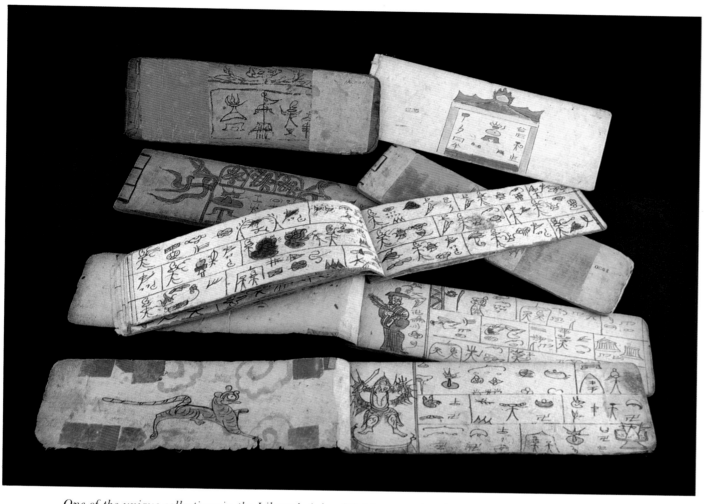

One of the unique collections in the Library's Asian Division contains these pictographic manuscripts of the Mo-so tribe that lives in the northwestern part of Yun-nan Province, southwestern China. Consisting of more than 3,000 volumes, they are sacred books written by hand by the tribe's sorcerers, and they deal with such subjects as sacrifices to the Dragon king, funeral ceremonies, and suppression of evil spirits. They were purchased for the Library by Joseph Rock and Quentin Roosevelt between 1924 and 1945.

about their values, their traditions, their needs and fears to live with them successfully.

Final possibility: "Because we have so many libraries and so many universities and so many governmental agencies and so many individual scholars seeking information about so many foreign places and cultures, it would be clumsy and wasteful to have all our experts competing against each other for materials. If all of them try to identify and bring back the fugitive and the ephemeral product of the out-of-the-way places it is an enormous waste of money and effort. The national library, which must do it for the government anyway, should be the central point of acquisition, and then produce lists and bibliographies and centralized cataloging so all the other institutions can pick and choose the

items that they need. They can then seek them out themselves, rather than floundering with everyone else through the bibliographic underbrush." Very good, the most convincing answer of them all.

But has the national acquisition policy ever really been so rational? Isn't the truth simply that from Jefferson's time on, the Library of Congress assumed that it would try to get one copy of everything from everywhere about everything and it is simply a part of the national expectation, its national role to do so? Probably. The Chinese and the Japanese and the Korean and the Indic collections certainly began that way, and most of the other now monumental holdings started in a similar manner.

Let me sketch out very quickly how the Library of Congress began to gather Chinese material and

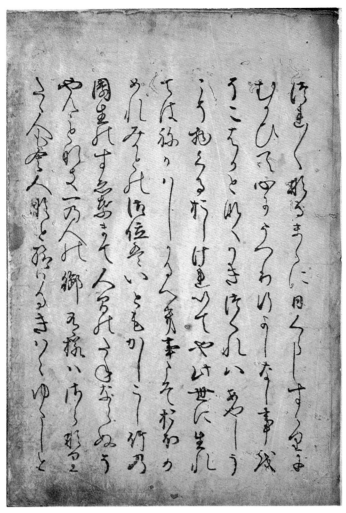

this can serve as a very legitimate model for most of the other Oriental collections.

Time and again what has really worked at the Library has not been a program or a library-wide plan but the effort of some single individual. This is proved true again with the actual beginning of its Chinese collection. General Caleb Cushing (from Massachusetts, of course) had served four terms in Congress when in 1843 he was appointed "Commissioner, Envoy Extraordinary and Minister Plenipotentiary of the United States to China." The Emperor Tao-Kuang had sent President Tyler a letter which read:

Now that the English barbarians have been allowed to trade, whatever other countries there are, the United States and others, should naturally be permitted to trade without discrimination, in order to show our tranquilizing purpose.

The President gave Cushing a frigate and a sloop-of-war so he could arrive in style and sent him out to make a trade treaty. Cushing spent the entire trip learning to read Chinese and, we are told, was fluent in Mandarin by the time he arrived in Macao.

Cushing stayed in China for three years and spent much of his time deliberately building an integrated book collection which would paint a com-

Above: Tsurezuregusa. *Well-known to the Japanese, these essays on such topics as manners, the arts, and nature were written about 1330. This block-printed version dates from the early seventeenth century and is in Saga-bon form, that is, books printed at a press in Saga, near Kyoto. Saga-bon are noted for the lavish attention given to the quality of paper, binding, calligraphy, and overall appearance.*

Right: *A rare manuscript edition of* Shigure (Romance of Autumn Showers) *from the early seventeenth century. An example of Japanese Nara-ehon.*

Soga monogatari, *manuscript of 25 volumes with 122 colored illustrations, is another example of Nara-*
ehon *from seventeenth-century Japan. These manuscripts, written in fine calligraphy on high-quality paper*
with brilliant illustrations, were all produced between the late sixteenth and early eighteenth centuries.
Nara-ehon *(fine manuscripts with illustrations) serves as a transition step between the ancient picture*
scroll and the modern illustrated book.

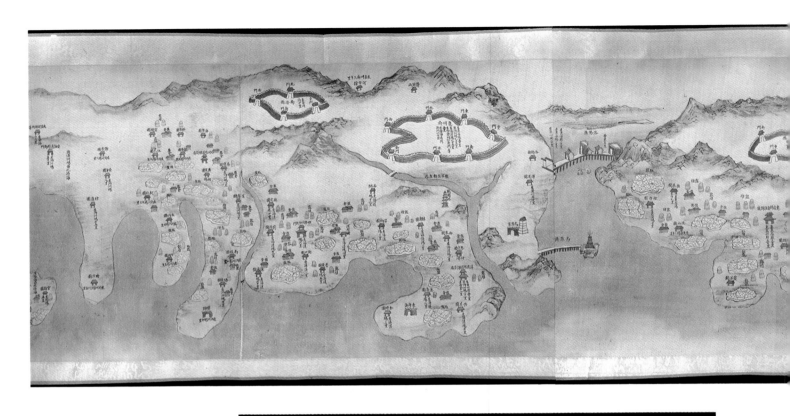

Right: Homyo doji *is a Japanese tale based on material from Buddhist scriptures. This manuscript, with eighteen brilliantly colored illustrations, dates from the latter half of the sixteenth century.*

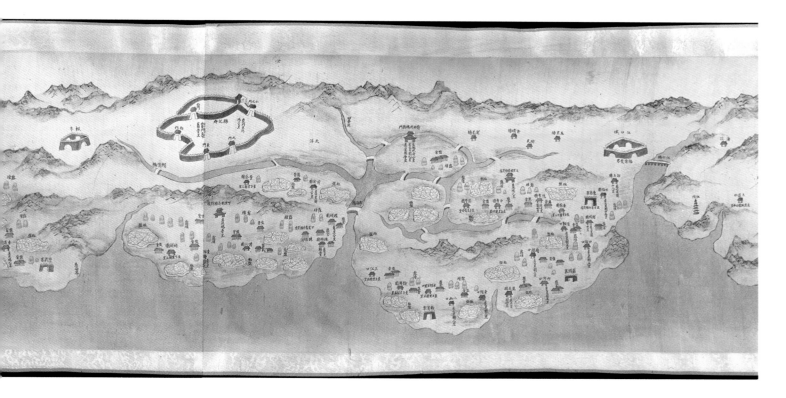

plete picture of all the aspects of the Chinese culture. Ultimately this basic group of books came to 2,547 unbound volumes (at a cost of 17 cents each in China!) and when it was auctioned off in Boston in 1879 on Cushing's death, Librarian Spofford recognized it as a genuine collection of treasure. Spofford bought it totally, using up 40 percent of the Library's book budget for that year on the single purchase. The Cushing collection can still be identified at the Library of Congress and Chinese scholars are still in awe at the precision and intelligence with which it was assembled. It has *all* the classics and essentially something of great value on all the parts of the then contemporary Chinese society.

At about this point, the Smithsonian Institution thought it was time to stir up some international exchange and set out to acquire Chinese books in general and Chinese botany books in particular (they especially wanted to identify plants that could be profitably imported into America—which roughly shares the same characteristic of temperature and rainfall with China). Secretary Joseph Henry wrote the United States chargé d'affaires in Peking suggesting that he negotiate a governmental exchange agreement so that documents could be traded on a regular basis. Henry filled three packing cases with U.S. government publications and offered them to the Emperor of China through the

Min sheng yen ch'ang ch'uan t'u, manuscript on silk scroll, oriented with north to the right, 1746. Since the salt industry was a government monopoly and an important source of revenue in imperial China, the distribution of salt fields along the coast, the method of shipping salt inland, and official quotas of salt in each province were a major concern to the ruling class. This drawing by an anonymous artist epitomizes the application of traditional landscape painting technique to the thematic mapping of the relationship between various salt fields and their major storages and administrative headquarters. The drawing covers both the coastal areas of Fukien and the west coast of Taiwan.

A colored woodblock by Suzuki Harunobu, printed with water-based inks on rice paper.

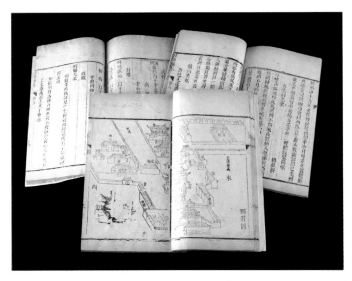

Above: *The Library of Congress has the largest collection of Chinese local histories outside China, with more than 4,000 titles in all. They are rich in historical data on local institutions, customs, geography, and plants and animals of the area. Shown here is a typical volume from the local history of Feng-tu County, Ssu-ch'uan Province, published in 1710.*

American diplomat. The diplomat examined the packing list and wrote to Henry:

At present I do not think there are a score of Chinese in the whole country who are able to fully understand them, but it is even more probable that there is not half that number of persons in the United States (not including Chinese) who could intelligently consult the works which this government might send to them in exchange. It is perhaps best then not to press the subject at present.

But the diplomat had misread the situation. In 1869, the Chinese government selected ten titles to send out—actually involving 934 of the folded Chinese paper volumes. The ten included *The Perfect Mirror of Medical Science* printed in 1740 and including 91 Chinese volumes; they sent 24 volumes on agriculture, 10 volumes on acupuncture, 10 on mathematics, and *Research into the Five Rituals* in 120 volumes and published in 1754. This dealt with marriages, funerals, military affairs, visits, and "joyful occasions." The diplomat had guessed right on the Chinese interest in materials from the United States, however. They told Secretary Henry that it would not be necessary to send any American materials in exchange. In fact, packing boxes accumulated in the Smithsonian warehouse for many years, waiting for information on where they should be sent, and they were ultimately discarded.

The next link to the Chinese culture came, surprisingly enough, from the Librarian of Congress himself, John Russell Young. Young had been a reporter who had gone around the world with General Grant (on a two-and-a-half-year voyage), and by the time he got back he had so impressed Grant that the latter got President Chester A. Arthur to appoint Young American minister to China from 1882 to 1885. The experience proved to be one of the most satisfying periods of Young's life, and he had surrounded himself with a group of young men who later became the "Old China hands" of the first half of this century. His personal secretary in Peking had been one William Woodville Rockhill who himself became one of the leading China experts in American history. Young became Librarian in 1897, died in 1899, and as a memorial to his mentor, Rockhill donated his entire China collection to the Library of Congress in 1902. This involved some 6,000 volumes in Manchu, Mongolian, and Tibetan.

Muhammad Amīn ibn Abī al-Husain Kazvīnī, *called* Amīna-i Kazvīnī Pādishāhnāmah. *This handsome Persian manuscript, part of the Rosenwald Collection, is believed to date from the early eighteenth century. It deals with the life of Shah Jahan, the Indian emperor during whose reign (1627–58) the Taj Mahal and other architectural glories were built in India. The text is written in Nastaliq script and the illustrations depict scenes from the emperor's private and official life shown against backgrounds of the unique architecture he created.*

I Tsung Kin Kien (The Perfect Mirror of Medical Science). *Printed at Peking in 1740 in ninety-one volumes, this is one of the ten titles that was part of the first exchange of publications between American and Chinese governments in 1869.*

Among the Library's first major acquisitions of Far Eastern materials is this collection of Tibetan books, donated by William Woodville Rockhill in 1902 together with his handwritten catalog of the collection.

Overleaf: *An 1841 Bengali manuscript in Sanskrit, from the* Mahabharata. *Scenes from the story of Krishna are painted on the inside of the wooden covers.*

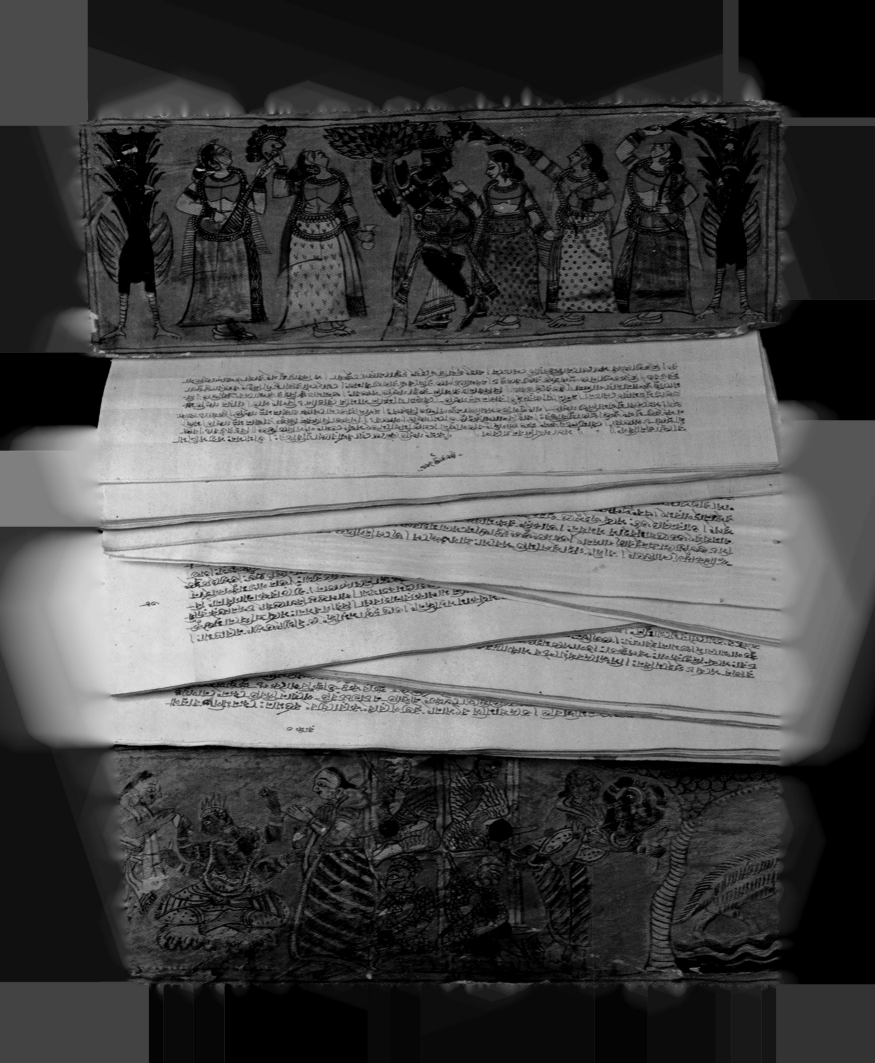

The first half of the twentieth century was filled with a steadily growing accumulation of Chinese books. As missionaries returned at the close of their careers they willed their collections to the Library, the United States invested its reparations from the Boxer Uprising to educating Chinese students and they donated materials, and the Library finally hired someone who could read Chinese to organize the growing number of volumes. (The American education of Chinese young people was truly astonishing. Between 1850 and 1950 Columbia University conferred nearly 2,000 degrees on Chinese graduates; the University of Michigan gave out some 1,300 and for a decade before World War II, the Nationalist Chinese government boasted that a majority of its cabinet members were Harvard graduates.) By 1925 the Library owned 5,850 Chinese titles containing 82,777 volumes "Chinese style" (as the annual report of the time calls them). By 1940 the titles had grown to 30,000 in 199,310 volumes. By 1975, 411,963 volumes—but since World War II, the collection has undergone a radical change of style and content.

Luther H. Evans became Librarian of Congress in 1945 and held the post until 1953 when he left to become Director General of UNESCO. Evans had been a professor of American history and political science, and was oriented to social research. As he took up his duties, he talked with his division chiefs throughout the Library and then concentrated on certain areas of his own interest. He was not overly enthusiastic with what he found in the Chinese Section. Methodically, through the years, the specialists in the unit had assembled a rich, balanced library which recaptured the history of Chinese society back for three thousand years. Most of the unit's purchases had been "retrospective" (seeking out ancient titles, or paying contractors to search for certain specific items). Evans cut this off in 1950. Thereafter, the unit could buy nothing older than two years (he finally made that five years when experience proved that it took two years for a book to be packaged, await shipping, and sluggishly work its way to Washington via a slow boat from China). But his purpose was consistent, and his attitude is still the one that prevails in all the Orientalia divisions: the Library wants current publications about the current activities of the governments and societies of Eastern nations. The materials should be found, processed in the issuing country, and moved directly to Washington via air freight.

To bring this off, the Library has set up its own acquisition offices in Jakarta, New Dehli, Karachi, and Bangkok. (It has similar units in Rio, Cairo, Nairobi, and Moscow as well.) Where there are booksellers, these are linked to the Library by contracts for "blanket orders." Blanket orders are in essence an agreement which says, "The Library of Congress wants *everything* that is published in your country which has substance and would provide significant information about your nation and your people." The agreement then says that for this the Library will pay up to such-and-such amount between one date and another. What is sent is carefully examined on receipt, and if it is unsatisfactory, new instructions are sent out, or the agreement is not renewed. Blanket-order houses buy books for the Library (by the tens of thousands) in Taiwan, Hong Kong, and Korea; and exchange agreements have been established with the Library of the National Diet in Tokyo, the University of Rangoon, the National Library of Vietnam in Hanoi, and the National Library of Peking.

What does the Library do when a country closes its borders to acquisition (as the People's Republic of China and North Vietnam did, for example)? It doubles its efforts and its rewards to acquisition agents in surrounding countries (in these cases, Hong Kong, Japan, Taiwan) and keeps right on acquiring.

The pattern we have seen here in the Chinese collection was repeated with startling precision in most of the Oriental collections—essentially libraries within a library. The Japanese holdings are based on the original gathers of Kan-ichi Asakawa of Yale University and Walter Tennyson Swingle. Swingle was a remarkable figure. He was a botanist who spent an entire lifetime criss-crossing the Far East looking for plants which would be useful to America. He brought the soybean from China, the tung oil tree, and introduced the fig insect to California, making the culture of Smyrna figs possible. He introduced the first date palms from Algeria on which the whole California and Arizona date industry is based. He brought Egyptian cotton to Arizona, he brought some twenty-two citrus strains from China to Florida, and then hybridized them into citranges, limequats, tangelos, and other new citrus fruits—and in all his travels he picked up literally tens of thousands of books, mainly in Chinese and Japanese, which he cataloged and gave to the Library.

There are similar figures who initiated the Armenian collection, the Ceylonese and the Nepalese

In 1907 the Library acquired an album of 333 drawings from the private library of a Siberian merchant, G.V. Yudin. It has since matted each drawing individually, producing a remarkable display of the costumes, furniture, vehicles, and building of the Chinese-Siberian border provinces in 1860. Who the many artists involved were or why the series was prepared remains a mystery. One picture has a notation in Russian, "Make the tree larger and move the bridge slightly to the right."

collections, Indic, Korean, and so on. Similarly, in each case, the collections started as gatherings of classical literature. Almost all of the "treasures" we have selected to show you are from this portion of the holdings. The initial collections were primarily religious, literary, or historical, but with the mid-twentieth century, all of them shifted to becoming libraries on the respective contemporary societies.

Undoubtedly there were times in the past 150 years when Librarians of Congress, pressed for space and staff, asked themselves whether they could afford so many resources being spent on areas of so little use. (When Librarian Putnam was asked, "Are these Oriental books used extensively?", he answered crisply, "No. They are used intensively.") But how right the early leaders have been proved!

With America's increased involvement in the Middle East, the Arabic materials are being used in an ever-growing curve. The Chinese reading room is packed on any day like a public library at term-paper time. Southeast Asian materials, America's linkage with Japan, our increasing ties to China, all make languages and information, which were once the dreaded "exotica" of which I was warned, now harsh daily data in the nation's growing thirst for information.

And there is one final anomaly to be noted. While the various collections all seem to have been started, developed, and used in astonishingly similar patterns, what the collections *are* is incredibly diverse. Geographically you can draw a neat circle around "the East" but within that circle and on the shelves of each differing social or language collection you meet mind-stopping extremes. Here is one society which even today is essentially medieval, the people clinging to prayer-wheel religions and sitting in the dust, while in a matter of minutes a plane (and in the Library, a matter of steps) takes you to another nation which with its cathode-ray tube and silicon chip society may be the most technologically advanced in the world. Here are nations still offering animal sacrifices around lagoons of off-shore oil rigs pumping high-grade, low-sulfur crude. The Library's books rest equally dramatically, juxtaposed between centuries and societies on adjacent shelves. Quite astonishing indeed.

CHAPTER IX

The Way Our People Lived

The national memory. Someone looking after the bits and pieces of our remembering—our houses, our clothes, our entertainments. The Library has acquired this responsibility, but it shares it with two other institutions. The Smithsonian tries to capture our artifacts, the National Archives preserves the memory of our government, leaving the Library of Congress responsible for images and concepts. We'll get to concepts in the last chapter; but right now let's look at the images.

These are visual images, of course, and the obvious vehicle is photographs, but photography is only one rather ordinary pillar of a multi-columned room. What are we after here? We are seeking the sense of the question, "What was it like *then*?" What was it like to be alive in, say 1880, or in any other decade or era or time? What did people do then? How did they work? What were they thinking about? What were they afraid of? Indeed, what mattered to them most?

I have selected fifty-odd images here to try to give an idea of the *ways* that the Library preserves our past, and we'll let the plates pretty much speak for themselves. But it might be interesting to underline a bit the kinds of collections (the hoards, an anthropologist would say) that they come from. Let's look at what they represent and then note some of the unexpected ways a single image can be used.

The first thing to recall is that so much of our memory is discarded as we go along. The whole field of packaging, labels, advertising appears to be so trivial at the time, so ephemeral, yet this becomes much of the memory of a time and place. At the present time, for instance, the most popular form of recall in the Library is newsreels for the period 1900 to 1940. Television producers are fascinated with the clips, as you might expect, but the second greatest target is less obvious: it is commercial design. Early Christmas cards, beer labels, calendars, cigar box lids, turn-of-the-century soft-drink trays, business letterheads and product advertisements are all being mined, copied, and carried off. Does the Library have *those* kinds of things? Of course. They were copyrighted; they were artistic designs. And they have been kept, and organized for retrieval, too.

But let's begin with something more substantial. How about buildings?

The Library has been collecting the records of historic and significant buildings for fifty years—quite apart from those captured in genre photographs and prints. The first organized effort began in 1929 when an architect and landscape designer by the name of Leicester B. Holland became head of the Library's Fine Arts Division. He promptly pursued one of his own dreams and got a substantial grant from the Carnegie Corporation to establish "a national repository for photographic negatives of early American architecture, to preserve and make available to students of history and others, pictorial records of our rapidly disappearing ancestral homes." With the money in hand, he bought advertisements in newspapers and magazines all over the country asking for pictures and blueprints and plans. He sent out letters to all the chapters of the American Institute of Architects; he queried every state historical society, and solicited material from any photographic club he could identify no matter how small. His pleas worked so well that by the end of the first ten years he had collected more than ten thousand negatives and the grant money had grown to twenty-six thousand dollars. Donations are still

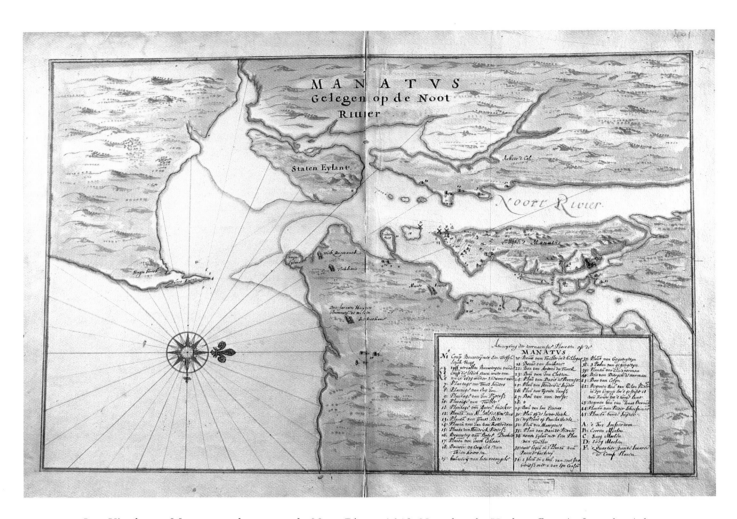

Joan Vingboons' Manatus gelegen op de Noot River, *1640. Note that the Hudson flows in from the right, and Manhattan Island lies at the center of the right panel. This early watercolor map, drawn on the site for the West-Indies Company of Holland, identifies each property owner by name and locates his farm or bourie and windmill. The artist accompanied the map with information about the Indians still living in and around the colony. An example of his comments is: "The life of these people is completely free....Marriages have no permanence, as a rule, every one has one woman, the chief has more and they lightly leave their wives...they cast out the women when they are with child or have given birth to a child, and because of this, the land stays sparsely populated."*

coming in today. Not long ago a snapshot of an old home on Staten Island was received stapled to a 1930s *New York Times* clipping with the headline, "Library of Congress Seeks Photographs of Historic Buildings."

The Pictorial Archives of Early American Architecture, as Dr. Holland's collection came to be called, was so successful that the same foundation decided to underwrite a "Carnegie Survey of the Architecture of the South." They hired the eminent photographer Frances Benjamin Johnston and sent her into the field. Between 1930 and 1943 she took nearly eight thousand photographs, being as interested in the "ordinary" dwellings on farms and along small town streets as she was in the aristocratic, pillared mansions from antebellum days.

Given this growing collection of architectural photographs (and the indexes to control and retrieve them), it was logical that the Library should be chosen by the National Park Service and the American Institute of Architects to be the home of the vast Historic American Buildings Survey. HABS (rhymes with "tabs") started as a depression project to tide over unemployed architects until the construction industry recovered. At the beginning of the project, some 750 architects worked their way through American communities measuring, drawing, and photographing. The product was so impressive that the program was continued in a smaller but more organized way and is now one of the major sources for restoration and preservation data in the nation. The files hold the documentation of over 20,000 American structures in 50,000 measured drawings, 44,800 photographs, and 15,450 pages of architectural narration. The material is presently one of the most heavily used collections of any in the Library of Congress. Builders, historians, theatrical designers, restoration specialists can approach it in many ways. One can search for a specific building by name, by geographical area, by type. If you are looking for adobe designs, onion-shaped cupolas, hotels or opera houses, California bungalows, or products of Frank Lloyd Wright, the in-

dexes will take you to the appropriate pictures and blueprints with astonishing speed. Few assemblies of knowledge in the Library work so well.

Fire insurance maps. One of the great unknown sources of historical detection anywhere. Amazingly, there are maps of your town, indeed of the block on which you live, which identify your specific dwelling, describe how many rooms it has, the kind of roof it carries, the number of windows, and the material the walls are made of. The map will tell anyone who looks at it who owns your house, where all the neighboring commercial buildings are located and what each is used for, the number of feet you are from the nearest hydrant (also how big the hydrant is, how far it is from the source of the water,

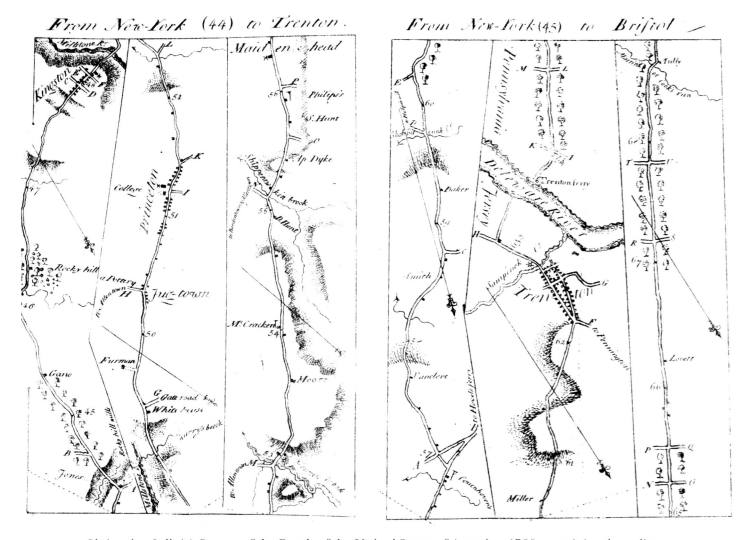

Christopher Colles' A Survey of the Roads of the United States of America, *1789, containing the earliest road maps of the U.S. The maps were based on surveys made by American engineers during the Revolution, and cover all of the major thoroughfares from Albany to Williamsburg.*

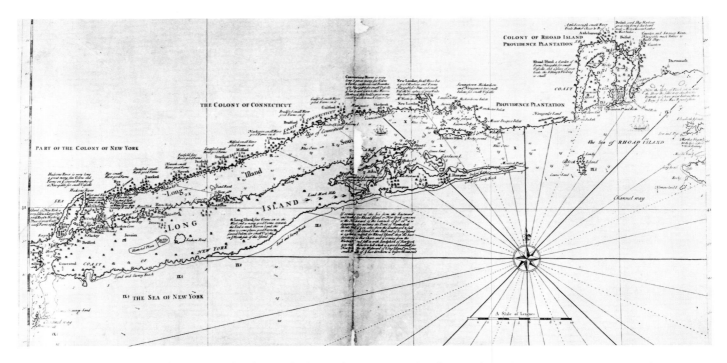

Cyprian Southack's "Long Island Sound" from The New England Coasting Pilot," *1734. Southack had "sailed for the King for 22 years" and put down his detailed knowledge of the waters from Sandy Hook to Cape Breton. Shown is one of the eight maps in the chart book.*

what the water source is, and how many persons are on call at the nearest firehouse).

This incredible collection of trivia began in 1850 (1792 in England) and since then has so proliferated that the Library of Congress owns 185,000 of these maps including thousands for towns that have long since evaporated from the face of the earth. What possible use are they to anyone but an insurance man? They are a gold mine for social historians. For instance, makers of literary maps love the sheets. You can take one for London in 1799 and identify precisely where each author and poet lived, where the coffeehouses were, the distance between a member of the royal family and his mistress.

With the quickest glance you can identify what businesses were in an American community at any particular time. How many available beds in how many hospitals. How many doctors' offices. How many churches (and what denomination). How many banks, groceries—how many saloons. ("Houses of ill fame" are identified on the maps as "ladies rooming houses" and the data will usually tell how many rooms are available for occupancy.) Simply by checking the maps (they were revised and updated frequently), you can trace who has owned the land on which you yourself live, for generations back. You can determine where all your kin lived in

the community at the time of the map, and the sheets are a great boon for genealogists. On page 236 is the insurance map for Tombstone, Arizona, 1886, showing the O.K. Corral, as it was located on the afternoon of the famous shootout between the Earp Brothers and the Clanton Family.

Colonial maps. Speaking of going back to find kin by reading contemporary land-use maps, we must not forget the original land-use records from colonial times. The very first maps we have were to record who lived where, and the parent "companies" who put up the money for early exploration were as curious about what it looked like out there as we are.

Joan Vingboons' drawing of New York City in 1639 is a good example. (Please see page 206.) If you rotate the scene so the fleur-de-lys points away from you, Manhattan Island (Manatus) is immediately apparent beside the Hudson (Noort River) and across from Staten Island (Staten Eylant). The forty-five Dutch boweries or farms are named and located, along with the position of the working windmills.

The Library has an even more elegant map engraved by Augustine Herrman in 1673. Its content is clearly stated in the splendid cartouche set in the sea off Hampton Roads; title: "Virginia and Maryland As It Is Planted and Inhabited This Present Year 1670 and Exactly Drawne by the Only Labour & Endeavour of Austin Herrmann Bohemiensis." (As for the spelling of his name, there are two different variations on the map itself, and no less than a dozen in the documents that accompany it!)

Similar maps appear for the Delaware colonies, the Massachusetts Bay settlements, and the Connecticut River settlements. For some reason, there are more maps of Quaker holdings in Pennsylvania than any other kind (although early Spanish records of California ranches are frequent, too).

Panoramic maps. Let's return to our own time and pursue the "how did it look then" with bird's-eye-views from the nineteenth century. These are much more common than is usually realized, and although they appear to have been done from a balloon, the artists never left the ground. (Please see pages 230, 246, and 249.)

Bird's-eye-views all start with certain accepted conventions. Apparently all the birds flew between 2,000 and 3,000 feet above the ground and were always looking across the narrowest part of town— thus the widest part goes from side to side. Astonishingly, the pictures were neither generalized nor faked. They actually *did* show every building as it was and frequently every tree. Itinerant artists would move into a town, go to the courthouse to get a plat of the streets, and then painstakingly walk through the city sketching the primary buildings with astonishing care and detail (exact number of windows, designs of doors, porches, cupolas). The artists' sketches and plans would then be taken back to the "home office" and drawn on stone lithographic plates for three or four color separations.

Most of the panoramas were commissioned. Usually the publisher himself would have "worked the area", getting a leading bank or merchant to underwrite the project or, in the small towns, getting all the merchants around the main square to contribute. The pictures would then be sold for anything from one to five dollars each—and they were enormously popular both for mercantile offices and wall hangings in private homes. The Library has 1,117 of these maps, with many showing how the same towns looked at ten or twenty year intervals. Los Angeles, for example, appears carefully detailed in 1857, 1877, 1894, and 1909. All of the major cities are represented (the Library has one of St. Louis done by Camille N. Dry in 1875 which involves 110 huge, multicolored sheets that, when as-

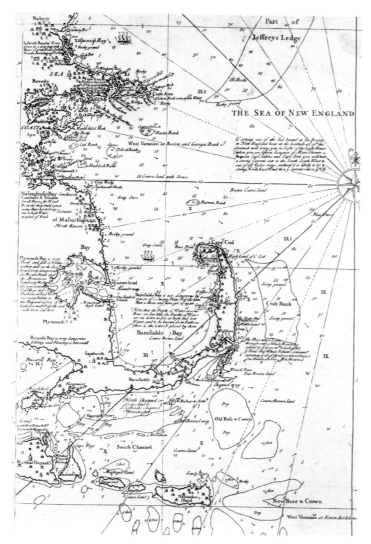

Southack's *"Sea of New England"* from the Coasting Pilot. *Some of his annotations: "Barnstable Bay is not dangerous by reason of so many Flatts. Vessells have run a Shoar and have got out again....Place where I came through with a Whale Boat being ordered by ye Gov/mt to look after ye Pirate Ship while Bellame Command/r castaway ye 26 of April 1717 where I buried one hundred & two men drowned."*

The Library's is one of two known copies of Coasting Pilot.

sembled, give a picture nine feet high and twenty-four feet long). But the small towns are covered too. There are carefully drawn images of Maysville, Colorado (1882), Winstead, Connecticut (1908), Clayton, Delaware (1885), Ocilla, Georgia (1908), Homer, Illinois (1869), Mexico, Missouri (1869), and many others.

While the street patterns and houses are very literally drawn, the streets themselves, the rivers

Right: *Jenny Lind, daguerreotype by Mathew Brady (taken between 1850–52). Phineas T. Barnum, the great nineteenth-century showman, brought Miss Lind to America to sing for 150 nights. "The Swedish Nightingale" was paid $1,000 a night—an astonishing sum at the time.*

Below: *P.T. Barnum's home near Bridgeport, Connecticut, hand-colored lithograph by Sarony and Major (drawn between 1847–54). Barnum called the building "Iranistan," kept an elephant on the grounds, and noted with pride its "90 foot central tower." It burned to the ground in 1858.*

A View of the Mansion of the Late Lord Timothy Dexter in High Street, Newbury Port, 1810, *hand-colored lithograph by John Bufford, c. 1840 (?). The figures were executed by a local carver of ships' figureheads and include Washington, Louis XVI, Nelson, and King George.*

The Library of Congress owns over 3,000 different Currier and Ives prints of an idealized world three-parts reality and one-part as the artist wished it were. Above: American Homestead, Summer. Overleaf: Left, top, Interior of Albany Steamer; Right, top, Trotting Cracks In The Snow; Left, bottom, A Cotton Plantation On The Mississippi; Right, bottom, Lower Broadway Street Scene.

and the harbors are filled with a world that never was. The roadways have more wagons, the ports more steamships, the tracks more trains than the sites ever saw. Here are traffic jams of every variety and the "turnpikes are clogged with commerce."

Currier and Ives. Such an embellished street appears on page 213, reminding us that for "how things were" the Currier and Ives scenes at least give us an idea of how our people *hoped* they would be.

Nathaniel Currier started his famous shop in 1835 and then continued on with James Ives as Currier and Ives from 1856. In the sixty-year lifetime of the business, they published more than 6,800 scenes of which the Library has roughly 3,000. Historically these are very useful since they reflect the aspirations of our people (how a fine farm should look, how a beautiful horse or emigrant wagon train *ought* to be), but artistically the

Library's holdings are frustrating for a strange reason. Thanks to the copyright deposit (which Currier and Ives adhered to religiously to protect their own product), the Library has some of the rarest prints there are. Many of these are to be found only in the Library's collections, but thanks to the reason for copyright, Currier felt no need to deposit any other than the basic plate to prove ownership. The result is that a substantial amount of the Library's collection is in black and white while the rest of the world's is in flaming color! What color sheets there are were the gifts of the prints scholar, Harry Peters, and others who shared their private collections with the nation. Together, the various sources have added up to one of the largest collections of Currier and Ives prints in the world.

Stereographs. Those double photographs on slightly curved cardboard that gave our great-grandparents a strange, three-dimensional view

211

of the world in flat planes. Stereographs started earlier and lasted longer than most people realize. The Library of Congress has approximately 150,000 different views beginning with Civil War battlefields and tourist shots of the 1860s and running right past World War II into the 1950s.

An unlikely source of the national enthusiasm for the device came from the poet, Oliver Wendell Holmes. In 1859 he wrote in the *Atlantic Monthly*, "The very things which an artist would leave out, or render imperfectly, the photograph takes infinite care with and so makes its illusions perfect... [There] will soon be such an enormous collection of [stereographs] that they will have to be classified and arranged in vast libraries as books are now." Holmes was so sold on the idea that he invented the

hand viewer we all recall when we think of "looking at those 3-D pictures."

The stereographs, in addition to the usual tourist scenes and Victorian whimsy, provided our ancestors with news photography coverage. They were pictures of disasters, candid shots of national leaders and European society, and (like the panoramas) views of local communities for local consumption. The two examples on pages 237 and 247 are, of course, one half of a stereograph card each. The Library has tens of thousands of these specimens in its special drawers and these have a strange numbing effect after one has looked at a few hundred, but this is gradually replaced with a shock of time. The views are stored geographically so a drawer of scenes of the Zambezi River produces

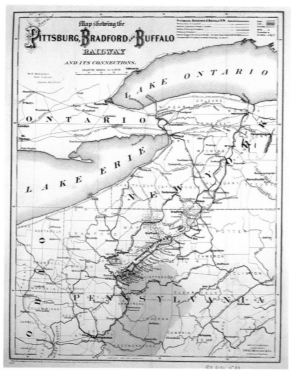

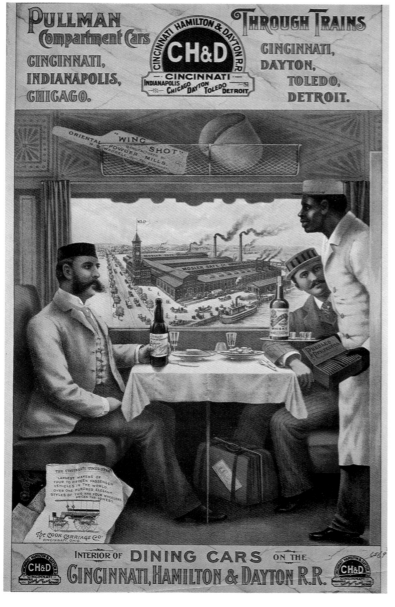

The nation's nineteenth-century preoccupation with railroads appears in dozens of forms. Top left: *Currier and Ives' American Railroad Scene—Train In Snow.* Top right: *Every railroad line had its official publicity map. In the case of the P.B. and B., its few miles of trackage take up only a tiny portion (center) of the routes shown.* Left: *Cooperative advertising. From the Library's tens of thousands of commercial plates comes this 1894 cooperative advertisement whose cost was shared by the firearms, cigar, lock, whiskey, carriage, newspaper, and railroad companies noted in the scene.*

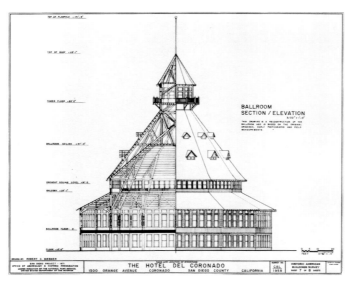

A typical "measured drawing," one of over 35,000 buildings so recorded in the Library's Historic American Buildings Survey. This is the Hotel del Coronado in San Diego; at top, the way it looked in the 1920s.

row upon row of multiplaned views each taken through jungle fronds and across torrential rapids—and little by little you are struck by the realization that there had to be a photographer, a tripod, and a bulky, twin-lensed camera peering through that jungle a full decade before Stanley ever heard of Livingstone. They are so *far* back in time. Here are the rocky passes of the Khyber Pass crisply photographed two full generations before the Bengal Lancers broke through for the first time! Here is a picture taken from the top of the Matterhorn long before most of us thought they had made a photograph from the bottom. "Way back then" suddenly gets closer to our own time.

Motion pictures. This sense of recency, of telescoping the distance to our predecessors, is even greater with the early motion pictures. Somehow we do not expect to see William McKinley campaigning for the presidency, Teddy Roosevelt opening the Panama Canal, the still-smoking ruins of the San Francisco earthquake, American troops in Peking during the Boxer Rebellion—American troops in the Spanish-American War, for that matter—yet all of these were photographed by the early movie cameras and all appear in the Library's vaults.

We have said that the Library has the earliest motion pictures in America, and the largest collection covering the longest span. Once again, it was the copyright deposit that brought this about.

No one really knows who invented motion pictures. A number of companies seemed to have hit the streets at about the same time, but the earliest prints to have survived were those belonging to Thomas A. Edison. Around 1887, Edison had perfected his phonograph and was trying to think of ways of linking his capture of sound to the duplication of a sight record of the source of the sound. His first solution involved a spiral of tiny pictures in grooves around a cylinder which you looked at with what was essentially a glorified microscope. The motion part was achieved by the already well-known phenomenon of persistence of vision, and Edison's machine had a tiny shutter to give you one picture at a time.

The cylinder was not successful, so he tried a drum of paper pictures which sped by too quickly and then he was saved by George Eastman's invention of a transparent gelatin film which Eastman had developed for the Kodak box camera (1889). Edison and his assistant, William Kennedy Laurie Dickson, took this new film, made their pictures on it lengthwise, invented a camera that would take the pictures serially (the Kinetograph) and another to view it with (the Kinetoscope), and motion pictures as we know them went commercial. The first films moved at the rate of forty-eight frames per second; Edison soon slowed that to sixteen frames per second and that was the speed used thereafter during most of the silent days. Our sound pictures run at twenty-four frames a second, and the difference accounts for the jerky appearance of the early images. When they are viewed on projectors of their own time, they are about as smooth as our own screenings.

The point of all this to the Library was that Edison immediately rented his films and equipment to vaudeville houses and then to Kinetoscope parlours, and he quickly felt the need for protecting his invention from piracy. He patented the machines and copyrighted the pictures. But the copyright practices of the time gave a copyright to each individual exposure. Edison therefore dutifully made paper positive strip prints of his films,

From Uncle Tom's Cabin, *1903, photographed by Edison and produced by Edwin S. Pater.*

There is no new scene under the sun. Here are some of the earliest motion-picture versions of what have become classic situations regularly restaged in television, motion picture, and video-tape plots. The copyright law in effect at the time of the invention of the motion picture required the deposit of a positive paper print of each individual frame photographed. The result of this ruling was the deposition of over 5,000 paper rolls between 1894 and 1912 when the law was changed. (In 1952 Kemp R. Niver and the Academy of Motion Picture Arts and Sciences reconverted 3,000 of the remaining rolls to safety film and thus recreated an astonishing number of the first films ever made.) The seven accompanying frames come from these early paper rolls. In Balked at the Altar, *the prospective groom is trapped by the sight of the girl reading a spicy novel by Elinor Glyn. He flees the church by jumping through a stained-glass window. In* Where Breakers Roar, *we are first given "beautiful young women frolicking in the sand," and later the seizure of the ingenue by a villain and her rescue by her boy friend in the second reel. Science-fiction appears in* The Primitive Man *in which a college man falls asleep at his club while reading Darwin. He dozes off to awaken in prehistoric times. Wings, horns, and tails were photographed taped on to living reptiles. In* The School Teacher and the Waif *we find one of the screen's first heroines threatened and alone.*

Top: Balked at the Altar, *D.W. Griffith's thirteenth picture, 1908.*

Middle and bottom: The Primitive Man *by D.W. Griffith working at Biograph, 1913.*

Top and middle: Where Breakers Roar, *D.W. Griffith's twenty-first film, 1908.*

Bottom: The School Teacher and the Waif, *Biograph, 1912.*

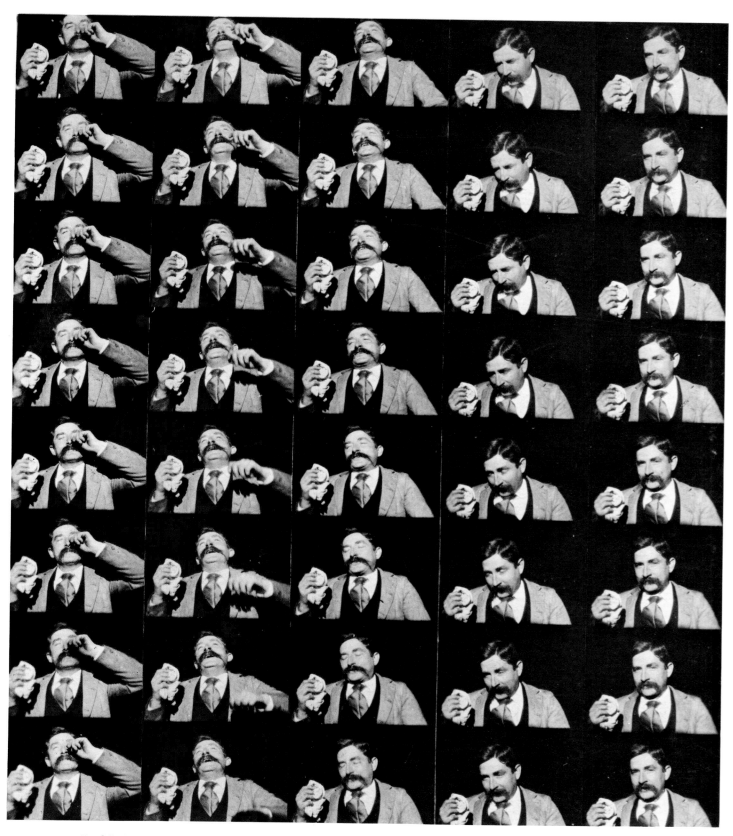

Fred Ott's sneeze. This is the earliest existing copyrighted motion picture. Fred Ott was an employee of Thomas Edison's Kinetoscopic company, and the picture was made in the Edison laboratory/studio in West Orange, N.J., 1893.

A typical bay among hundreds in the motion picture division containing film, television tapes, video discs, et cetera.

deposited these, and the by-product was that the record has been preserved beautifully right into our own time. The clumsiness of the positive to positive printing, however, got the rules changed in 1912, whereupon the nitrate film itself was deposited—and great quantities of these have deteriorated into solid blocks of potentially explosive nitrocellulose. (The Library has a full-time laboratory converting these nitrates onto modern day safety film, but much has already been lost and more is disappearing every day. Modern safety film was embraced by the industry in 1950, and the production since that time is chemically stable.)

Fred Ott's famous sneeze was taken by W.K.L.

Dickson for Edison in 1893 and is the earliest known motion picture. (Please see page 219.) It was deposited as a paper print—a picture of the picture—and was photographed at the Edison laboratory/studio in West Orange, New Jersey. The early movies we have of Edison himself were taken by Dickson and with this same camera.

The importance of the motion picture archives to social history is so obvious it need not be described. The Library has over fifty thousand film titles preserved on safe, modern film which is kept in special, fireproof vaults, several miles from the Library. All the color film is refrigerated to thirty-three degrees to retard its fading. About ten percent of the collection is silent film from the turn of the century to 1930, and in addition to newsreel and dramatic material, enormous quantities of educational and documentary footage are retained. Nowadays, of course, the copyright deposit of television videotape far exceeds the footage of "movie" material, but the television reels are so important an archive of the life of our people from 1950 on that the chief users of this hoard are the television companies themselves. They are now creating retrospectives of their own industry, so the *Thirty Years of Lucille Ball* or *Two Decades of Ed Sullivan* programs often come out of their own copyright deposits.

Speaking of Lucille Ball, an odd footnote to the story of copyrighting television series was that for years these were not deposited until they went into re-run syndication. At that point all the parts were deposited simultaneously and the Library would open its mail room to discover that three truckloads of *I Love Lucy* had arrived during the night, or that five hundred reels of *Gunsmoke* had appeared in a single batch. With the invention of the home television recorder, individual network shows are now copyrighted at the time of screening. If you are surprised to hear that the Library preserves such items as these, consider: can you think of a better single explication of the social issues of the sixties than *All In The Family* when viewed by our successors a hundred years from now?

Indeed, what is the Library doing for the social historians of a century hence? Is this generation accumulating the visual hoards for our successors as effectively as the early librarians collected for our use?

I approached several of the curators on this and I found a fairly reassuring consensus. The feeling was that yes, our posterity will have even more material to work with than we do. The difference will be that it will appear in a different form. Just as our present newsmagazines and deposited evening news television shows are richer records than stereographs and Currier and Ives lithographs, so the next generations are surely going to find digitally preserved images on discs and tapes even richer than anything we know today. The trick, the curators believe, is not to fear that our generation will rest on its past accomplishments and collect less vigorously than its predecessors, but that it will fail to recognize technological improvements in the capturing of the image and thus collect the wrong thing. Although they are in no way sure this is indeed what will happen, they want to be certain that simply because they have traditionally collected photographs—fixed silver salts on paper—they do not miss a better device for storing records in the laser and the aluminum plate or the home cathode ray tube when or if it comes along.

Fortunately these are our successors' problems. We can relish the images our present devices have held for us and are reproduced herein.

As we turn to these images, let me suggest a device which may be new to you. Many of the specialists who use the Library's collection look at pictures quite differently from the rest of us. When we see a picture of the interior of a river steamer (page 212) or a line of prospectors climbing a mountain to reach the Klondike (page 247), we may think of how very large the steamer was and how very many prospectors there were going to the goldfields. A specialist may look at the very same pictures and be intrigued with how a riverboat was illuminated inside at night, how women in bustles sat down, beard styles, the etiquette of wearing hats indoors for men and women, all the places one could find to put a ribbon. One may want to see precisely what tools the prospectors carried, what kinds of footwear were used in the snow, the age and sex of the explorers. One expert in pictorial social history says that his device for looking at a picture is to examine it in two-inch squares. If the complete picture was only what appeared in that two-inch window, what would you see? You may find the technique amusing (try it in the middle of the intersection in that scene on lower Broadway, for example, page 213).

The way our people lived....

Charles H. Currier (opposite top left; *no relation to the lithographer) was a Boston jeweler from 1872 to 1888, and then a professional photographer to 1909. These pictures are from the Library's collection of 550 glass plates found in his shop after his death. They are photographs he took for his customers of their Boston homes at the turn of the century. In a day before flash bulbs, photofloods, and exposure meters, his interiors are technically astonishing, and provide a remarkable record of a proverbial "vanished past." Note the fully equipped bathroom* above, *the family room filled with mementoes at* top right, *the cycle standing on the walk at* mid-right, *and the complexity of gables and porch roofs in the lower pictures,* right *and* opposite.

Signs of the times. Above: *A suggested solution to all that wasted space over Trinity Church.* Top right: *Clam seller in Mulberry Bend, N.Y.;* Center right: *City Hall subway station;* Bottom right: Bathing Hour on the Beach *at Seabreeze, Florida.* Opposite top: *Anti-scab badges worn by children in sympathy with street car strikers.* Opposite bottom: *The headquarters of the National Association Opposed to Woman Suffrage.*

Design details from the Historic American Buildings Survey. Above: *A fire alarm call box, a bird bath and lamppost, and a coal chute cover.* Right: *The Roxy Theater in New York City.*

The West As It Really Was:
An Album

It is surprising how complete a record we do have of the Opening of the West. Our sense of the mountain men, the discovery of gold, wagon trains, and cattle drives feels so distant, yet all the steps and stages were remarkably well captured by engineers, accompanying artists, and on-site photographers present at the very time the events occurred. The camera overlapped a great deal of the period. The artist Albert Bierstadt accompanied an expedition in 1859 traversing the overland trails from Puget Sound to South Pass (present-day Wyoming) taking stereoscopic camera views along the way. He later painted many of his monumental Western scenes from his stereo pictures using a hand viewer as he

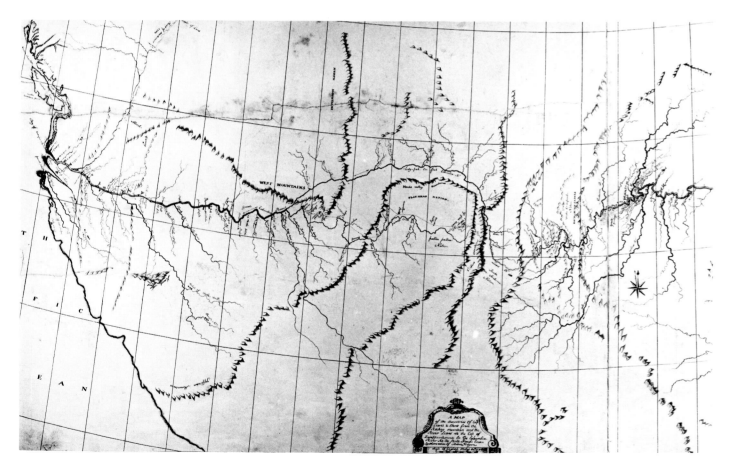

Robert Frazer's pen-and-ink map from the Lewis and Clark Expedition, 1807. Frazer was an army private who accompanied the explorers and recorded each day's travel (as he says) "from the Rockey mountains and the River Lewis to the Cap of Disappointment On The Coloumbia River At the North Pacific Ocean." The only features he really knew were near the rivers' banks; the mountain ranges across the Southwest were from Indian reports— and the explorers' conjecture.

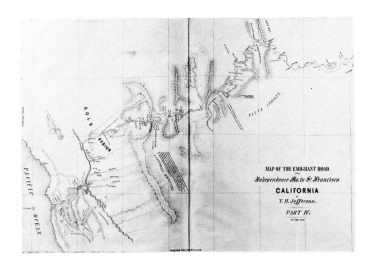

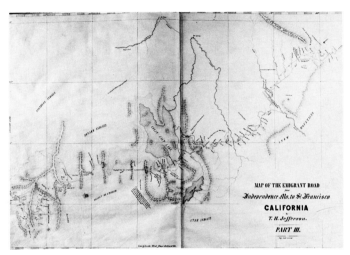

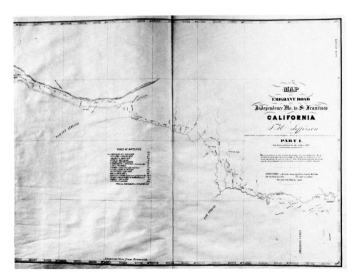

Above: *Three portions of* A Map of the Emigrant Road from Independence, Mo. to St. Francisco, *by T.H. Jefferson, 1849. Among the annotations beside the recommended route are: "This is a bad Canyon," "The fearful long drive 83 miles no grass nor water," "On this drive a party should go in advance with a shovel and collect the water of the Boiling spring in vats to cool."*

Opposite: Cañon de Chelle *(as he called it) by Timothy O'Sullivan. The tents of the Expedition of 1873 can be seen in the lower left. The surveyors reported rock walls 1200 feet high.*

Below: Melish's Map of the United States with Contiguous British and Spanish Possessions, *1816. Note that remarkably detailed knowledge of the rivers draining into the Mississippi was available so soon after the acquisition of the Louisiana Purchase.*

Bottom: *A rare manuscript map (one of only two extant known copies) of a Spanish map of the Southwestern missions, 1823.*

worked. As early as the 1850s, Carleton E. Watkins was making a comfortable living taking daguerreotype portraits in San Jose just as he would have been in Boston or New York, and many of the San Francisco photographers who would record the gold rush had arrived by ox team carrying their chemicals and cameras with them in the same covered wagons with which they themselves crossed the prairie.

A great deal of our own, present image of the nineteenth-century West comes from motion-picture and television recreations, of course, but none of the following scenes is synthetic. Every one of the maps and pictures following was made on the spot at the "real time," and as always they represent only a tiny sample of the kinds of materials accumulated in the Library's broad holdings on the American West.

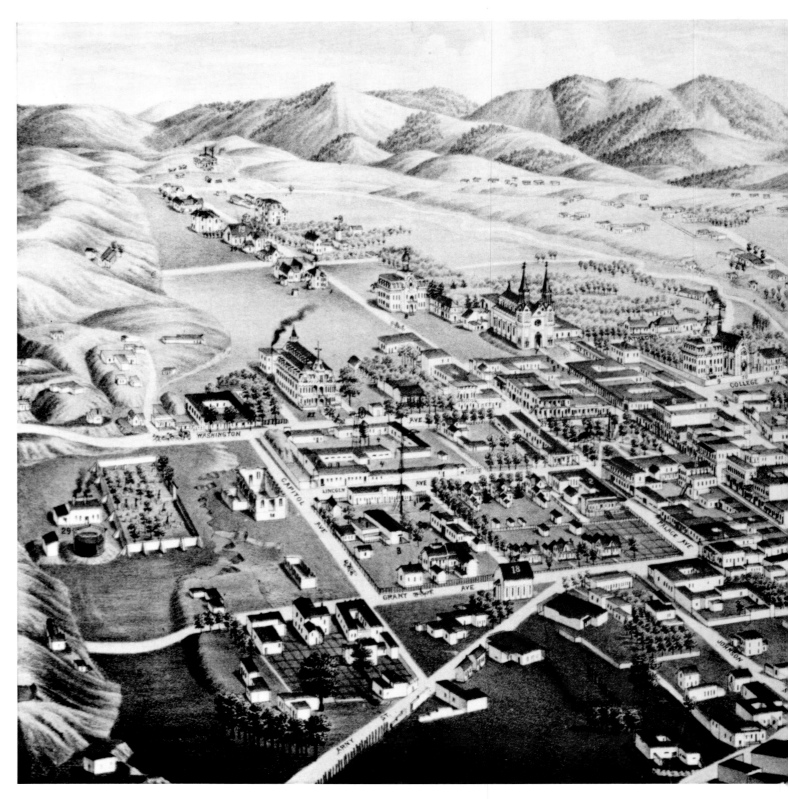

Bird's Eye View of the City of Santa Fé, N.M., 1882, *lithograph drawn by Henry Wellge.*

John C.H. Grabill of Sturgis and Deadwood, Dakota Territory, has left us an astonishing record of his part of the world for the years 1887–91. Here are eight examples. He titled the picture above Villa of Brule. The Great Hostile Indian Camp on River Brule Near Pine Ridge South Dakota. *The last great battle of the Indian Wars took place at Wounded Knee, South Dakota, on December 29, 1890, leaving 150 Sioux dead as well as 25 dead and 39 wounded soldiers. The Indian bands had exploded in all directions, but Gen. Miles drew them back to the above camp and a general surrender on January 15, 1891. This picture was taken a few days later when the camp held some 4,000 people (800 to 1,000 warriors), over 1,000 horses, 500 wagons and 250 travois. Left: Red Cloud and American Horse, 1891.* Opposite top: *Two Deadwood coaches.* Opposite bottom: Freighting in the Black Hills. Overleaf: top left, *The Wade and Jones Railroad Camp in Whitewood Canyon, 1890;* top right, *Washing and Panning Gold in Rockerville, Dakota, 1889;* bottom left, *Hose team, 1888;* bottom right, *Western ranch house, 1888.*

No. 2853 "The Deadwood Coach."
Photo. and copyright by Grabill, '89.

Freighting in the Black Hills Copyright by Grabill

No. 1007. Whitewood Canyon, With a Train on Railway, Black Hills, Dak.
Made and copyrighted by Grabill. 'X9

No. 1204. HOSE TEAM.
The Champion Chinese Hose Team of

#357. "We have It Rich." Washing and panning gold. Rockerville. Dak. Old timers, Spriggs.Lamb and Dillon at work. Photo and copyright by Grabill. 1889.

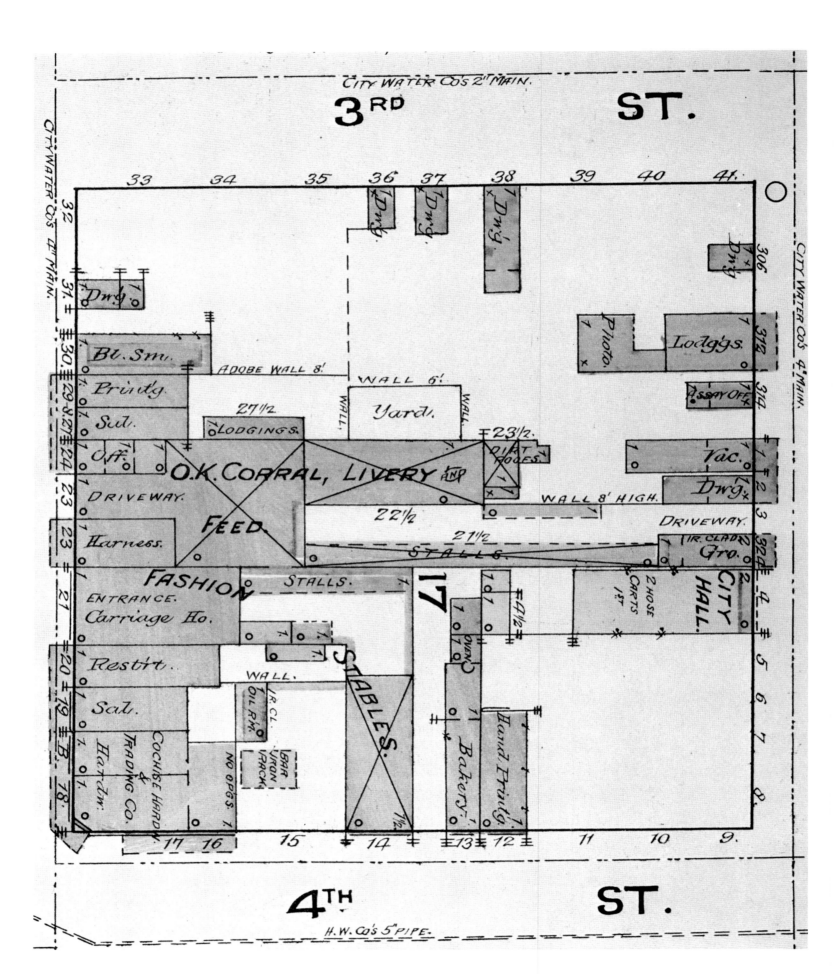

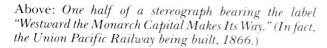

Above: *One half of a stereograph bearing the label "Westward the Monarch Capital Makes Its Way." (In fact, the Union Pacific Railway being built, 1866.)*

Right: *One of the richest collections of Westerniana is the Erwin E. Smith Collection of Range-life Photographs. Smith was acutely conscious that the time of the cowboy was destined to be brief and transitory. He therefore lived on the range and recorded hundreds of scenes of the cattle industry at the turn of the century.* Top: *Sam Whittaker, wagon cook for the LS Ranch (Texas) getting breakfast in the dawn.* Middle and bottom: *Jack Wofford of the Shoe Bar outfit "bronc riding" and "flanking the trail herd."*

Opposite: *Tombstone, Arizona, July 1886. A single block from a large fire insurance map; this portion shows the O.K. Corral, scene of the famous shoot-out between the Earps and the Clantons. The map carries index notes for the Catholic Church, Contention Consolidated Mining and Milling Co., Episcopal Church, Rattle Snake Mining Company's Stamp Mill, the Variety Theatre—and the Public Library.*

Erwin E. Smith. Top: *R.M. Niece of the Bar Diamond Ranch (Texas, 1905) lounging on his horse "Chappo."* Above: *Cowboys of the Turkey Track Ranch (Texas) letting their horses drink while crossing the Wichita River.* Left: *Cattle cooling off in the river.*

Erwin E. Smith, Matador cowboys in for dinner at the Turtle Hole Division roundup camp.

The same Carleton E. Watkins who did the earliest Yosemite pictures (here the Valley with Half Dome on the right) recorded daily life in California from the 1850s through the 1880s.

In timbered country it was frequently easier to lay flat track on a built-up trestle than grade a roadbed on the broken terrain. It also avoided the earliest snow drifts in the Fall.

Following are five pictures, typical of Watkins' scenes and subjects.

The Tejon Ranch.

Buena Vista Farm.

A block in Bakersfield.

Carleton E. Watkins. Above: *The front porch of the superintendent's residence on the McClung Ranch.* Left: *The Avenue to the superintendent's house.*

Opposite: *William Barnhill's* Children Had Few Toys.

Overleaf: *Currier and Ives lithograph of San Francisco Panorama, drawn by Charles R. Parsons, 1878.*

242

243

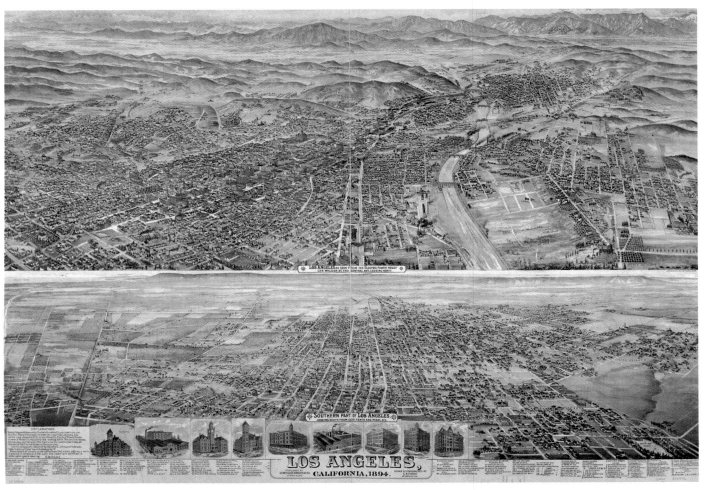

Top: *View of Los Angeles, 1877.*
Above: *Los Angeles, California, 1894.*

Above: *One-half of a stereograph carrying the title,* Bound for the Klondike Gold Fields, Chilcoot Pass, Alaska, 1898.

Top right and above: *Arnold Genthe was not only an early, fashionable photographer, but one who went on to become a leading portraitist of motion picture and Broadway theater notables. On the day of the San Francisco earthquake and fire, however, he seized his camera and rushed into the streets to make many of the scenes by which the national memory recalls the catastrophe.*

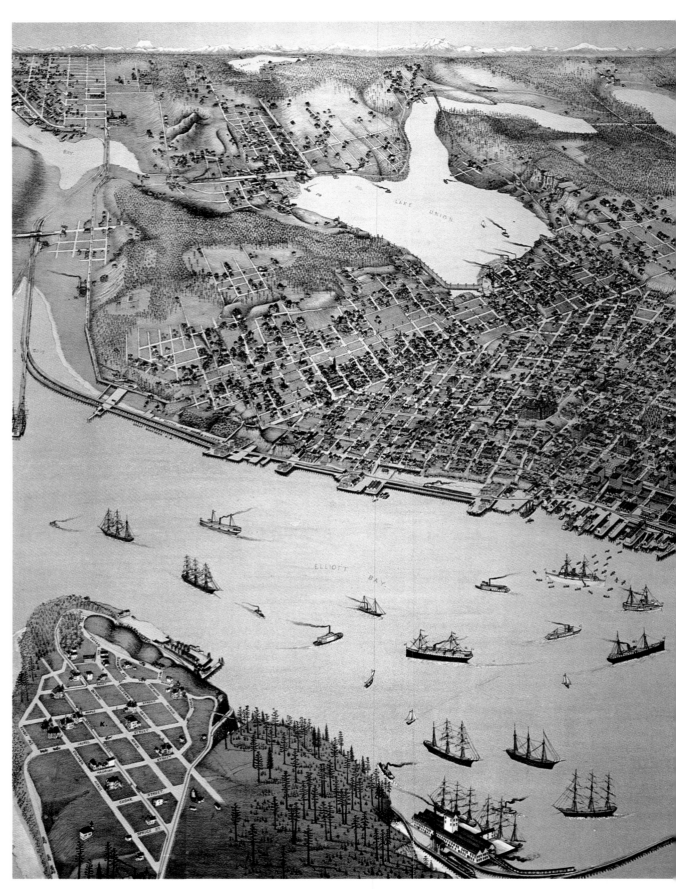

Bird's eye view of Seattle and environs. King County,
Washington, 1891. "Eighteen months after the great fire."

LAKE WASHINGTON.

CHAPTER X

Joyful Noise

Is it really true that the Library of Congress owns *five* Stradivari violins? It does—or, to be precise, it owns three Stradivari violins, one Stradivarius viola, and a Stradivarius cello. It also owns one of the finest Guarnerius violins ever made, and an Amati. But that is excess—crass ostentation! Do they show them off as a museum does? No, they are played. All of them are played every week or so, and during the concert season most of them are played every day. Can they be seen? Of course, if they are not being played right now.

Music at the Library of Congress—where do you start? With the nation's largest collection of jazz music? Manuscripts, thousands of hours of wire and tape recordings made in jails, with chain gangs, in music halls, and literally on that oft-saluted levee. Shall we consider the opera collection of 25,000 librettos, the handwritten original manuscript of *I Pagliacci*, of *Peter Grimes*, of *Wozzeck*? Or the American manuscript holdings of John Philip Sousa, George Gershwin, Leonard Bernstein, Jelly Roll Morton?

No, the first question is always about the Strads, so let's begin there, too.

What is so great about a Stradivarius violin? Is there really some mystical secret about it that makes it impossible to duplicate in our own time? We might establish a few things about Cremonese violins in general before we turn to the Library's instruments specifically (all of which, by the way, have names, personalities, and elaborate pedigrees which musicians can recite with the speed and enthusiasm of a baseball statistician).

The Library's curators tell us that the building of violins reached its peak of development be-

Chansonnier de M. le Marquis de Laborde, fifteenth-century vellum manuscript. A nobleman's songbook of French secular tunes, interesting both for its early music and for the illuminations, fanciful animals, and coats-of-arms that embellish the pages. While the hand-lettered notation illustrated was somewhat primitive (our present devices for showing notes and tempo are a product of the invention of printing itself) the techniques used here worked very well for the singing needs of the time.

The Library owns five Stradivari instruments—three violins, a viola, and a cello—and a Tourte bow to go with each. The instruments were a gift from Gertrude Clarke Whittall who also provided accompanying money so they can be played in free concerts throughout the year. They are displayed here in front of an early eighteenth-century tapestry, Apollo and the Muses. The tapestry was also a gift of Mrs. Whittall who furnished a pavilion in the Library in which the Stradivari are shown to the public.

tween 1650 and 1780, and although some instruments since that time have been as good, they have never been better than the product of the violin makers of Cremona, Italy. Indeed, violin makers have been diligently following the designs of those Italians for nearly three hundred years now, copying some parts down to the last centimeter. The first great violin-making family were the Amati and most of the other famous names worked in Amati shops and were taught their skills by the Amati brothers (who apparently were completely open about their so-called "secrets" of wood and varnish and design, teaching them to anyone on their payroll).

The violins that the Amati designed and built are characterized by their very high backs and bellies. There are still many Amatis around, and violinists can easily identify them by their unique shape and small size. They were considered the finest instruments in the world in the seventeenth century and they were noted for having a beautiful, very responsive tone of sufficient volume to handle a German castle or an English manor house—although present taste feels they are not quite up to our modern concert halls. The Library of Congress permits its Amati to be played on the premises by any visiting musician who is searching the collections for new musical material for his repertoire.

A violin is made of sixty-eight separate wooden parts, each one cut to a specific pattern shape, carved, and dressed out individually. It is not "formed" or bent over a molded model with clamps. All the shapes are carved out of solid wood to make the various lines that are apparent. The front of the violin is called the belly and this is made from a single board. A violin maker will use chisels, then planes, and ultimately shapers to cut away the wood, leaving the center under the bridge half again as thick as the wood out at the edges of the instrument. The front and back are carved to exactly the same shape, but they are made from different woods: the belly wood is very lively (usually spruce) and the back is of some hard, stiff variety like maple or poplar. The vibrations of the strings are transferred to the belly and the magnified tone is thus produced. An even wider variety of woods goes into the ribs, finger board, neck, scroll, pegs, et cetera.

We first hear of Antonio Stradivari when he goes to work for the Amati family in his teens; he stayed with them until the senior Amati died in

1684, when Stradivari was forty. Stradivari then moved out on his own, and his first innovation came in 1690 with a new, considerably enlarged model of his own design. These violins were no wider than Amati's but longer and considerably flatter. The flat face made the sound stronger, more resonant, and gave it a much more brilliant tone. (The flat face also made it harder to play single notes on a single string but simpler to play chords across two strings at a time, since the bow could stroke them in pairs across a flatter bridge.) Stradivari experimented with F-shaped sound holes and ultimately moved them farther back and also made the corners of the violin more sharply pointed.

In 1700 Stradivari modified his pattern for the last time (he was then fifty-six years old), and he began what the music historians call the "Golden Period" of Strad production—which continued on until his death at ninety-three. He worked right up to the day he died and ultimately produced 1,116 instruments. These were not casually or creatively formed; they were all made to his very precise patterns. The difference in their various tones and personalities does not come from different shapes but from three kinds of variables—the variations of grain and texture in the wood, the variations in the way the varnish was mixed and absorbed by each instrument, and the inevitable variations involved in carving wood by hand. There are 600 Stradivari instruments still in existence—540 violins, 10 violas, and 50 cellos.

There was nothing particularly mystical about the way the Library's five instruments came together. Back in the twenties and thirties the Library was blessed by the ministrations of two very firm, very wealthy women, who wished to do good things for music and for the Library, and who wished their own memories to be kept alive by continuing, creative philanthropies. We'll get to the rather amazing result of their efforts later, but it's enough to say at this point that Mrs. Gertrude Clarke Whittall simply went to a dealer in antique musical instruments, told him to go out and buy her a string quartet of Stradivari instruments, and he did. They all came from different sources, the dealer's judgment has proved to be flawless (the instruments are universally praised as forming a sublime playing ensemble), and the whole project could probably never be duplicated again. The cost of the five in 1938 was far less than any *one* would be today, and the possibility of now acquir-

ing this many instruments of this quality even in a lifetime is most unlikely.

The most famous violin of the group is called the Betts and was named after a famous English violin maker who owned it for many years. Stradivari made it in 1704 and it is considered to have a very strong personality with a splendid, "royal" tone, according to the cognoscenti. The Castelbarco Violin (1699) is also named after one of its former owners, Count Cesare Castelbarco of Milan, whose family sold it in 1862. It passed through a number of owners until it reached America in the late 1800s. Approximately half of all known Strads are now in the United States. The Castelbarco has been characterized as being "feminine" and is easy to identify among the three from its golden orange varnish.

The Ward Violin (1700) was named after its first recorded owner, an Englishman, and it has been called "sophisticated"; the Cassavetti Viola (1727) was once owned by the Wanamakers of Philadelphia, although its name comes from a Greek family who lived in England and owned it during the nineteenth century. (You recall that this is one of the ten known Stradivari violas. A viola is approximately one-seventh larger than a violin and is tuned five tones lower.) The final instrument of the group is the Castelbarco Violoncello (1697), which was owned by the same Milanese count as the violin. A cello is about twice the size of a violin and is tuned twelve notes below the viola.

Now let's test some myths. Is it true that it is impossible to duplicate a Stradivarius? The experts say no, a violin can be made to the exact same dimensions and indeed tens of thousands are. The difference is in the wood, its seasoning— the way it dries, takes the varnish—and the complications of cross strains in all the dimensions of the instrument. The variables make the odds against success very high, but fine, carefully constructed modern instruments are becoming just as great as Stradivaris as they mature. Indeed, the experts tell us, it is simply that time has proved the Strads. It will take decades—at least a century—to find out which of our present instruments are the real masterpieces (and unfortunately none of us will be around to find out who the winners are).

Is it true that if you alternate playing a Strad and a fine modern instrument behind a screen, a real musician can spot the Strad every time? The Library has a constant stream of the world's finest string players coming through the building so this

The Juilliard String Quartet performing on the stage of the Coolidge Auditorium. The Auditorium was a gift from Elizabeth Sprague Coolidge and is internationally known for its exceptionally fine acoustics.

question is frequently debated on the premises. There is a vigorous difference of opinion. Some say any expert can identify the Strad immediately; the others claim the claim is a myth.

Is it true that a fine violin has to be played to keep it "alive?" Definitely yes. One of the greatest violins of all time was the Guarnerius that Paganini played thoughout his career and then gave to Cremona as a gesture of returning it to its home. It was placed in a glass case as a museum piece and it sat there too long before someone realized what was happening, and it is now quite useless as a concert instrument. What makes the difference? The violinists who use the Library's Strads say it is a non-rational combination of human sweat, the warmth from hands, the flexing of the wood fibers by the vibrating tones, and the adjustment of the glue to changes in rooms and cases, lights and handling. Some believe that the wood of a violin is still alive (being organic it still has living characteristics which, given the proper conditions, continue to renew the wood). (Preservationists who are baffled at the way antique paper from the sev-

enteenth and eighteenth centuries seems to last beyond logical limits are exploring the same phenomenon.)

Because of all these dangers, Mrs. Whittall decreed that her five Stradivari must be played regularly (she was also eager to make chamber music available to a broader audience, of course) so she gave additional money to see that free concerts are given with the instruments throughout the year, and that the Library keeps a continual, resident ensemble under contract to play them. There have been only three such groups in the half century of the endowment, each staying on for years. The second, the famous Budapest String Quartet, was so associated with the instruments and the concert series that in most people's minds they were all created at the same time. When these noted performers retired, the Juilliard String Quartet took their place and are presently carrying the role. Mrs. Whittall also insisted that the instruments must never leave the Library except for repairs, so the free in-house Library of Congress concerts have become not only a traditional part of the

Washington musical scene, but a stock property on "fine music" stations around the world.

There is one characteristic of the Library's Strads that leads us on to another variety of treasure; it is well known to the specialists but rarely noted by the general public. The fact is that in spite of the way the Library and the music world go to great ends to preserve the violins precisely as they were when they left the Master's hands, every one of the violins has been altered with a longer neck; the strings are longer than they were in Stradivari's time, they are pulled harder, and the pitch is higher. And on this phenomenon hangs a tale.

It can best be illustrated by the flutes. From among all the statistics and superlatives that one stumbles over throughout the Library of Congress, I must admit the one that I find the most unlikely is this: the Library owns the greatest—defined either as the largest, the most significant, the most elaborate, or the most complete—collection of a single musical instrument in the world. And this collection is, of all things, the Dayton C. Miller collection of flute and flute-like instruments. It started with only 1,300 examples that Miller had accumulated, but since its transfer to the Library in 1941, flutists and flute makers have been donating both their instruments and their oddities to it so that it has continued to grow without interruption.

This unexpected situation came about in the following way: Dayton C. Miller was a physicist who first specialized in sound waves in general, but soon became fascinated with wind waves produced by human breath, and finally got down to his real specialty, wind waves in straight tubes blown across round holes. He first gathered the world's largest collection of books, articles, and research papers on the subject, and then set out to accumulate the world's greatest collection of examples. He collected them by material: bamboo, jade, ebony, ivory, clay, and ultimately one of solid gold. He collected them by culture: Mayan, Chinese, Eskimo, a flute made from a human skull in Micronesia, the personal flute made for Frederick the Great (with its magnificent porcelain case, lined in compartmented velvet and decorated in high baroque).

His primary preoccupation was with the development of the instrument. He traced it in microscopic detail from the Renaissance to the present, searching out how the tone had changed,

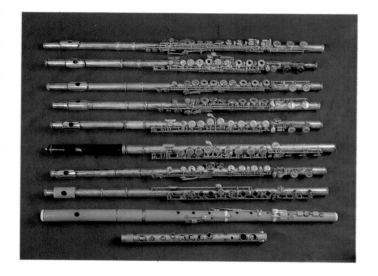

Flutes from the Dayton C. Miller Collection. Opposite: *A two-key instrument by Johann Joachim Quantz which belonged to Frederick the Great. The porcelain case contains extra joints used to change the pitch of the instrument.* Above: *Examples of the development of the flute from the eighteenth century to the present.*

Above: *Examples of primitive flutes and flute-like instruments made from such materials as pottery, bamboo, and soft woods. The decoration on the North American Indian piece at right from the Arkansas Osage tribe is a human scalp.* Opposite: *Examples showing the range of the collection, by time and by place. From left, a notched flute from Peking, China, made of jade in the seventeenth and eighteenth century, a gold flute designed by Dayton C. Miller himself, and a wooden Renaissance recorder. Other varieties shown include instruments of glass and ivory.*

how the finger holes had been shifted to make it easier to play faster, how its size had been altered to affect its pitch. He researched the interior of the tube—the bore, the feature that is essential to timbre and tone—and traced its modifications through different societies. The flute is not simply a hollow pipe, but has different profiles inside, and Miller drew interior silhouettes going from the perfectly cylindrical to the eccentrically conical, noting where different designers had placed careful narrowings at various points. This led him into the scientific analysis of instrument making that was so prevalent for all of the musical instruments in the nineteenth century. As is obvious, Bach never heard his music as it sounds on a modern organ. Haydn wrote for a small orchestra, yet we still play his symphonies with a stage full of instruments collected to do justice to Richard Strauss—and get a sound that even Beethoven could not conceive. Each one of the instruments went through dramatic development during this

period: trumpets and horns that left the 1700s as simple, flared tubes of different lengths came out with finger valves that made each single instrument several instruments-in-one capable of producing a full chromatic scale. (The valves on wind instruments were perfected in the 1840s by a man named Adolphe Sax, who ended up being known for a reeded novelty he designed as a sort of after-thought, the Saxophone.) This sort of experimentation was going on all across the symphonic spectrum, and the designer Theobald Boehm (1794–1881) was the "name" in flutes.

He too was trying to increase the range and the flexibility of his instrument, and Miller acquired Boehm's complete collection illustrating a lifetime of experimentation. Boehm's prototype is there, a simple tube with holes in various places but made of slides and sleeves so the spacing can be changed, the relationships can be adjusted, the mouth hole shifted back and forth. You can then watch the development through a hundred silver instruments from a simple tube to one with a few keys and pads operated by levers for closing multiple holes—on to incredibly complicated pivots and hinges and overlapping, cantilevered apparatuses so a flutist can sweep up and down the chromatic scale to highs and lows that would astound an eighteenth-century composer.

The Library has its connection with this roomful of gadgets because of Miller's book collection. When he was preparing to retire from his scientific work in the 1920s, he offered his collection of books and instruments to various schools, institutions, and libraries but insisted that it be maintained so that all of its parts would be equally accessible to the general public. Only the facilities offered by the Library of Congress satisfied him, and the whole collection was therefore moved to Washington. Miller intended to follow it and spend his retirement writing from its material—but he suddenly died without having a chance to tell its story.

From the Library's point of view, the books on acoustics and patents for new instruments were a splendid addition to its already broad collection of the history and physics of musical instrumentation, but as the years have passed, the Miller collection has proved to be used in an intriguing way. In our time, the *development* of musical instruments has to all intents been completed, but the *historical interest* in how each one of these highly mechanized gadgets looked and sounded in the

In 1951, the noted violinist Fritz Kreisler gave the Library his Guarnerius, his Hill bow, and the autograph manuscript of the Brahms Violin Concerto.

time of the early composers has become a center of great attention. Thus the Miller collection is now being mined for his data and measurements of the early wind pieces. The two-thousand-odd items in the Library's collection are being carefully preserved in the state of their original receipt, with a few examples of each development kept ready for concert use. These are thus used by visiting ensembles and recital musicians to give authenticity to period music, but even these instruments are carefully measured and photographed, and when any element (such as a pad or pin) has to be renewed, the original part is kept in perpetual storage with the instrument itself.

All of this links us back to the Stradivari, because these too sounded different in their own time. The music now written for the violin requires more extended range, a louder and more brilliant tone, and, so that the Library's Strads can be used for any of the music of the past three centuries, their necks have been extended. In a few cases they have been completely renewed; in others, blocks have been inserted between the body of the violin and the neck to move it farther out but retaining the original wood. The finger boards have been extended so higher notes can be played, and the bridges are rounder for greater flexibility.

We have been looking at the instrumental treasures of the Library as they are now, but these, of course, came fairly late in the Library's life. (Professional violinists, by the way, are as impressed by the Guarnerius that Fritz Kreisler gave the Library in 1950, as they are with Mrs. Whittall's Stradivari. The Guarnerius is considered to be one of the very finest violins ever made and it is the instrument usually used by guest soloists in the Library's recital programs.) The foundation stones of the music holdings are the music on paper, and the treasures of these are the composers' manuscripts. By now, these holdings—and recall, these are the scribbled original sheets in the masters' own hands showing the incremental changes, the rejected solutions, the autograph notations...these are not the resulting printed versions, these are the manuscripts from which the first editions were made— these holdings have produced an awesome, one-stop research center for musicology.

It is almost impossible to capture the breadth of the material in the vaults. Some of the composers are represented by individual pieces as in the case of Bizet, Tchaikovsky, and Sibelius. In other instances, almost the entire production of a composer—the works of a lifetime—are in the collection. The family of Leo Delibes presented the full, handwritten scores of *Lakme, La Source*, and *Sylvia*. Herbert Witherspoon gave the full manuscript score of Leoncavallo's *I Pagliacci*. Fritz Kreisler gave the manuscript of Brahms' Violin Concerto in D Major (of which more later). Mrs. Whittall gave the original draft of Brahms' Third Symphony. Robert Schumann's First Symphony (the *Spring*) and Mendelssohn's String Octet op. 20 are here. Incidentally, it is interesting to note that the personality of a composer—the image with which he is usually remembered—rarely has much correlation with the appearance of his working scores.

Pencil sketch for the second movement of Robert Schumann's First Symphony (the Spring*). The opening measures of the symphony were transposed up a third at Mendelssohn's suggestion. Corrections appear at numerous points in the manuscript in Schumann's hand.*

Schumann and Mendelssohn are neat, clean, and easily understood by any amateur pianist, but Brahms is a fearful mish-mash of smeared, hurried, free-flowing script. Beethoven (the Library owns the original manuscript of the famous Piano Sonata in E Major op. 109, for example) appears hurried, but completely controlled, and the notes are thin and spidery like snippets of black thread thrown on the page. Beethoven looks the way you'd expect Brahms to be, and vice-versa. The Library owns Haydn's 52nd Piano Sonata, his Symphony No. 90 in C Major, and the andante movement of his 94th, the *Surprise Symphony*. Haydn looks like Haydn would be expected to look.

These great monuments of eighteenth- and nineteenth-century music are just an introduction to the Library's musical treasures. The Library's holdings are equally strong in the early twentieth-century moderns and vastly rich in works of our own day. Sergei Rachmaninoff's wife donated a huge collection of rare musical material relating to the composer himself, but even more from his friends and the performers of his period. Included in his collection are the manuscript of his *Rhapsody on a Theme by Paganini*, the score of his Third Symphony, and the two-piano transcript of his Prelude in C Sharp Minor. The Library owns Prokofiev's String Quartet op. 50, Ravel's *Chansons*

Right: *The Library's oil portrait of Ludwig van Beethoven, age forty-five, by Christopher Heckel. Below: Autograph manuscript of the slow movement of Beethoven's Piano Sonata, opus 109. Bottom: Joseph Haydn's Symphony No. 94 (the* Surprise*). This version, an authentic autograph score, lacks the famous "surprise" chord introduced by the composer for its startling effect.*

A corner of the music reading room where Sergei Rachmaninoff's writing desk is used by scholars; here it is shown with the composer's autograph score of his Symphonic Dances. *A portrait of Rachmaninoff is seen on the shelf behind.*

Madecasses, Respighi's *Trittico Botticelliano*. It has unbelievable quantities of Franz Liszt's worksheets, correspondence, and final drafts. To extract a handful at random, the letters between Liszt and Henry Wadsworth Longfellow are unexpected and extensive. Liszt set Longfellow's poem *Excelsior* to music, and Longfellow commissioned a portrait of Liszt to give the composer as a present. A typical Longfellow letter includes passages like:

After dinner, went to the opera and heard "Norma," whose beautiful music I like; but

Top: *The copyist's score with composer's corrections of Franz Liszt's First Piano Concerto.* Above: *A scholar examines the music, here looking at one of the many "paste-overs" Liszt used to correct or change the original draft.*

the opera itself—its Druids and Romans and sheeted chorus and prima donnas, looking as if they had just jumped out of bed—has grown very tedious to me. I was in an ab-Normal condition.

It is not surprising that the Library's collection of contemporary music is so rich, since so much of it was commissioned and paid for by Library foundation funds. The Koussevitzky Foundation, the McKim Fund, the benefactions of Mrs. Elizabeth Sprague Coolidge have produced dozens of the pieces that have become an indispensable part of the modern repertoire. Mrs. Coolidge herself had been a pianist of recognized stature in the Chicago area, but in time she became better known for her philanthropies to the musical world. She founded the Berkshire Chamber Music Festivals; at the Library she gave the money for the building of the five-hundred-seat concert hall which now operates under her name, and she gave a substantial amount of money to the Elizabeth Sprague Coolidge Foundation for commissioning work from established, modern composers. As a result of this, not only did the Library have a role in bringing into being such memorable works as Aaron Copland's *Appalachian Spring*, Béla Bartók's Fifth String Quartet, Arnold Schoenberg's Third String Quartet, Benjamin Britten's *Peter Grimes*, Heitor Villa-Lobos' *Madona*, Alberto Ginastera's *Bomarzo* Cantata (and many more); but since the pieces were written for the Library, the Library has received the original manuscripts for its permanent collections. In most cases, the personal papers of the composers follow close behind. (I have always wondered whether the heavy literary content of the Library's commissioned works is due to fashion or to the library connection, but such innovative titles as George Crumb's *Ancient Voices of Children*, Gian Carlo Menotti's *The Unicorn, the Gorgon, and the Manticore*, and Igor Stravinsky's *Apollon-Musagète* must have some larger explanation!)

It is hardly startling to find that, in spite of the awesome majesty of the musical monuments mentioned above, the greatest strength of the Library—the holdings that simply cannot even be approached in any other institution—are the materials relating to American music. They would be genuine treasure under any condition; they certainly are in the context of the national culture. Let me suggest a checklist to give you a feel for the *kinds* of rarities that are here.

Above: *The Library's portrait of the opera singer—and silent film star—Geraldine Farrar. The oil painting was executed by E.A. von Kaulbach, 1904.*

Right: *Benjamin Britten's opera,* Peter Grimes, *commissioned by Serge Koussevitzky.*

First, there are the essentially historical materials. The works of the first American composers like Francis Hopkinson, signer of the Declaration of Independence and the first American to publish music; the colonist William Billings, Boston singing master, writer of patriotic and religious songs, of whom the Library has not only his printed sheets, but the only known autographed manuscript.

There are the early copyright materials. You will remember that during the nineteenth century people bought sheet music to play on their home pianos just as we buy single records and albums today. Stephen Collins Foster copyrighted his songs—many more than the dozen that are commonly sung. The minstrel shows of mid-century produced the hints of coming Dixieland, ragtime, and jazz. These are in the Library by the tens of thousands—you will recall that the institution already owned over 300,000 pieces of sheet music even before it left the halls of the Capitol. This is all "popular" music, if you can make the question-

Night on Bare Mountain, *by Modest Mussorgski as re-orchestrated and arranged by Leopold Stokowski for the Walt Disney animated motion picture,* Fantasia.

able distinction between "everyday" music and "serious" or "classical" music. The Library's musicologists note that this is a division that is essentially American. In Europe Mendelssohn, Grieg, Verdi, Smetana, Dvořák all just wrote music and their melodies were embraced by all classes; neither they nor the man in the street would have understood the distinction. In this country, "popular" music was shoved off to the side, and even "serious" music was denigrated. The American composers like Edward MacDowell, John Knowles Paine, Horatio Parker went off to study under Liszt and Joseph Rheinberger and returned to be patronized in an atmosphere of academic snobbery brought on by a national inferiority complex. No American could ever be taken as seriously as European composers were. The Library has broad collections of the personal papers, unpublished music, plus the better known works of these American composers and the Library staff is convinced that they will be recognized for their stature and skills in the years to come.

Next we come to the one part of the American musical tradition that has always been a source of pride and commercial success: the theater. The Library has great holdings of Victor Herbert, John Philip Sousa, and thousands of pieces in manuscript as well as print from Jerome Kern, Irving Berlin, George Gershwin, Richard Rodgers.

Going down a parallel path is the ragtime, blues, jazz, and folk-music tradition. Not only does the Library have whatever happened to get into print, but through the imaginative efforts of Library staff, thousands of hours of field work were invested during the first half of this century to capture mountain music, railroad music, prison music, Indian music, ethnic festival music, and similar un-written, traditional songs before they were lost from memory.

All of this is in the Library's vaults—in excess of three million pieces of printed material, plus thousands of discs, reels of tape, and kinescopes. The process of identifying the enduring from the trash is fascinating. It seems to appear in every kind of

The Library's portrait of Arnold Schoenberg painted by George Gershwin.

The autograph piano score by Gershwin of his Rhapsody in Blue.

Recording folk music in southern Georgia. John R. Griffin, an 80-year-old resident of Cook County, shows a Library folklorist how to "beat the straws"—adding a staccato rhythmic drone by striking the fiddle strings with a broom straw. The resultant tape went into the Library's American Folklife Center collection.

music. Some of the gold is there and is simply un-recognized. Individual performers search the files; Joan Baez and Harry Belafonte got much of their repertoire from previously ignored materials in the Library's holdings. But other examples are distilled out by use. Most of what is discarded or forgotten deserved to be, but it is interesting to note how many of the avant-garde experiments, the protest songs, the attempts at being out-rageous have proved to have qualities that have given them immortality.

One final thought relating to the great holo-graph rarities in the vaults. What practical good are they really? Most of them are next to impossi-ble to read by anyone but an expert, and it's the music that makes the difference, not the paper and ink it's written with. Isn't a good, clean, printed copy what is really worth caring about?

The answer is that the great historical, musical monuments are useful in two very real ways. The first has been gracefully expressed by the concert violinist Yehudi Menuhin, who has written:

I have always felt a peculiar frisson upon see-ing for the first time the actual handwriting of a master composer, alive with its irregularities, its visible impulses, its detectable moments of ease and worry, of joy and despair. It leads one straight to the heart of the matter, to the mind of the man who wrote the composition. No printed score can offer one such insights.

This is an intangible condition, very real to the specialist or virtuoso, but harder for the rest of us to sense. But the other application is clear even to those of us who cannot respond to the "presence"

Opposite, top: *Bluegrass music on the Neptune Plaza.*
Opposite, bottom: *David Raksin conducting the score for* Laura *in synchronization with the film.* Above: *Raksin's original score for the film. Also shown from the Library's collection of dramatic music are,* top, *Leonard Bernstein's* West Side Story, *the love duet;* top right, *Aaron Copland's score for the* Red Pony; *right, Bernard Hermann's manuscript for* Citizen Kane—*this the famous flashback to the scene in the snow.*

of the master musician: the manuscripts provide an enormous amount of information.

First. As you can see by the examples illustrated, they are indeed very difficult for a non-musician to read; astonishingly, they are almost as difficult for the specialist! These sheets are worked over and over by the composer until he finally—usually reluctantly—passes them to his publisher who gives them to his editor who gives them to the engraver. Oddly enough, the editor and the engraver don't know much more about it than we do. They really only do the best they can. They guess, they assume—frequently they clarify—and then the printing proof is returned to the composer for checking. Many composers are genuinely grateful for elements supplied by the publishing staff. Others seem to argue back and forth, but most surprisingly, an astonishing number of errors creep in which, usually because of traveling, concert schedules, or general distraction, the composer never sees at all. The comparison between printed material and original manuscripts goes on all the time.

A second application of the holographs comes simply in answering questions. Mozart's famous *Serenade for Thirteen Wind Instruments* was so scored for generations until the missing original was acquired by the Library and its staff discovered that Mozart had scored it for twelve wind instruments and a stringed bass viol. John Philip Sousa felt required to write new songs for every season, but as his years accumulated, this pressure (plus short deadlines) forced an enormous amount of composition. In mid-career he developed a technique of shortcuts that involved lifting portions of works that "worked" and recycling them into new forms. The result was a distillation process that kept skimming off the best elements so the products kept getting better and better rather than less and less imaginative. Since only a fraction of his product was ever printed, only his manuscripts provide the real story of where the pieces came from.

The Library's manuscript of Haydn's *Surprise Symphony* corroborates the story that the "surprise" in the slow part was an afterthought. The Library copy has no evidence of it and shows how Haydn originally pictured the passage in his own mind.

And thus, third, the manuscripts give an insight into what the composer was trying to express—frequently by pointing out what he had rejected and thereby rather firmly pointing out what he did *not* want by way of notes, emphasis, and treatment. The manuscript of the Brahms Violin Concerto is a classic demonstration of this phenomenon.

Brahms was a pianist. When he wrote for the violin he wrote as well as he could, as a professional composer and musician would, but he questioned his ability to wring out the highest potential of the violin instrument itself. What fingering would be the most effective (even possible)? What qualities of tone should be exploited or minimized?

The greatest concert violinist of Brahms' day was Joseph Joachim, with whom the composer developed an increasingly close friendship. In August of 1878 Brahms sent the first score of the violin concerto to Joachim asking him to examine it, to make any comments which he believed would improve it, and to comment on passages "that are difficult, uncomfortable, or impossible." From this started a year of correspondence during which two complete movements were abandoned at Joachim's suggestion. The violin solo part was worked and reworked by the violinist, which caused the piano part to be changed and strengthened, and then ultimately brought the piece to a series of refinements producing the masterpiece that has become an established part of the symphonic repertoire.

The astonishing thing is that major portions of this distillation and refinement process are revealed in the manuscript copy itself. The first draft is clearly stated by Brahms' use of brown ink on a smooth, white paper. Variations in the speed of his strokes and pressure on his pen are remarkably apparent and revealing even to the layman.

Next, dark red ink in notations by Joachim's hand revises passages for the soloist and indicates very careful additions and changes.

The next layer is gray-pencil changes in the orchestration which seem to be the product of Brahms *and* Joachim. Their prime purpose (according to the Library's musicologists) appears to have been to make the orchestra "more transparent" and to emphasize the bass themes. The gray pencil also adds a neatly written violin part in the margin and then crosses it all out at the end.

Overlaid on this are blue pencil notations in Brahms' handwriting which were clearly put there for the conductor to tell him where the emphasis

Stars and Stripes Forever, *John Philip Sousa's (indeed possibly America's) most famous march.* Left: *A page of the autograph score.* Above: *Various published forms including a music-box disc, an Edison wax cylinder, a song arrangement, and a set of marching-band parts.*

The manuscript copy of Johannes Brahms' Violin Concerto in D Major, op. 77, with corrections by Joseph Joachim. The first page of the score shows the warning by the musical editor to the engraver to be certain he does not abbreviate certain passages written in musical shorthand.

The adagio, showing typical pencil corrections in Brahms' hand of the orchestral parts.

in playing should be applied, and for keying reference points for the premier performance in Leipzig.

Finally, a soft red crayon or pencil in Brahms' hand makes final changes in the dynamic markings and appears to set the final form of the piece for first playing, and then for engraving and publication.

The importance of all of these elements is so obvious it need not be described. The one footnote about it all that should be underscored is what the Library has done with this information. It becomes a demonstration model for our understanding. One, the manuscript was a gift to the Library by the great concert violinist, Fritz Kreisler, another example of the institution's dependence on the generosity of its donors. Two, the Library's staff spent many months researching Brahms' correspondence and linking the various changes in the manuscript to the written dialogue between composer and musician and then to the performance history, criticism, and traditional commentary. Three, money from the McKim Fund was used to support Yehudi Menuhin in a study and commentary on the piece. The commentary was then published by the Library with a complete, six-color facsimile of the manuscript so that the research and treasure could become available to the music world in general. Similar facsimiles have been issued of the Library's holograph copies of Mendelssohn's String Octet, Mozart's *Serenade*, and so on—and the activity adds up to the best possible application and dissemination of the contents of these national treasures. The exercise is a classic demonstration of what a national library is supposed to be here for.

CHAPTER XI

Give Us Victories

And so we come in conclusion to what Archibald MacLeish called "the chief jewel" of the institution: the personal papers of "those men and women who, throughout the centuries, have most profoundly influenced the lives and destinies of their countrymen." Here are the fibers of our traditions, the agonies of those who took the nation down new paths and across new horizons in politics, war, literature, civil rights. There are over 10,000 of these collections with every one revealing a slightly different picture of the individual from the generalized silhouette passed on to us by traditional history. There are so many of them and the materials are so splendid; the best we can do is simply walk through the riches, seize a few handsful off the shelves to demonstrate who the people are, note how their private secrets got here, and spot a few of the surprises—astonishments, even—that lie among the pieces.

Where to start? Anywhere will do. The Lincoln papers? Very rich. Here are all the drafts as he struggled through the Emancipation Proclamation, the First Inaugural, letters about politics, his domestic troubles, the two copies of the Gettysburg Address in his own hand. *Two* copies of the Gettysburg Address? Yes, the Library owns two; he actually wrote out five—all of which are scattered around the nation, and each of which differs slightly from its neighbors. But we've always heard that he wrote it at the last minute on the train to Gettysburg; we thought he scribbled it on his knee on the back of an envelope. Not so; let me explain.

The Battle of Gettysburg ended on July 3, 1863. Governor Andrew Gregg Curtin of Pennsylvania asked David Wills, a leading Gettysburg citizen, to be his agent in caring for the Pennsylvania wounded. Wills made his first report on July 24, telling the Governor that the wounded were being

Abraham Lincoln's preliminary draft of the Emancipation Proclamation issued after the Battle of Antietam (1862). Here he warns the opposing forces that if the rebellion is not ended in four months, "I, as Commander-in-Chief of the Army and Navy of the United States, do order and declare that on the first day of January in the year of our Lord one thousand, eight hundred and sixty-three, all persons held as slaves within any state or states, wherein the constitutional authority of the United States shall not then be practically recognized, submitted to, and maintained, shall then, thenceforward, and forever be free."

Timothy O'Sullivan's photograph of a meeting of General Ulysses S. Grant's field officers, June 2, 1864. The scene is in front of Bethesda Church, Virginia. Pews have been brought out of the church and Grant's staff is conducting a council of war. Grant can be seen leaning across the back of a pew to examine a map held by a seated officer.

John Reebie's photograph of a burial party collecting dead on the Cold Harbor, Virginia, battlefield, April 1865. (Print by Alexander Gardner.)

Abraham Lincoln aged 51. This ambrotype made in Springfield on August 13, 1860, was taken for Mr. J. Henry Brown who used it to paint a miniature on ivory. The photograph itself later ended up with Lincoln's son, Robert.

Probably the most famous photograph of Lincoln, this was made by Mathew Brady on February 9, 1864, three-and-a-half years later than the one on the left. Robert Todd Lincoln considered this the best likeness of his father; an engraving from the picture appears on U.S. currency and thus this is known as the Five Dollar Bill portrait.

treated as well as could be expected, but the situation with the dead was horrible. There were 5,000 bodies, most of them being buried where they fell in shallow graves, barely covered with soil. Wills suggested that all the states that had lost men should quickly get together to build a cemetery. The governor sent letters, the states agreed, seventeen acres were purchased and landscaped, bodies began to be moved, and plans for a suitable consecration were put in motion.

In the 1860s, the nation's leading orator was Edward Everett of Boston, so he was asked to make a speech of dedication, and the date of October 23 was set for the event. Everett replied to the request in three days, "The occasion is one of great importance not to be dismissed with a few sentimental or patriotic commonplaces" but he said he could not possibly be ready before November 19; would they

wait? Everyone agreed that in order to get Everett, they would.

Thus far, all the activity had been done at the state level. On November 2, apparently as a near after-thought, Wills wrote to President Lincoln asking him if he would like to come and, "after the oration," make "a few appropriate remarks." By the time Lincoln had received the letter and accepted the invitation, the time was down to ten days and he appears to have begun working on the speech at once.

On the 15th of November, Lincoln was going to Alexander Gardner's studio for some photographs accompanied by a friend, Noah Brooks, and as they started out of the White House Lincoln stopped and then returned to get an advance copy of the speech that Everett was planning to give. Brooks recalls Lincoln saying, "It was very kind of

Mr. Everett to send me this. I suppose he was afraid I should say something that he wanted to say. He needn't have been alarmed. My speech is not long."

Brooks asked, "So it is written, is it, then?"

Lincoln replied, "Well, no. It is not exactly written. It is not finished, anyway. I have written it over two or three times, and I shall have to give it another lick before I am satisfied. But it is short, short, short."

Ward Hill Lamon, the U.S. marshal for the Dis-

trict of Columbia and a former law partner, remembers Lincoln reading a completed draft "a day or two before the dedication." Writing in 1887 he recalls, "From his hat (the usual receptacle of his private notes and memoranda) he drew a page of foolscap, closely written, which he read to me, first remarking that it was a memorandum of what he intended to say. It proved to be in substance, and I think in *haec verba*, what was printed as his Gettysburg speech."

But James Speed, a friend who would become

The wagon park at Brandy Station, Virginia, May 1863. The picture was taken by Timothy O'Sullivan and printed by Alexander Gardner.

Attorney General in 1864, reports that Lincoln had written "about half a speech" before he left Washington for Gettysburg.

In any event, none of it was written on a train. (The Library of Congress owns the draft of Lincoln's farewell speech at Springfield, February 11, 1861, and it *was* written on the train and it very much looks it.) The story that the Address had been scribbled on his knee began very early and was being refuted very early. His personal secretary, John G. Nicolay, and Gen. James Barnet Fry, both of whom sat near Lincoln all the way to Baltimore and then on to Gettysburg, denied it in writing and in print.

Nicolay does recall that Lincoln may have finished the speech in the Wills house in Gettysburg the night before the ceremony. Thus page one of the First Draft is in ink on White House letter paper, and the other half is in pencil "on a half sheet of foolscap (diplomatic size)" as Nicolay describes it.

There seems to be general agreement that the

In 1937 Lincoln's granddaughter gave the Library a leather-covered box containing the contents of President Lincoln's pockets the night of his assassination. They consist of a pair of gold-rimmed spectacles with sliding temples and one of the bows mended with string, another pair of folding spectacles in a case, a pocket knife, a watch-fob of gold-bearing quartz, and a linen handkerchief. There is also a single sleeve button with a gold "L" on dark blue enamel, and a wallet containing several interesting items: the only money is a five dollar Confederate note, and there are nine newspaper clippings, obviously long-carried, each praising Lincoln for an achievement during his presidency.

First Draft is the one he held in his hand at the dedication. Everett orated for slightly over two hours and then Lincoln was called on, and all accounts describe him "drawing a copy from an inner pocket." Of the five drafts, only the First shows any sign of being folded.

So what are the other four? The Second Draft was given to the Library by John Hay, Lincoln's other secretary, and Library tradition says that when Lincoln left Gettysburg, his host, David Wills, asked if he might have a copy of the Address as a keepsake. Lincoln is supposed to have agreed and written out a copy at the White House shortly after he returned from Pennsylvania. Why it was not given to Wills is never explained. There are fifteen variations in capitalization and punctuation between the First and Second drafts, and some

sixty-five variations in wording as the President "improved" it on second thought.

On November 20, Edward Everett wrote Lincoln, "Permit me…to express my great admiration of the thoughts expressed by you, with such eloquent simplicity & appropriateness, at the consecration of the cemetery. I should be glad, if I could flatter myself that I came as near to the central idea of the occasion, in two hours, as you did in two minutes." And some time later, Everett asked Lincoln if he would write out a copy to be sold at the Metropolitan Fair to be held in New York in April 1864; Lincoln did, and this copy is now in the Illinois State Historical Library at Springfield. It differs slightly from drafts one and two. (It also reminds us that the legend that no one noticed Lincoln's speech at the time was quite

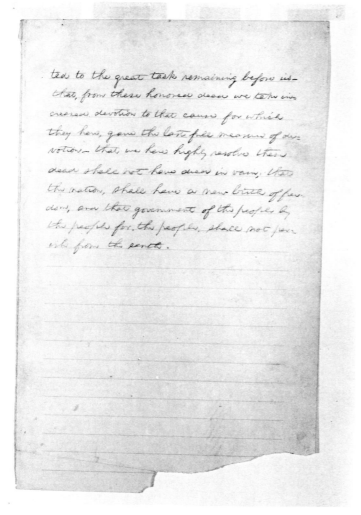

The Gettysburg Address as written by Abraham Lincoln, November 1863. It is believed that these are the sheets Lincoln held in his hand at the dedication ceremony. The Library owns two such holograph drafts.

untrue. It was immediately recognized as one of the masterpieces of the English language. The Associated Press put it on their wires at once and it appeared in newspapers all over the country within days.)

The next request came from the historian George Bancroft who asked Lincoln to give him a handwritten copy for the benefit of the Baltimore Sanitary Fair. It was to be a part of a bound set of autograph letters from contemporary authors, and the paper Lincoln wrote it on proved to be the wrong size, so the Bancrofts kept the Fourth Draft for themselves and it remained in the Bancroft family until 1929. It is now in the Cornell University Library in Ithaca. Lincoln then wrote the Address out again on proper-sized paper and sent this to Bancroft, and this version, amazingly enough, is 1) considered to be the official and correct version of the Gettysburg Address since it was the last one written, 2) soon left the country and for years was owned by Oscar B. Cintas, a businessman of Havana, Cuba, but who willed it to the Federal Government, so it is now 3) in the Lincoln Room in the White House.

The Library owns 14,000 such pieces of Lincoln manuscripts, absolutely filled with fascinating items revealing his multi-faceted personality. A few samples:

A letter to James Henry Hackett, a Shakespearean actor. "I think nothing equals Macbeth....Unlike you gentlemen of the profession, I think the soliloquy in Hamlet commencing, 'O, my offence is rank' surpasses that commencing 'To be, or not to be...'"

The files are jammed with requests for government jobs, and Lincoln says he has "fewer oats than horses" to offer them and then, in a letter to his old law partner, William Herndon, says "If our American society and the United States Government are demoralized and overthrown, it will come from the voracious desire for office, this wriggle to live without toil, work and labor from which I am not free myself."

Any author will understand Lincoln's joust with the Public Printer, John Defrees. Defrees had objected to Lincoln's use of *sugar-coated* in a message to Congress as being an "undignified expression" and suggested that Lincoln select one more appropriate for the permanent government archives. Lincoln replied, "Defrees, that word expresses exactly my idea, and I am not going to change it. The time will never come in this country when

people won't know exactly what sugar-coated means."

Every draft shows linings-out and insertions that strengthen—or deliberately weaken—a text as he works with it. His original sheets of the First Inaugural, for example, close with the war-like challenge: "*You* can forbear the assault upon [the government], I cannot shrink from the defense of it. With *you*, and not with *me*, is the solemn question of 'shall it be peace or a sword?'" He ultimately lined that out and substituted the "We are not enemies but friends..." paragraph that he finally used.

The greatest majority of the Lincoln papers came to the Library of Congress from Lincoln's son, Robert Todd Lincoln. Ten days after the assassination the papers were taken from the White House by Mary Todd Lincoln who shipped them to Illinois where they were closed to everyone but the two secretaries, Nicolay and Hay. When Mary died, Robert inherited them. He went through them carefully and (to the horror of historians) burned all the "useless" parts and deposited the rest with the Library of Congress on May 7, 1919. His instructions were that they were to remain sealed to everyone until twenty-one years after his death. Robert Todd Lincoln died in 1926, so they were not made available to scholars until 1947. The Library has since microfilmed all its Lincoln papers and sells them as a set of ninety-seven reels, at cost.

One final example of a Lincoln manuscript which, as a sometime bureaucrat myself, I cannot leave un-noted. It is Lincoln's letter to General Hooker and is a part of the Library's collections as an item in the Alfred Whital Stern gift. In a world in which obfuscated bureaucratese has become a high art form and nothing is so opaque as a military directive, consider the clarity of Lincoln's instructions to his newly appointed general:

I have placed you at the head of the Army of the Potomac. Of course I have done this upon what appear to me to be sufficient reasons. And yet I think it best for you to know that there are some things in regard to which, I am not quite satisfied with you. I believe you to be a brave and skilful soldier, which, of course, I like. I also believe you do not mix politics with your profession, in which you are right. You have confidence in yourself, which is a valuable, if not an indispensable quality.

You are ambitious, which, within reasonable bounds, does good rather than harm. But I think that during Gen. Burnside's command of the Army, you have taken counsel of your ambition, and thwarted him as much as you could, in which you did a great wrong to the country, and to a most meritorious and honorable brother officer. I have heard, in such way as to believe it, of your recently saying that both the Army and the Government needed a Dictator. Of course it was not *for* this, but in spite of it, that I have given you the command. Only those generals who gain successes, can set up dictators. What I now ask of you is military success, and I will risk the dictatorship. The government will support you to the utmost of its ability, which is neither more nor less than it has done and will do for all commanders. I much fear that the spirit which you have aided to infuse into the Army, of criticising their Commander, and withholding confidence from him, will now turn upon you. I shall assist you as far as I can, to put it down. Neither you, nor Napoleon, if he were alive again, could get any good out of an army, while such a spirit prevails in it.

And now, beware of rashness—Beware of rashness, but with energy, and sleepless vigilance, go forward, and give us victories.

Lincoln's letter to General Joseph Hooker displayed between a bronze life mask of Lincoln made by Clark Mills and a cast of his right hand made in Springfield, Illinois, the Sunday following his nomination to the Presidency in 1860.

The Lincoln papers are but one of the twenty-three presidential collections from Washington to Coolidge which add up to a total of two million manuscript pieces. They are incredibly different in "feel" and even in appearance. Andrew Jackson and Zachary Taylor are even rougher and readier than we have been led to expect. A poignant letter from Jackson's frontier wife, written slowly and painfully to Andrew then off to war, somehow tells more about the two of them than the words denote:

My Dearest Life. I received your Letter by Express....My Dear pray Let me Conjur you by every Tie of Love of friend ship to Let me see you before you go againe. I have borne it untill now....I never wanted to see you so mutch in my life...you have been gon a Long time six monthes in all that time what has been your trials daingers and Diffyculties hardeships oh Lorde of heaven how Can I beare it...once more I Commend you to god his providential Eye is on you his parental tender Care is garding you. my prayers my tears is for your safety Day and night. farwell my I fell two much at this moment our Dear Little Son is well he sayes maney things to sweet papa which I have not time to mention. the chest blessings of Heaven awaite you Crown your wishes. health and happy Dayes untill we meete. Let it not be Long from your Dearest friend and faithfull wife untill Death.

Rachel Jackson

Many of the sainted leaders, all-wise and imperturbable, reveal themselves as being just as irritated and frustrated as the rest of us—thereby adding to the reality of their stature in an appealing way. Consider the letter from Thomas Jefferson to Dr. Benjamin Rush (September 23, 1800) that contains the magnificent credo: "for I have sworn

The Capitol as it looked in 1806. This watercolor, painted by the architect Benjamin Latrobe himself, was given to Jefferson with Latrobe's note: "In presenting to you this perspective of the Capitol, I have no object but to gratify my desire, as an individual citizen, to give you a testimony of the truest respect and attachment." Jefferson and Latrobe had argued about the three domes which Jefferson thought inappropriate to the facade.

Probably the rarest treasure in the Library of Congress, this is the Rough Draft of the Declaration of Independence in Jefferson's own hand. It bears some 80 emendations made first by John Adams and Benjamin Franklin, and later by the whole Congress. All of the changes debated on the Floor were entered on this copy as votes were taken.

upon the altar of God eternal hostility against every form of tyranny over the mind of man." This marvelous phrase is embedded in a fulmination against Episcopalians and Presbyterians and his fury at the attacks being made on him by the press and the clergy—"…all the lies which have been preached or printed against me"—but the letter opens on quite another subject. He begins by congratulating Rush "on the healthiness of your city," and notes:

when great evils happen, I am in the habit of looking out for what good may arise from them as consolations to us: and Providence has in fact so established the order of things as that most evils are the means of producing some good. the yellow fever will discourage the growth of great cities in our nation; & I view great cities as pestilential to the morals, the health and the liberties of man. true they nourish some of the elegant arts; but the use-

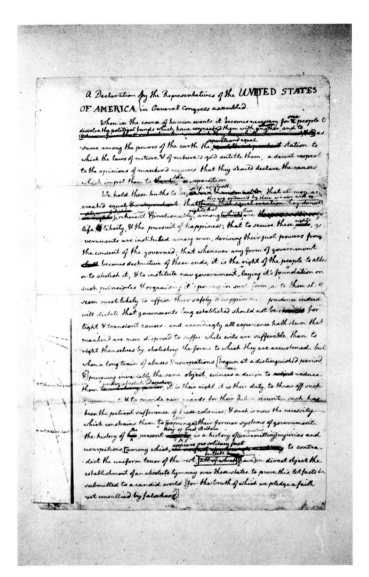

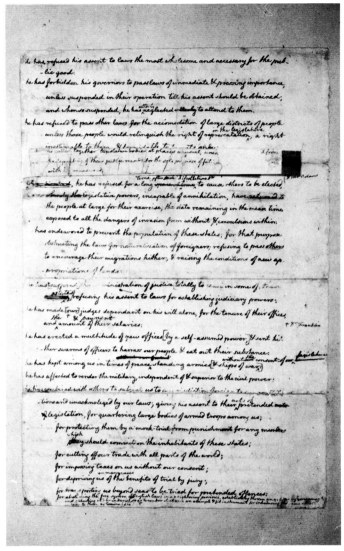

These are the four pages which make up the complete Declaration. Jefferson wrote it alone while in his bedroom at Market and Seventh Street, Philadelphia, the last week of June 1776. He claimed he "turned to neither book nor pamphlet" while sketching it out, producing the entire text from his own thoughts. He later said he was not trying to be novel or original, but was trying "to place before mankind the common sense of the subject, in terms so firm and plain as to command their assent, and to justify ourselves in the independent stand we are compelled to take."

ful ones can thrive elsewhere, and less perfection in the others with more health virtue & freedom would be my choice.

Even our most prescient leaders are occasionally overtaken by changing perceptions of time, and the beautiful Thomas Jefferson Reading Room in the Library has a fine mural bearing the Jefferson quotation, "The earth belongs always to the living generation. They may manage it then and what proceeds from it as they please during their usu-

fruct. They are masters too of their own persons and consequently may govern them as they please," which is somewhat at variance with our present attitude toward generational responsibility for natural resources.

The Library's holdings of Jefferson manuscripts were purchased in 1848 from Thomas Jefferson Randolph for $20,000, and they include approximately ninety percent of all known Jefferson material. It is interesting to note that just as Jefferson's Monticello book collection began the Li-

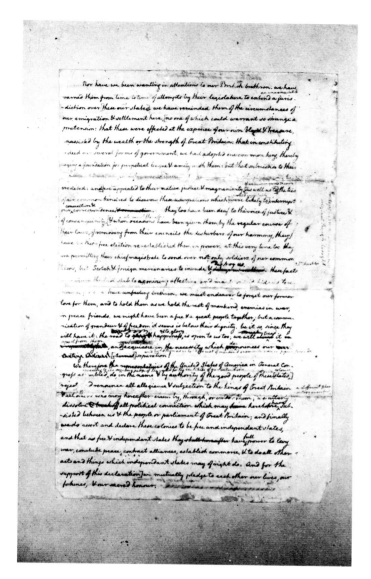
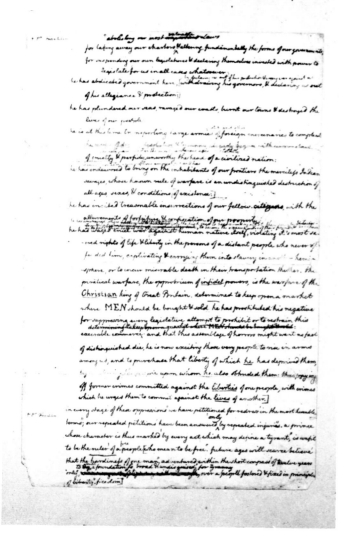

It will be noted that Jefferson wrote "inalienable rights" but either Congress or the printer changed this to "unalienable." He originally called them "sacred and undeniable" truths, but changed this to "self-evident." Jefferson himself became increasingly proud of the work and showed these four sheets to endless visitors at Monticello in his later years. Most political scholars agree that this first public paper of the Republic also remains its finest.

brary's present book collection, among those boxes were the first manuscripts the Library was to own. They contained written drafts of the laws of Virginia, Jefferson's manuscript of "Notes on Virginia," and two manuscript record volumes of the Virginia Company of London for the years 1619–25. All of these survive today.

The George Washington papers are the most complete of all personal collections from the eighteenth century, and provide a genuinely comprehensive view of his life nearly day-by-day from the time he was a schoolboy of about fourteen until his death in 1799. The years of the Revolution alone amount to 25,000 pieces, but what is news about the whole collection is the precision with which it was preserved and organized by Washington himself. You have the sense that he knew from the very beginning that he was going to be "an historical figure." He kept every scrap of paper by year and within the year by name and subject. Once he began to hold public responsibilities, he referred to his papers as a "public trust." He kept them

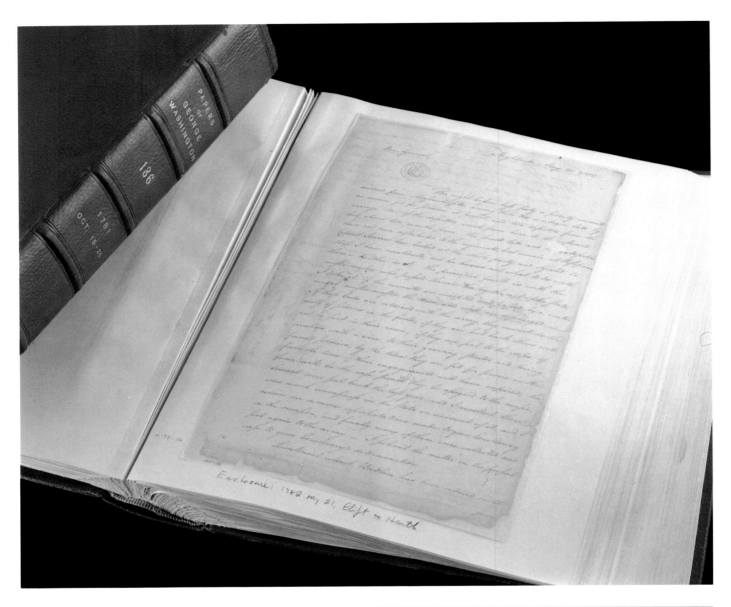

Above: *A typical letter in a bound volume of George Washington's papers. Each letter is mounted on a single page, the multiple sheets hinged at left. There are 163 linear feet of Washington papers and the Library sells the complete set on 124 reels of microfilm.*

Right: *A powder-horn map made 1757–60. The lines, in the manner of scrimshaw, show New York City at the bottom, the Hudson and Mohawk rivers, and Lake George and Lake Champlain.*

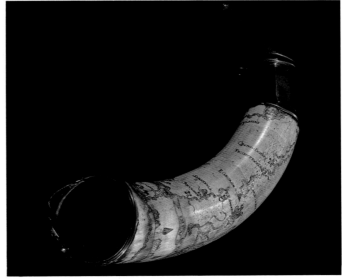

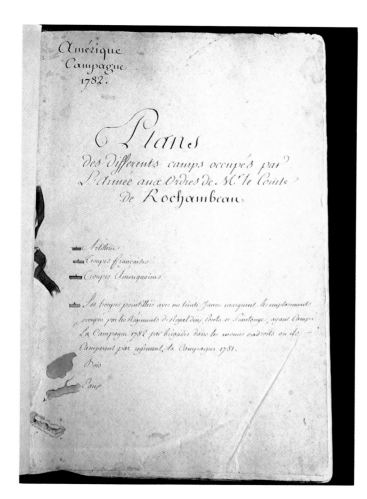

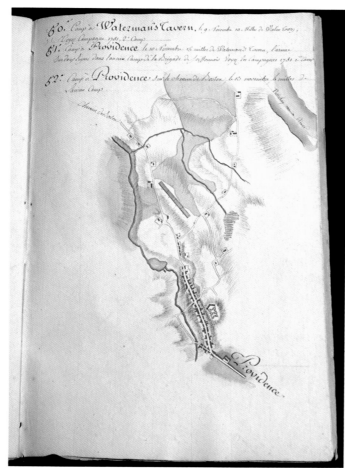

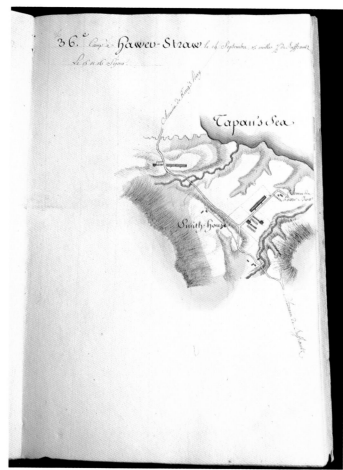

The American Campaign, 1782, *a collection of fifty-four watercolor maps, drawn on the sites of the different camps occupied by the troops under Count Rochambeau.* **Above:** *The area near Providence, Rhode Island, occupied in early November 1781.* **Left:** *The camp at Haverstraw, New York, on the west bank of the Hudson below West Point.*

with him on military assignments, and one of the constant duties of the Commander-in-Chief's Guard was to see to the papers' safety. If his headquarters were threatened, the papers were rushed to a more protected area. When he became president, they had a full-time secretary, and when he left office they were moved en masse to Mount Vernon. After Washington's death, Jared Sparks took them away to Boston, and they were there when in 1832 Congressman George Cochin Washington (a nephew of Justice Bushrod Washington) sold them to the Government. Sparks dutifully shipped them off to the District of Columbia as ordered.

This practice of buying out widows and heirs keeps turning up in these matters. The most important James Madison papers were bought from Dolley Madison in 1838 for $30,000, in 1848, being pressed for cash, Dolley sold another portion for $25,000. A final portion was purchased from Dolley's son from an earlier marriage by, surprisingly, Marshall Field of Chicago. The famous store owner gave them to the Chicago Historical Society which ultimately sold them to the government. Hamilton's and Jefferson's were purchased from heirs in 1848. (As late as 1882, Librarian Spofford was begging $20,000 from Congress to buy the Revolutionary papers of the Marquis de Rochambeau from the then current Marquis de Rochambeau—successfully.)

The Washington papers have endless scraps of papers accounting for purchases in pennies, and soporific letters complaining about slow promotions and suspected slights—but they also have such awesome monuments as his Commission as General and Commander-in-Chief (June 19, 1775, countersigned by John Hancock), the Articles of Capitulation concluded between himself and Earl Cornwallis (October 19, 1781, signed by both at Yorktown), and his twelve-page ink draft of the First Inaugural Address. I also recall, while looking for something else, coming on a crisp letter from Count Casimir Pulaski telling him what was wrong with his cavalry and what to do about it.

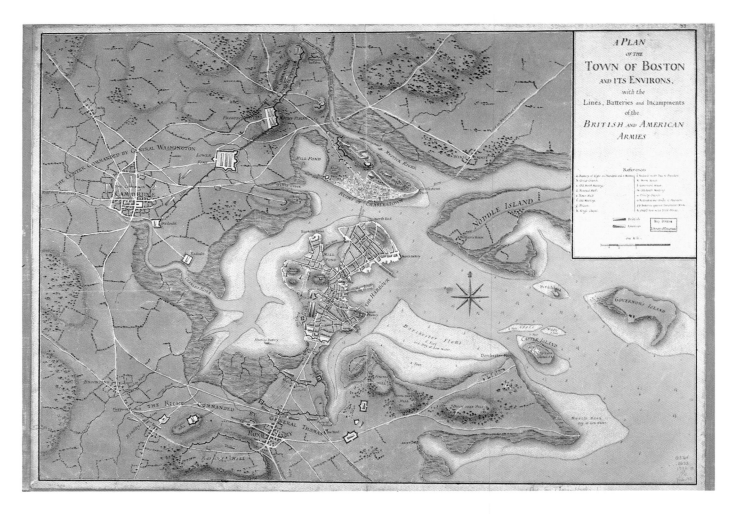

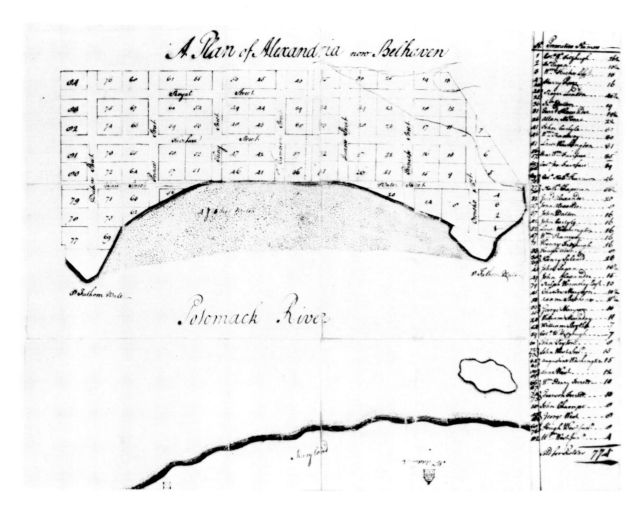

A Plan of Alexandria now Belhaven

Potomack River

Maryland

Above: *The lots laid out on John Alexander's farm in 1749 by George Washington, then seventeen years old. This is Washington's manuscript drawing of Alexandria, Virginia, with the list of winners in the drawing-by-lot with numbers and names at right.*

Opposite: *A carefully detailed watercolor map drawn during the siege of Boston by Sir Thomas Page (then Lieutenant Page of His Majesty's Engineers). Done in 1776, the map became a part of the personal holdings of William Faden, mapmaker to King George III; the Library owns almost all of the maps surviving from that large and extraordinarily valuable collection.*

Right: *The end of the nine-page Articles of Capitulation concluded between George Washington and Earl Cornwallis at Yorktown, October 19, 1781. Washington's description of the event appears in his diaries, also owned by the Library.*

for Security during the Siege

Article 14th

No Article of the Capitulation to be infringed on pretext of Reprisal, & if there be any doubtful Expressions in it, they are to be interpreted according to the common Meaning & Acceptation of the Words.

Done at York in Virginia this 19th day of October 1781

Cornwallis
Thos Symonds.

Article 14th

Granted.

In 1783, when James Madison was a Virginia delegate to the Continental Congress, he lived at a boarding house with Col. William Floyd, a delegate from New York. Floyd's youngest daughter, sixteen-year-old Kitty, attracted Madison (then thirty-two years old and a bachelor) and he proposed to her. She accepted, and they exchanged the above miniatures painted by Charles Willson Peale in Philadelphia. Kitty took a trip to visit relations in New York State, thought better of the engagement, and returned her picture of Madison. (She went on to marry a medical student and later said she never once regretted her decision. Madison remained a bachelor until he was forty-three when he married the widow Dolley Payne.) Madison returned her miniature as well, and the two portraits were re-united in 1976 when his picture was given to the Library, and the Floyd portrait was loaned by its present owners for extended display in the new Madison Memorial Library Building.

Speaking of monuments, simply walking down the aisles of this portion of the stacks is to feel the same sense of exhilaration one gets from reading the tombs of Westminster Abbey or from an hour's walk in The Forum. Here is the pantheon of American politics: here are George Mason's papers, including his scribbled draft of the Virginia Bill of Rights; here is Jefferson's first, handwritten draft of the Declaration of Independence itself with amendations by Adams and Franklin; here are James Madison's autograph notes of the debates in the Constitutional Convention. Here are four sheets from the Committee on Style, September 12, 1787, carrying the discussion draft of the Constitution (the Library has nine versions of the Constitution-in-progress) and the above sheets have autograph annotations by a dozen different hands, including Washington's. Here are two volumes of *The Federalist* papers which belonged to Jefferson with notations in Jefferson's hand on the back of the cover saying, "Numbers [so-and-so] by Mr. Jay. Numbers [so-and-so] by Mr. Madison. The rest of the work by Alexander Hamilton."

Here is Hamilton's written draft of his "Report on Manufactures," Jefferson's handwritten First Inaugural Address, and Monroe's draft of the Louisiana Purchase Treaty.

It may fairly be asked, Why are these treasures in the Library of Congress, not in the National Archives? The distinction, of course, is that the latter is responsible for *official* papers of the U.S. Government. These are the private documents, the initial drafts, the not-yet-decided-ons—and the personal letters of these men. Once the action becomes an official act of the government, the paper goes to the Archives. Traditionally, "private papers" have been defined in the following way:

Personal papers are an individual's or an organization's correspondence (both letters received and retained copies of letters sent), memoranda, notebooks, journals and diaries, logs, orderly books, commonplace books, drafts of speeches, articles and monographs, trial lines, scrapbooks, reports, press releases, ephemera; in short, writings (inherently unique) of whatsoever sort or kind that possess evidential value, illuminate a personality, or provide a basis for scholarly judgment on actions and events.

With the invention of carbon paper, more copies of "personal papers" stayed in government and were *also* taken home; and now, with the presence

The Library owns the two manuscript volumes of James Madison's "Notes of Debates in the Federal Convention," our best window into the famous proceedings in Philadelphia. The notes were intended for his own use and reflect such a purpose. Top: A typical page from a day's proceedings. Left: A portion from the final day, September 17, 1787, on which the Constitution was actually signed. The complete collection covers May 14–July 25, in the first volume, and July 26–September 27 with various miscellaneous papers from his files in the second.

or in any department or officer thereof.

Sect. 9. The migration or importation of such persons as ~~the several~~ states now existing shall think proper to admit, shall not be prohibited by the Congress prior to the year one thousand eight hundred and eight, but a tax or duty may be imposed on such importation, not exceeding ten dollars for each person.

The privilege of the writ of habeas corpus shall not be suspended, unless when in cases of rebellion or invasion the public safety may require it.

No bill of attainder shall be passed,

No capitation tax shall be laid, unless in proportion to the census herein before directed to be taken.

No tax or duty shall be laid on articles exported from any state.

No money shall be drawn from the treasury, but in consequence of appropriations made by law.

No title of nobility shall be granted by the United States. And no person holding any office of profit or trust under them, shall, without the consent of the Congress, accept of any present, emolument, office, or title, of any kind whatever, from any king, prince, or foreign state.

Sect. 10. No state shall coin money, nor emit bills of credit, nor make any thing but gold or silver coin a tender in payment of debts, nor pass any bill of attainder, nor ex post facto laws, nor laws altering or impairing the obligation of contracts; nor grant letters of marque and reprisal, nor enter into any treaty, alliance, or confederation, nor grant any title of nobility.

Working draft of the Constitution of the United States. This text-in-progress is the Report of the Committee of Style, September 12, 1787. These are George Washington's annotations on his own copy. The Library has nine versions of the Report, as it appears in as many of its collections of participants at the Convention.

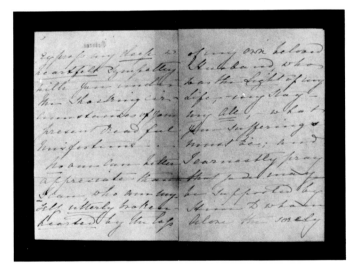
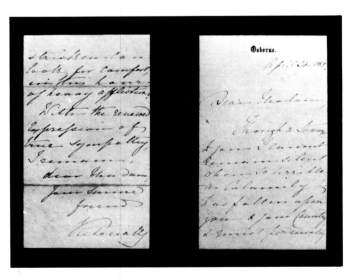

Queen Victoria's letter of condolence to Mary Todd Lincoln on the loss of her husband. In the letter, dated April 29, 1865, Victoria referred to her own distress at the sudden death of Prince Albert four years before.

of the ubiquitous copying machine, a cabinet secretary may leave his entire files in his outer office at the agency (and have his assistants copy a complete set to retire with—and, hopefully, in time give to the Library of Congress).

But even in the files of the mighty, the personal letter of tenderness has an impact a thousand times greater than the declaration of state. Queen Victoria's black-edged letter to Mary Todd Lincoln is here, sharing her experience at the recent loss

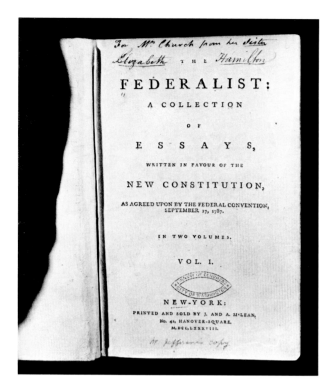
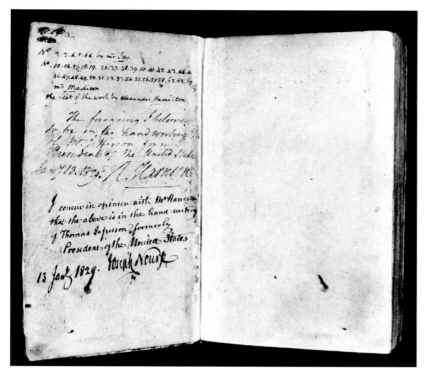

Thomas Jefferson's personal copy of The Federalist *papers (which had originally been owned by the Alexander Hamilton family). At right, the front endpaper on which Jefferson had noted the author of each of the unsigned essays.*

of a husband. Here is Jefferson gallantly closing a twelve-page letter to Maria Cosway with the assurance that though her letters to him might be "as long as the bible, they will appear short to me, only let them brim full of affection." Or Alexander Hamilton writing to Elizabeth Schuyler, September 6, 1780, about the perils confronting the Revolutionary Army and then suddenly interrupting his text with, "Pardon me my love for talking politics to you. What have we to do with anything but love?...If America were lost we should be happy in some other clime.... What think you of Geneva as a retreat?"

Enough of politics. The Library has enormous quantities of military papers, too—but we will ignore these completely, and let's consider some literary figures instead. The Library is as proud of its collection of poets, novelists, dramatists, and critics as it is of cabinet members and "public figures."

Its very large collection of Walt Whitman papers is probably a convenient access point. The Whitman holdings begin with what has been called "the most famous letter in American literary history"— the original holograph that Ralph Waldo Emerson wrote on receiving the anonymous copy of *Leaves*

of Grass. Whitman sent a few early copies of his poems to leading contemporary men of letters, and Emerson responded to this unknown author with "I greet you at the beginning of a great career...." The Library also owns, as a matter of fact, the only surviving page of the original manuscript of *Leaves of Grass.* It is a fragment (and barely readable—Whitman's script is only theoretically legible) of "Song of Myself." The page managed to survive because Whitman had turned it over to write a list of words on it. The rest of the manuscript was used "to kindle the fire or to feed the rag man." And speaking of *Leaves,* the Library owns the copy of the printed book that Whitman gave Henry Thoreau on an 1856 visit to Brooklyn. Thoreau returned the gesture by giving Whitman an inscribed volume of *A Week on the Concord and Merrimack Rivers,* which the Library also owns.

The Library has a fascinating manuscript of "Mowgli's Brothers," the first tale in Rudyard Kipling's *Jungle Book,* which Kipling wrote while living in Brattleboro, Vermont, during the winter of 1892–93. The text starts out in neat fountain-pen script, and then as he proceeds through its seven pages there are increasing changes, more insertions; he is obviously writing faster and faster un-

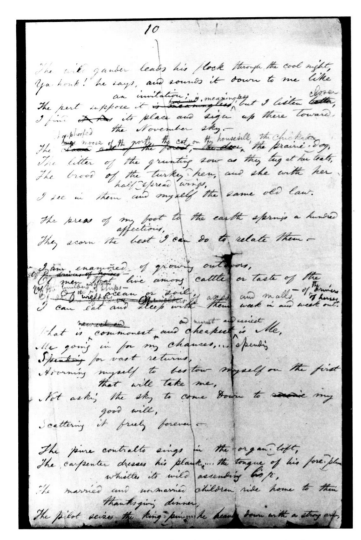

The only surviving page of Walt Whitman's original manuscript of Leaves of Grass. *The poem, of which these lines are a part, was titled "Song of Myself." This rare piece is a part of the comprehensive Feinberg Whitman Collection.*

The first sheet of the first draft of "Mowgli's Brothers," the first story in Rudyard Kipling's Jungle Book.

til, by the end, the lines are slanting dramatically up the page. The top of the first page reads "Susan Bishop from Rudyard Kipling." Susan Bishop turns out to have been a neighboring farm girl who helped Mrs. Kipling at the birth of their first child. Miss Bishop later reported that she had told the author how much she had enjoyed the story and Kipling had given her the manuscript telling her to sell it if she ever got "hard up." Miss Bishop reported she had done just that and done very well on it, too. (It had brought $25,000 in a sale just before it was given to the Library.)

The Library has all of A.E. Housman's notebooks from 1890 to 1936. It has John Steinbeck's manuscript of *The Grapes of Wrath*, which is more notable for the scribbling in the margins than for the text itself. Steinbeck was feuding with his editor, and the repeated bickering appears along the edges.

The Library owns the fifty-five volumes of diaries and notebooks deposited by Edna St. Vincent Millay, covering the years 1908–50. Robert Frost was closely associated with the Library as one of its most active Poetry Consultants (a two-year residency in the institution) and he therefore gave great quantities of material to the Library. Archibald MacLeish, Librarian of Congress from 1939–44, has deposited his materials, as would be expected. Maxwell Anderson, Edwin Arlington Robinson, Vladimir Nabokov, James Michener,

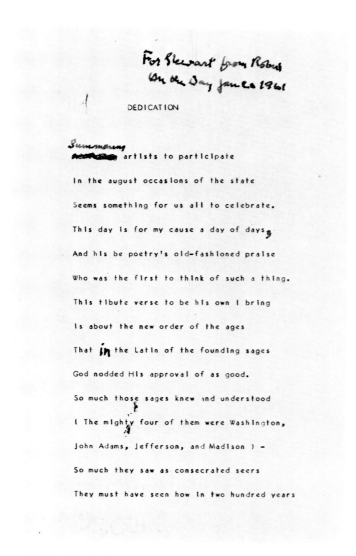

For Stewart from Robert
On the Day Jan 20 1961

DEDICATION

Summoning artists to participate

In the august occasions of the state

Seems something for us all to celebrate.

This day is for my cause a day of days.

And his be poetry's old-fashioned praise

Who was the first to think of such a thing.

This tibute verse to be his own I bring

Is about the new order of the ages

That in the Latin of the founding sages

God nodded His approval of as good.

So much those sages knew and understood

(The mighty four of them were Washington,

John Adams, Jefferson, and Madison) –

So much they saw as consecrated seers

They must have seen how in two hundred years

"Dedication," the poem Robert Frost read at John F. Kennedy's inauguration. Frost autographed the sheet and gave it to Stewart Udall after the ceremony; Udall presented it to the Library.

John Updike —it is frustrating to be able to recite only the names when the materials are so filled with intriguing insights. Even the most insignificant piece of correspondence gives a tiny window into the personality of the figures. Three examples:

From the playwright Tennessee Williams to the critic Joseph Wood Krutch:

October 21, 1948

Dear Dr. Krutch:

I have just read your article on "Summer and Smoke" in The Nation and want to give you my thanks most earnestly. The play has re-ceived such an avalanche of adverse notices that our gratitude for the good ones is almost tearful. Yours and Brooks Atkinson's are the best critical support that we have received—I speak for the entire company—and there are certainly no two critics in the world that we would rather have pleased. I liked particularly your allusion to "a morality play" which was very much what I had in mind. Few other critics seemed to feel how much less realistic my intentions were in this play than in "Streetcar" and that an overall romantic or Gothic quality (at the expense of realistic plot progression) was the primary aim in the writing and staging. At any rate, I am not unhappy over the general effect. There are marked deficiencies and disappointments, particularly in the script itself, but the reception, particularly the understanding shown by you and Mr. Atkinson, have assured us that the production is worth while.

Ever,
Tennessee Williams

From architect Frank Lloyd Wright to architect Ludwig Mies van der Rohe:

My dear Mies:

Somebody has told me you were hurt by remarks of mine when I came to see your New York show. And I made them to you directly I think. But did I tell you how fine I thought your handling of your material was?

I am conscious only of two "cracks." One: you know you have frequently said you believe in "doing next to nothing" all down the line. Well, when I saw the enormous blow-ups the phrase "Much ado about your 'next to nothing'" came spontaneously from me.

Then I said the Barcelona Pavilion was your best contribution to the original "Negation": and you seemed to be still back there where I was then.

This is probably what hurt (coming from me) and I wish I had taken you aside to say it to you privately because it does seem to me that the whole thing called "Modern-Architecture" has bogged down with the architects right there on that line. I didn't want to classify you with them—but the show struck me sharply as reactionary in that sense. I am fighting hard against it myself.

But this note is to say that I wouldn't want to hurt your feelings—even with the truth. You are the best of them all as an artist and a man.

You came to see me but once (and that was before you spoke English) many years ago. You never came since, though often invited.

So I had no chance to see or say what I said then and say now.

Why don't you come up sometime—unless the break is irreparable—and let's argue.

Affection,
Frank Lloyd Wright   October 25th, 1947

From the poet T.S. Eliot to the comedian Groucho Marx:

26th April 1961

Dear Graucho Marx,

This is to let you know that your portrait has arrived and has given me great joy and

During the 1930s, the main headquarters of the National Association for the Advancement of Colored People were located at 69 Fifth Avenue in New York City. The name of the association's official organ, Crisis, *can be seen spelled out on the windows. Each time there was a lynching in the United States the "Lynching Flag" was flown. Threatened with the loss of their lease because of the practice, the Board of Directors reluctantly gave it up in 1938. The Library has the office files of the* NAACP *from its founding—both the national records and many of the "Branch Files" from the state units as well.*

The Library owns all of the Woodrow Wilson papers from his initial draft of the Fourteen Points through such memorabilia as his gold Nobel Peace Prize medal. It also includes such items as the following statement expressed by Wilson in 1887 when he was teaching at Bryn Mawr: "Lecturing to young women of the present generation on the history and principles of politics is about as appropriate and profitable as would be lecturing to stone masons on the evolution of fashion in dress. There is a painful absenteeism of mind on the part of the audience. Passing through a vacuum your speech generates no heat. Perhaps it is some of it due to under-graduation, not all femininity."

will soon appear in its frame on my wall with other famous friends such as W.B. Yeats and Paul Valéry. Whether you really want a photograph of me or whether you merely asked for it out of politeness, you are going to get one anyway. I am ordering a copy of one of my better ones and I shall certainly inscribe it with my gratitude and assurance of admiration. You will have learned that you are my most coveted pin-up. I shall be happy to occupy a much humbler place in your collection.

And incidentally, if and when you and Mrs. Marx are in London, my wife and I hope that you will dine with us.

Yours very sincerely,
T.S. Eliot

Eliot said in a postscript two years later:

P.S. Your portrait is framed on my office mantelpiece, but I have to point you out to my visitors as nobody recognises you without the cigar and rolling eyes. I shall try to provide a cigar worthy of you.

Things keep turning up, by the way. A long lost Emerson journal worked its way to the surface recently with certain elements of interest. Emerson's family had frequently referred to one of his manuscript books called *Liberty*, and Edward Emerson had described it as "one of the most interesting" of all his journals—but no one had ever seen it.

In 1929, the Moorfield Storey papers were acquired by the Library to record his role as the first

I do not choose to run for President in nineteen Twenty eight

Left: *The holograph copy of the famous statement of President Calvin Coolidge's political intentions in the summer of 1927. He wrote the above in the presence of his secretary, Everett Sanders, in late July. On August 2, he asked Sanders to make copies and it was handed to the press at 11:30 the same morning.*

Opposite: *Among the records relating to various organizations in the Library's Manuscript Division are those for the Society of Woman Geographers (SWG). Founded in 1925 to bring together women active in exploration, geography, and the allied disciplines of anthropology, geology, and biology, the Society offered support and encouragement to women in these fields at a time when society did not. Such familiar names as journalist May Craig, writer Pearl Buck, and First Lady Eleanor Roosevelt have graced the rolls of the Society over the years. At top: Marguerite Harrison, one of the four founders of the Society of Woman Geographers, partakes of a meal of broiled wild goat in the Taurus Mountains of southern Turkey. At bottom: Sculptor Sally Clark, who "shoots for science, not for sport," is shown here with an eland, an African antelope, she brought down in an expedition to the Serengeti Plain near Lake Victoria.*

president of the National Association for the Advancement of Colored People. The papers since then have been heavily used by scholars, but since most of the researchers were lawyers or civil-rights specialists, they were not aware that the item by Emerson had any particular literary significance. In fact, it has been identified as the missing journal and contains Emerson's thoughts on the topic of liberty for a period of over twenty years. For some of us non-specialists, the picture it reveals of the calm, almost glacial Sage of Concord fuming with frustration is reassuring. He writes that he is convinced most Americans are "quadrapeds." He declares bitterly that his rule of political prophecy is "to ascertain which is the worst party, & the meanest action," expect them to prevail, "and I am seldom disappointed." He refers to those who disagree with him as "waspish egotistical Ishmaelites" and those who are ineffectually on his side such as to "let them neigh, & bray, & follow a handful of oats, as they genuinely will."

Just because we are trying to find the "treasures" of the Library, we must be careful we don't confuse age with value. There are few people who would challenge the founding figures we have noted above as having great impact on the nation. But it must be noted that the personal papers of the Library are growing steadily in quantity, richness, and variety with each successive year, and they are growing with the materials of *contemporary* leaders. So we come to the question, How does the Library get these particular manuscript collections? Answer: It goes out and solicits them individual by individual. While so much of the Library's book and serial receipts are acquired passively—copyright material is sent in by the publisher, exchange material comes as a result of long-established agreements—in the case of personal papers, committees of curators decide which contemporary leaders meet the requirements of having "profoundly influenced the lives and destinies" of the rest of us, and then the Library goes directly to the individuals or their immediate heirs and discusses the possibility of their giving the papers to the nation through the custody of the Library. In this way, a balanced program of materials from scientists, performing artists, jurists, newspaper editors, and so forth is pursued.

The papers of Frederick A. Cook, the doctor/explorer who said he reached the North Pole on April 21, 1908, a full year before Robert E. Peary claimed to have achieved the same goal on April 6, 1909, were given to the Library in 1989 by Cook's granddaughter, Janet Cook Vetter. The collection, comprising approximately 8,000 items, includes Cook's diaries from his 1908 assault on the North Pole, measurements he took of the angle of the sun at the Pole, as well as annotated maps of the polar region and an extensive number of photographs. The Cook-Peary controversy—which of the two men, if either, set foot on the North Pole first—has raged since 1909 when Peary returned from the Pole only to learn that Cook had returned a month earlier claiming he reached the Pole in 1908. With "Cook's own account" now at the Library of Congress, scholars will be able to examine these primary documents and other relevant papers for themselves to determine whether they provide any new keys to help unlock this almost century-old historical mystery.

CHAPTER XII

Tomorrow's Treasures

For the past ten chapters we have been hurrying through the treasures of the Library, seeing pieces of great value as if they had been illuminated by a long-intervaled strobe light. A rarity is revealed for a moment of our attention, and then dozens more are missed as we rush past them in the darkness. I would like to change our approach in this final chapter to avoid compounding an error of perception:

This is not a museum. The three buildings are not monumental mausoleums holding the artifacts of our society. There is nothing passive or static about this place, and, if anything, the institutional image should be more one of a wide, relentless river, constantly changing, endlessly being added to and growing, different for each generation watching it from the banks and drawing on it for nourishment.

This pontification is fairly obvious for the quarter million books and documents that are added annually for use in the "regular library," but it is equally true of the kind of unique rarities we've been looking at in this book. New "treasures of the Library" are coming in every week—one-of-a-kind pieces of creativity that keep the Library in the business of preserving the nation's experience and providing resources for the nation to draw on as it goes along.

For this reason, I would like to devote this final chapter to examples of treasure that have been acquired in just the last decade—a bit over a hundred months. These pieces were not handed down by our forefathers but gathered in our own time. We will start with a half dozen items deliberately chosen for their extremes of form and purpose.

First, Maya Lin's dramatic design for the Vietnam Veterans Memorial in Washington. The Library has received her original drawing, along with images of the thousand-odd also-rans. The antecedents were as follows.

In 1979, a Vietnam veteran by the name of Jan Scruggs had just returned from seeing the anti-war film *The Deer Hunter*. Scruggs had himself come from the Pennsylvania area depicted in the film and it added to his despair over the way the Vietnam participants were being depicted in American literature and drama and the rejection the Vietnam veterans were receiving from the nation. He decided he was going to see that their efforts were recognized. He decided he wanted a monument to those who fought in Vietnam, and he wanted it in the Nation's Capital.

He began completely alone, soon got the help of a few friends who turned to other Vietnam veterans who had access to the Washington scene, and then to those who could help with a nationwide campaign. Within a year he had begun to collect money, and the group had decided that they were going to insist that their monument be located on the Mall between the Capitol and the Lincoln Memorial. They called themselves the Vietnam Veterans Memorial Fund, and at this point they decided it was time to have the specific monument designed. Each member had certain images in his mind of war memorials he had seen—the Iwo Jima memorial to World War II marines, the Tomb of the Unknown Soldier, local Civil War monuments, and colonnades in national cemeteries. Most were stately and in white marble, and the men veered between hiring a famous sculptor to give them a single design versus holding a nationwide competition. They opted for the latter for its more democratic involvement of the nation, and they got recommendations for people who might serve as a jury. The judging panel was ultimately composed of eight renowned sculptors and landscape architects, and they were immediately recognized as flawless choices. It was the last decision about the Memorial that generated no criticism.

The requirements for the monument went out, and anyone who would pay the twenty-dollar entrance fee could submit his drawing. The judges expected a flock of oddities (there were indeed a few: a twenty-foot-high steel helmet, a helicopter on pylons) but they were very few; the submissions were overwhelmingly in good taste and done by almost all of the recognized artists in the field of monument design.

A professor at Yale outlined the requirements to his students as a class project, and three of them drove to Washington to examine the site. It was a narrow, two-acre plot beside the newly opened Constitution Gardens at the Reflecting Pool end of the Mall. One of the students used all of the remaining six weeks designing her entry, and she took it to the New Haven post office on the last day it could be postmarked.

When the judging committee examined the submissions, it discovered to its horror that there were 1,421 of them which, when set side-by-side on racks at eye-level, ultimately stretched 1.3 miles in line. The veterans sent out a plea for help, and the Air Force offered a huge, empty hangar at Andrews Air Force Base east of Washington, D.C. Once the submissions were set up, the jury entered the closed building and for two days worked their way individually and in silence back and forth down the long rows. Without comparing notes or reactions, when the final ballots were opened every single judge had selected No. 1026 as his choice for the design to be built.

Instead of its being a gleaming white marble symbol of triumph, it was a long, black wall cut down into the earth, covered with the names of those who had died in Vietnam. The walls were set at a slightly encircling angle, and started with a narrow point at each end and then the panels grew larger and larger toward the middle. The names of the dead increased and increased until the center when they began to be fewer and fewer until they also disappeared into the sod at the opposite end. The 58,000 names were to be listed in chronological sequence as they had died. (Ultimately the first became Major Dale R. Buis, who had been killed by machine gun fire at Bien Hoa, July 8, 1959, and the last was Richard Vandegeer, killed in the rescue of the U.S.S. *Mayaguez,* May 25, 1975.) The artist proved to be a twenty-one-year-old architecture student by the name of Maya Ying Lin. She was the daughter of two naturalized Chinese (a literature professor and a ceramicist from Athens, Ohio), and she was thoroughly American. She had been born the year of the first American casualty in Vietnam, had never seen a movie or read a book about Vietnam, nor, as the press noted, had ever had anyone she had known personally die.

The design jury's choice got unanimous approval from the Fine Arts Commission and the National Capital Planning Commission but from few other bodies. The press began calling it "the black gash of shame." The *Chicago Tribune*'s critic called it inane, an erosion control project; others declared it a body count on the Mall. The Secretary of Interior, James Watt, said it had to have a flagpole and the American flag at the center where the walls came together. H. Ross Perot, who had already given over $150,000 start-up money for the project, declared he would withdraw it all unless a plain old, recognizable bronze statue of a soldier went beside the flagpole.

One agency of the government demanded that the site be removed from the Mall so as not to desecrate the sacred ground; another withheld its approval unless the black marble be replaced with white and the names be incised in gold. As the pressures for change grew, Maya Lin was told she would have to yield on first one aspect and then another or it would never be built. Everyone had some elaboration or an element to be added. Lin held grimly firm, often in front of dozens of media reporters and governmental delegations. She said the design "evokes feelings, thoughts, and emotions....It does not scream anything. It is strong in its understatement. It is strong in its simplicity." She would make no changes. In her mind it was not a wall hidden in a hole of shame but a wall where the ground had subsided, leaving the rock of names for all to read and remember. She held to her black marble so the person reading the names would be reflected and become a part of the memorial, and the clouds and trees behind them would be a part of a distant picture seen on the wall before them.

Slowly the Congress and the veterans came around to her view against the bureaucracy and the press. And ultimately, on Veterans Day 1982, Maya Lin's memorial was dedicated, with threatened injunctions and government interference occurring right up to the morning of the event. Her design has proved to be a total success. Now, nearly a dec-

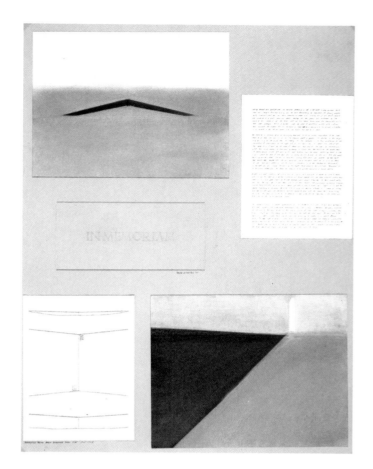

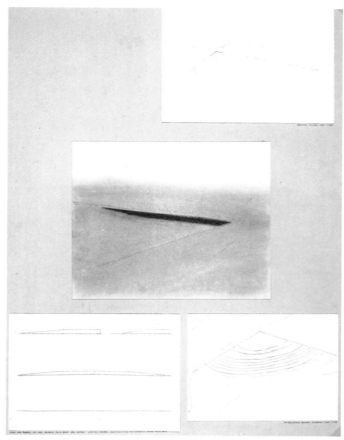

Although these panels are as large as card tables, they are all the judges had to go on to choose Maya Lin's now famous design for the Vietnam Memorial in Washington, D.C. They were among 1,420 competing drawings.

ade later, it is the second most visited memorial in Washington (only the Washington Monument exceeds it). Whether seen by day or night, it has a compelling mystical effect on those who view it. Everyone seems to touch it involuntarily, and Maya Lin's every defense of her vision has proved to be true.

How did the design materials come to the Library of Congress? As the Vietnam Veterans Memorial Fund came to an end having achieved all of its purposes (the Memorial was built without a cent of government money being spent), the founders wanted a place where the story could be preserved and available to future scholars. The Fund called the Library of Congress and asked if it would accept the materials and give them a home. The Library was overjoyed and sent a senior curator of its Manuscript Division to the VVMF offices. Here he found photographs and slides of the hundreds of designs, as well as filing cabinets full of both personal endorsements of the idea and residues of the innumerable legal roadblocks thrown across its path—all adding up to the history of the Memorial. As preparations were made to send the materials to the Library, the curator discovered the original Lin design thrown on top of some cabinets back against a wall, and was asked whether he would like that, too. He would, and it now rests carefully mounted and preserved among the donations.

Consider next the Gary Yanker Collection of modern political propaganda posters. Since the late 1960s, Yanker has been collecting what he calls "prop art"—some 4,500 items—from groups as diverse as the National Association for Irish Freedom and the League of Women Voters. The materials come from nearly fifty countries including China, Russia, and Cuba, although they are strongest in North American materials.

For our purposes, while they represent current history and vigorous contemporary poster design, they are an example of new technology making fragile materials available for use. How would you examine 4,500 of these very large and very colorful items? By sitting down in front of a color monitor in the Library's Prints and Photographs Division, and keying in either the subject or the country you are seeking. You want anti-rape posters from Brazil? You type in the appropriate codes and the color images come up, one at a time, on the screen before you. The 4,500 elements are kept on an optical disk beside the screen, and, in the same manner as a commercial motion-picture laser disk, projects the contents of the collection. You move back and forth, skipping among nations and topics, until you find what you seek, and then either request the original, full-sized poster via call slip from the stacks, or identify the image's serial number and buy a color slide from the Library's Photoduplication Service.

How did the Library come by this unlikely collection? Gary Yanker had first collected the material and then used it as research sources for a book. In the course of creating this work, he had learned of the longtime strength of the Library's collection of political posters, and felt that his materials would both elaborate the accumulated holdings and make his own collection more meaningful to scholars of the future. He then gave the original 4,000 pieces outright, but has continued to add newly printed items.

The Yanker Collection is a unique treasure, there being no other accumulation of such art forms in the world, and represents thousands of artists. The Shelton maps are equally unique, but in this case all done by a single man in an art form unique to his own genius.

Hal Shelton created what is now recognized as a new and singular style as a way of making maps for the non-technical layman. He is the man who created all those beautiful, double-page spreads in the backs of airline magazines to show the routes the company flies. You know the ones, all looking like a single photograph of the country taken from a passing satellite, the cultivated land green in black soil, the mountains dry and gray, the deserts red

These two and overleaf are examples of the meticulous, hand-drawn images of the earth's surface as created by mapmaker Hal Shelton. Shelton works with a tiny, oscillating-needle airbrush, and paints to precise measurements of contour lines that he has previously projected onto his etched zinc plates. At right, an imaginary satellite view of the Middle East; below, a drawing of the Grand Canyon as it would appear at ground level; and overleaf, an image of Europe. The paper patches are register marks for printing reproduction. Thousands of airline travellers have become familiar with Shelton maps as the passengers consulted airline route maps in the ubiquitous flight magazines found in airplane seat pockets. The Times Mirror Company, parent owner of the company for which Shelton worked, gave thirty-two of the original Shelton drawings to the Library.

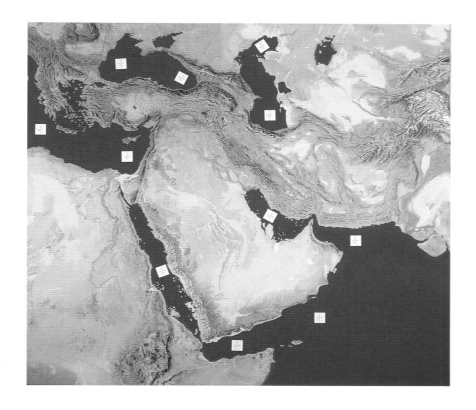

sand, and the forest trees growing green with black trunks and snow showing above the timberline. You don't have to know anything about cartography to understand what you are seeing, but if you do have a technical understanding, you could use the self-same maps to plot flight paths, index satellite photographs, and do land-use studies.

The maps are both beautiful pictures and absolutely accurate to the tiniest bend of a stream bed or an outline of a lake or pond. Shelton invented the way of doing it. He first took thin zinc plates and projected cartographic base lines—contour lines, geographic outlines—on them. He then etched the surface of the metal so it would take his acrylic and casein paint, which he air-brushed on, giving the three-dimensional effect of landforms in relief. The end result is a map so realistic that you simply assume he painted "what it looks like"—what's there. In fact the image existed only in Hal Shelton's mind, as unique as a Dürer, but as accurate as a photograph.

Shelton developed his technique over some forty years, primarily while working for the Jeppeson Company of Denver. Jeppeson became part of the H.M. Gousha Company, which in turn is part of the Times Mirror Company, and it was Times Mirror that gave the collection of thirty-two hand-painted original Shelton maps to the Library of Congress. The maps include such choices as an image of the hemisphere of the earth as seen from above the North Pole; a continent like Africa; an area like the Near East; a state like California; or a city like Salt Lake or Reno. And possibly most startling of all, Shelton has painted natural wonders such as the Grand Canyon seen not from above, but as viewed by a person standing on the canyon rim—with every detail as precisely accurate as if drawn by a laser mounted on a surveyor's sextant. Thus the maps are another treasure, unique, bearing information and beauty like nothing else of its kind anywhere.

And while we're considering maps and the face of the world, let us note some of the people who live there: The Cultures of Oceania preserved in the

This is the schooner Director II, *in which Margaret Fahnestock Lewis and her husband and brother sailed the South Seas in the early 1940s. The Fahnestock Expedition made 143 large disk recordings of Tahitian, Fijian, Balinese, and Samoan music (the first electronic recordings of Oceanic culture), many reels of color film, and notebooks of observations throughout the Marquesas, Madura, and the Kangean Islands. The expedition, which had been sponsored by the American Museum of Natural History, captured its materials within months before the impact of World War II hit the South Sea cultures, thus preserving information that can never be duplicated. This unique collection was presented to the Library's American Folklife Center by Mrs. Lewis and members of the original crew. The schooner itself ultimately struck a shoal and sank on the Great Barrier Reef of Australia.*

rare Fahnestock Collection of the South Seas. In the early 1940s, with incredible luck just before World War II swept over the islands and changed them forever, Margaret and Sheridan Fahnestock bought a three-masted schooner and with Sheridan's brother, Bruce, sailed into the South Seas to capture the rhythm of the daily life of Tahiti, Fiji, Samoa, Bali, Java, and New Caledonia. They made 143 16-inch disk recordings (the first electronic recordings to be made in Oceania), five reels of color film, filled cabinets with reports and documents of the travel. All of this has ended up with the Library's Folklife Center, but the 137-foot schooner *Director II* rests on the Great Barrier Reef of Australia where it struck a shoal and went to the bottom. The crew survived the disaster, and forty-five years later Margaret Fahnestock Lewis deposited the rare materials with the Library for the use of the nation.

It is the Fahnestock's breadth and unique variety that makes it a treasure; the Edith Rosenwald Book of Hours, on the other hand, is not only a single, one-of-a-kind work of art, but it is so tiny, so jewel-

309

The Rosenwald Book of Hours, at left, *is in fact only slightly larger than a matchbook, but it contains 163 leaves and twenty-three tiny paintings. One of these is greatly enlarged* below. *The book was created in Paris between 1340 and 1360.*

The rare-book collector Lessing Rosenwald, who has given so many treasures to the Library, gave this gem as a personal present to his wife as a birthday gift in 1951. Thirty years later, Edith Rosenwald in turn gave it to the Library for the nation.

like that if anyone were to drop a business card or matchbook across it it could disappear from sight. We met books of hours in Chapter II of this volume, and although they are six hundred years old, thanks to the generosity of the Library's donors they still come into the collection.

The one illustrated on the opposite page was originally given by her husband as a private gift to Edith Rosenwald on her birthday in 1951. The tiny vellum volume was created between 1340 and 1360 in Paris. It has 163 tissue-thin leaves, and of these 9 are full-page painted miniatures with 14 smaller illustrations of exceptional quality. The latter are scarcely larger than a fingernail, but are fully developed scenes and figures surrounded with the typical medieval embellishments of birds and vines and butterflies. It used to be traditional to say such paintings were painted by eyelashes dipped in pigments floating in tears. Examining these miniatures makes one think that an eyelash would have been too gross to make the lines.

We have seen examples from the Lessing Rosenwald gift to the Library of the world's finest book illustrations in many places in this book. Like the Stern Collection of Lincolniana, the Feinberg Collection of Whitman memorabilia, and the Colt Kipling Collection, the Rosenwald Collection continues to be added to each year although both Lessing Rosenwald and his wife are now gone. Mrs. Rosenwald gave the Library her birthday Book of Hours in 1982, shortly before her own death. Since then, the Library's Rosenwald curator has traded duplicates and research materials to buy and secure additional pieces (such as *Jazz*, the only book that Henri Matisse both wrote and illustrated), so the Collection continues to grow and include the finest of illustrated volumes as they become available.

Let's go from a matchbox-sized book of hours to something as big as a...courthouse. In 1981 the Joseph E. Seagram and Sons distilling company gave the Library 11,000 photographic negatives, 8,000 reference prints, and 2,500 master prints of

King William Courthouse, Virginia, from the Seagram County Courthouse Archive.

To mark the Bicentennial of the United States, the Joseph E. Seagram and Sons corporation commissioned twenty-four photographers to record more than 1,100 county courthouses across the nation. The idea was to capture the hundreds of buildings which were the clearest embodiment of law, justice, and continuing governmental records in every local community—the places where the courts met, taxes were paid, births and deaths recorded nearest to the individual citizen.

Ultimately, the Seagram corporation gave the 11,000 negatives and 8,000 reference prints to the Library of Congress to join the Library's Historic American Buildings Survey (HABS) Collection, where they could be easily available to historians and scholars.

From the Seagram County Courthouse Archive:

Opposite, top: *Hopkins County Courthouse, Sulphur Springs, Texas.*

Opposite, bottom: *Interior Rotunda of the Jay County Courthouse, Portland, Indiana.*

Right: *Davis County Courthouse, Bloomfield, Iowa.*

1,100 American county courthouses. This astonishing archive was created by Seagram as their contribution to the U.S. Bicentennial celebration. Its purpose was based on the following assertion:

> The county courthouse has been central to the democratic system of government since the beginnings of this nation. It continues to be the place where citizens debate and vote on the conduct of the populace and the legal issues affecting their daily lives; where they settle their differences, keep the peace, record their property, pay their taxes, and set down births and deaths. Over the last 200 years the scale, form, and materials of these structures have reflected the prosperity, aspirations, and geographic and cultural diversity of the nation's people....The development of the architectural heritage of the United States can be observed in its courthouses.

The project was directed by Phyllis Lambert and edited by Richard Pare; it resulted in the most comprehensive survey of a single type of American building ever done in this country. The archive was given to the Library by Seagram, where it joins the rich architectural holdings of the HABS collection we saw earlier on pages 216 and 226 of this book.

THE GERRY-MANDER.

A new species of *Monster*, which appeared in *Essex South District* in Jan. 1812.

" O generation of VIPERS ! who hath warned you of the wrath to come ?"

THE horrid Monster of which this drawing is a correct representation, appeared in the County of Essex, during the last session of the Legislature. Various and manifold have been the speculations and conjectures, among learned naturalists respecting the *genus* and origin of this astonishing production. Some believe it to be the real *Basilisk*, a creature which had been supposed to exist only in the poet's imagination. Others pronounce it the *Serpens Monocephalus* of Pliny, or single-headed *Hydra*, a terrible animal of pagan extraction. Many are of opinion that it is the *Griffin* or *Hippogriff* of romance, which flourished in the dark ages, and has come hither to assist the knight of the rueful countenance in restoring the gloomy period of ignorance, fiction and imposition. Some think it the great Red Dragon, or Bunyan's *Apollyon* or the *Monstrum Horrendum* of Virgil, and all believe it a creature of infernal origin, both from its aspect, and from the circumstance of its birth.

But the learned Doctor Watergruel who is famous for peeping under the skirts of nature, has decided that it belongs to the *Salamander* tribe, and gives many plausible reasons for this opinion. He says though the Devil himself must undoubtedly have been concerned, either directly or indirectly in the procreation of this monster, yet many powerful causes must have concurred to give it existence, amongst which must be reckoned the present combustible and venomous state of affairs. There have been, (says the Doctor) many fiery ebullitions of party spirit, many explosions of democratic wrath and fulminations of gubernatorial vengeance within the year past, which would naturally produce an uncommon degree of inflammation and acrimony in the body politic. But as the Salamander cannot be generated except in the most potent degree of heat, he thinks these malignant causes, could not alone have produced such diabolical effects. He therefore ascribes the real birth and material existence of this monster, in all its horrors, to the alarm which his Excellency the Governor and his friends experienced last season, while they were under the influence of the Dog-star and the Comet—and while his Excellency was pregnant with his last speech, his libellous message, and a numerous litter of new judges and other animals, of which he has since been happily delivered. This fright and perturbation was occasioned by an incendiary letter threatening him with fire-brands, arrows and death : (if his proclamation is to be credited) which was sent to him by some mischievous wight, probably some rogue of his own party, to try the strength of his Excellency's mind. Now his Excellency being somewhat like a tinder-born, and his party very liable to take fire, they must of course have been thrown into a most fearful panic, extremely dangerous to persons in their situation, and calculated to produce the most disastrous effects upon their unborn progeny.

From these premises the sagacious Doctor most solemnly avers there can be no doubt that this monster is a genuine Salamander, though by no means perfect in all its members ; a circumstance however which goes far to prove its illegitimacy. But as this creature has been engendered and brought forth under the sublimest auspices, he proposes that a name should be given to it, expressive of its *genus*, at the same time conveying an elegant and very appropriate compliment to his Excellency the Governor, who is known to be the zealous patron and promoter of whatever is new, astonishing and erratic, especially of domestic growth and manufacture. For these reasons and other valuable considerations, the Doctor has decreed that this monster shall be denominated a *Gerry-mander*, a name that must exceedingly gratify the parental bosom of our worthy Chief Magistrate, and prove so highly flattering to his ambition, that the Doctor may confidently expect in return for his ingenuity and fidelity, some benefits a little more substantial than the common reward of virtue.

That astute naturalist Lucricostus however in the 26th section of his invaluable notes upon the Salamander, clearly shews that this word is a corruption of the Latin *Salimania*, expressing the characteristic dislike and almost hydrophobic antipathy of that animal for sea salt : " Oweinge (to use the words of the author) to the properties and virtues of the sayde " mineralle, as is well knowen to moste folke, in dampeinge the heate of that elemente of fyre, wherein the sayde beaste " doth abide, so that if a piece of salt, or any marine thinge be placed neare it, it clothe fret it sorely, and enrage it to such " madnesse that it dothe incontinently throw from its mouthe a venomous spittle, which dothe tarnishe and destroy all that " is of worth or value that it falleth upon. A further and most manyfest proofe of which deadlie hatred appeareth in " that, whereas, on and neare the renowned salt mountayne, so called, amydst alle the marvells and wonders with which " it dothe abounde, not any of this Lizarde species hath been discoverable thereyne." We therefore propose, with the utmost deference to the ingenious Doctor's opinion, that the term *Gerry-mania* be substituted for Gerry-mander, as highly descriptive both of the singular ferocity of the monster in question, and the influence which the moon at certain periods, more especially on the approach of April, is supposed to exert over it.

A friend of ours has further suggested that there is a peculiar felicity at the present time in adopting the term Gerry-mania, as according to his definition, Gerry is derived from the French *Guerre*, or the Italian, *Guerra*, (war) and that it therefore possesses the double advantage of expressing the characteristic ferocity of this monster, and that magnanimous rage for war which seems to have taken such possession of our worthy Chief Magistrate and his friends. But we mention this merely as an ingenious speculation, being well convinced ourselves, notwithstanding appearances, of the truly pacific sentiments of that great man, whose *mild* and *charitable* denunciations of his political opponents have had such a wonderful effect in convincing their reason, allaying the spirit of party, and in reconciling all conflicting opinions.

While the Gerry-Mander is well known in the American political vocabulary, the fact that it got its first wide distribution as a belligerent political broadside is not so well known. The Library now has one of the rare originals from 1812.

The rare picture of the original Gerry-Mander (opposite) is an unlikely piece of Americana that the Library's rare materials scouts heard might finally be coming on the market, and when the golden moment arrived in 1985, they pounced, making an unusually cost-effective purchase. All the way back to the very founding of the republic, state legislatures have been designing electoral districts to perpetuate the "ins" and frustrate the "outs." If you have a city that votes strongly for the Urban Party completely surrounded by four agricultural districts that always vote for the Farm Party, when the Farm Party controls the legislature it cuts the city into four parts and attaches a quarter slice to each of the agrarian districts. At voting time, the Urban votes are thus scattered and dissipated to nothing since the winner takes all. But if the Urban Party manages to seize control of the legislature, the city suddenly becomes an unbeatable single district, a sure thing for the Urban Party, and if the surrounding farm counties can be stretched to hang off other Urban towns, sometimes they can be so thinned the Urbans can win multiple seats. This practice went into the American political vocabulary with the Gerry-Mander districting of 1812.

Governor Elbridge Gerry, Democrat of Massachusetts, signed a bill that created a single district in an area that traditionally went two-thirds Federalist. Via an inspired linking of super-strong Democrat counties with traditionally not quite so strong Federalist ones, the Essex district was taken into the Democrat fold. Tradition has it that Benjamin Russell, editor of the Boston *Centinel,* was going to run a map of the imaginative design when the painter Gilbert Stuart sketched on a head, wings, and claws, and said, Now it looks like a salamander. No, said the editor, it looks like a Gerry-Mander, and Governor Gerry became part of political history.

In fact, as is so often true in these cases, the Governor didn't deserve the reputation. He himself had been a signer of the Declaration of Independence, James Madison's vice-president, and he pronounced his name "Gary" (though the beast is pronounced Jerry). He strongly opposed the electoral manipulation of counties but the Legislature stuck him with the oddity, and he reluctantly signed the bill. The Gerry-Mander's progeny are just as vigorous today as they were two hundred years ago. The exercise now concentrates on splitting apart or pulling together ethnic neighborhoods, or linking suburban housing developments or college communities to offset industrial or farm counties. While the

Supreme Court says electoral districts are supposed to be compact, the ability of the computer to come up with minutely fashioned configurations still makes gerrymandering a major sport after each national census. The Library now has one of the rare original broadsides of the animal.

As we have seen, some of the richest collections in the Library came from dedicated—and usually wealthy—collectors who had devoted their lives to assembling rare materials on a single topic. The Hans and Hanni Kraus Collection on Sir Francis Drake is an intriguing variation on this theme.

Hans P. Kraus was the world-famed antique bookseller who assisted so many bibliophiles in putting together their own specialized collections, but the Drake assemblage was his own. It was started by a casual item in a sentence that Kraus was reading which noted that Drake's three-year circumnavigation of the world not only was a sailing triumph but a signally successful business venture as well. As Drake went from continent to continent, he plundered towns and stripped ships until he had gathered literally millions of dollars' worth of gold and an equal amount of silver and jewels. This triumph captured Kraus' romantic interest in pirates and deeds of derring-do, and he set out to gather everything he could find about Drake which described Drake as he would have been revealed to the people of Drake's own time.

It took Kraus twelve years to put together over a million dollars' worth of Drakeiana which he would ultimately give to the Library of Congress, and as he said:

> I had not realized how difficult it would be to build up a Drake collection. I wanted to gather only original and contemporary sources, in printed books, in autographs and manuscripts, in maps, in portraits, or in medals. The motive for my collecting was to learn about Drake in the same way as anyone living in Europe during his lifetime would have done....This is a beautiful conception, but the material seemed to be so scarce that at times I felt inclined to give up the whole idea.

The challenge he faced came not only from the materials being four-hundred-years old, but that they were equally rare in Drake's day for an intriguing reason. Drake had got his nautical start as a captain sailing under Adm. John Hawkins. In 1567 they were in the process of raiding Spanish ports

The famous rare-book dealer Hans P. Kraus helped many bibliophiles to accumulate their own themed collections, but the five pieces illustrated here are from Kraus's own specialty: Sir Francis Drake. Ultimately Kraus gave a collection of sixty Drake rarities to the Library of Congress, the largest such single collection in the Americas.

Left: The earliest book describing Drake's voyage of circumnavigation of the world, with a contemporary portrait of the admiral; a second contemporary book describing Drake's role in the defeat of the Spanish Armada; and the original deed of the manor that Drake sold to finance the Circumnavigation voyage. The wax bears Drake's personal seal.

Above: An original watercolor map of St. Augustine, Florida, 1589, which is the earliest existing view of any city in the territory of the present United States.

Overleaf: The rare Van Sype map (1581), the earliest known revelation of the route of the Circumnavigation.

and managed to get themselves caught inside the breakwater of Vera Cruz when a large convoy of armed merchant ships arrived from Spain. The English worked out a truce that would permit the convoy to enter the harbor in safety in return for letting the English reprovision and repair their vessels and make a safe passage out. Once inside the harbor, however, the Spanish fleet broke the truce, and destroyed most of Hawkins' men and ships. The two captains managed to get back to England (separately), but Drake never forgot or forgave the incident.

When he set out on what became the circumnavigation in 1577, Spain and England were officially at peace, so Drake's depredations throughout Spanish colonies could not be admitted, and when he finally got home in 1580, he gave his maps and journals directly to the Queen and they were never seen

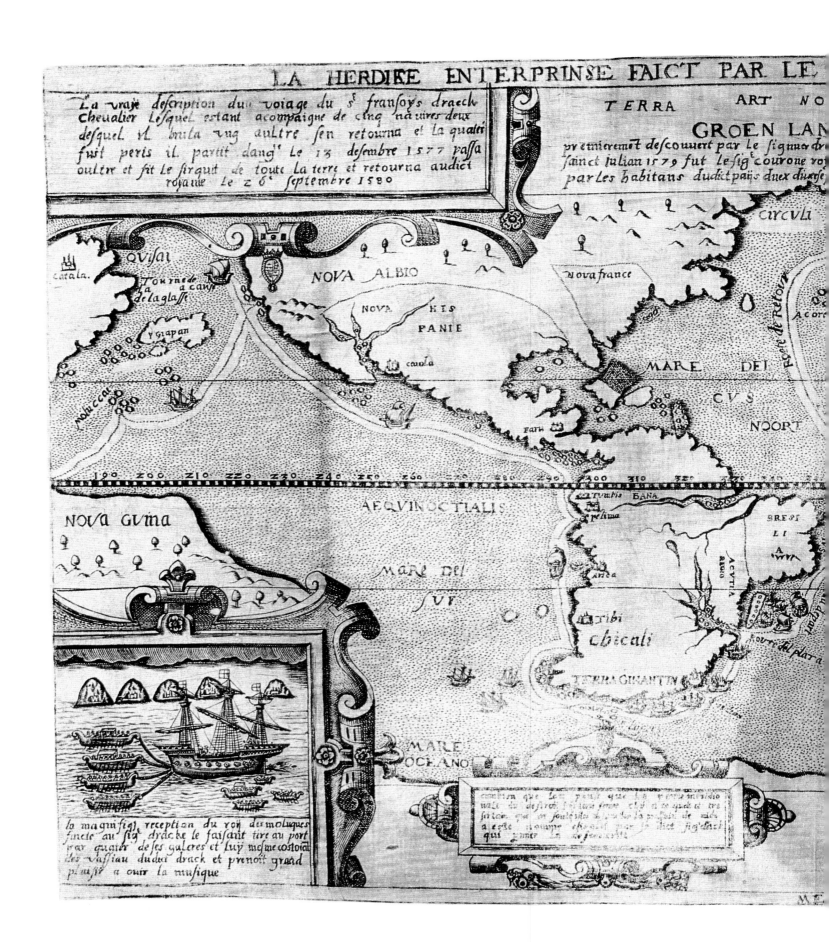

La vraje description du voiage du s fransoys draeck
Cheualier lesquel estant acompaigne de cinq nauires deux
desquel il brula ung aultre sen retourna et la qualet
fuit peris il partit dang Le 13 desembre 1577 passa
oultre et fit le sirquit de toute la terre et retourna audict
royaume Le 26e septembre 1580

TERRA   ART NO

GROEN LAN
premieremet descouuert par le signue dre
sainct iulian 1579 fut lesig couroue roi
parles habitans dudict païs duex diuese

CIRCVLI

QVISAI

catala.

Tournede
la   a caus
de la glasse

NOVA ALBIO

nova france

A core

Ygiapan

NOVA   HIS

PANIE

MARE   DEL

moluccai

caula

CVS

NOORT

farn

190 200 210 220 230 240 250 260 270 280 290 300 310 320

AEQVINOCTIALIS

BANA

BRES
LI
A

NOVA GVMA

ACVTIA
REGIO

Arica

MARE DEL

SVR

ribi

chicali

TERRA GIGANTIV

Route del plata

MARE
OCEANO

la magnifiq reception du roi des moluques
finete au sig drycke le faisant tire au port
rar quater deses galeres et luy mesme costoia
des vassiau dudci drack et prenoit graud
plaisir a ouir la musique

ME

318

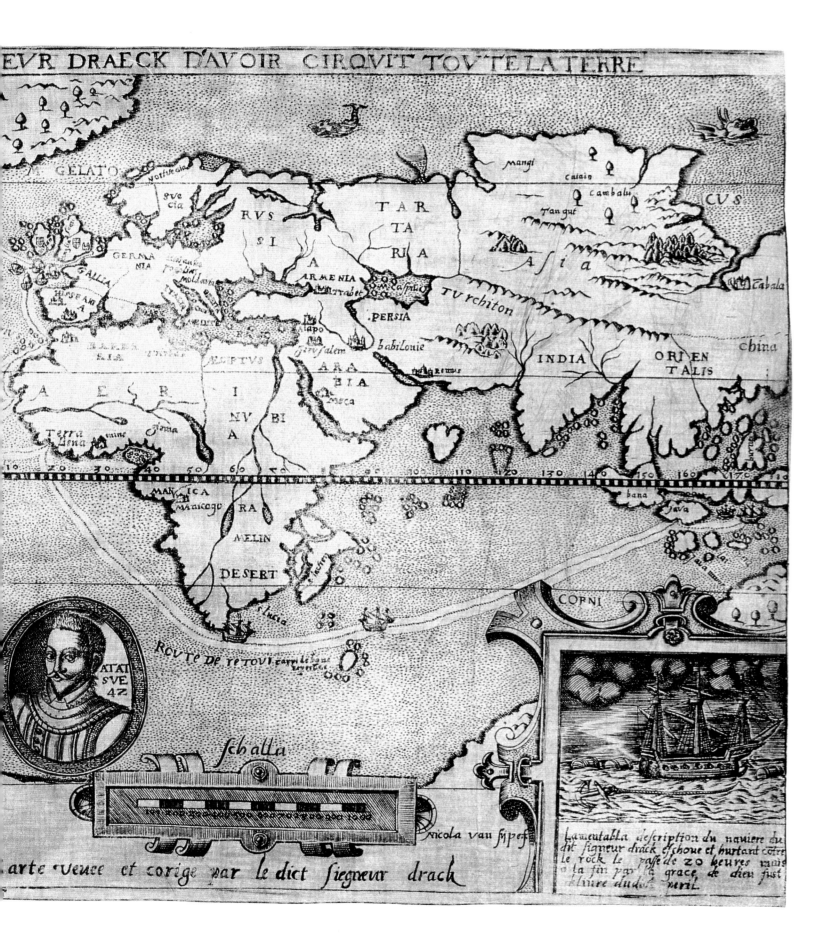

M GELATO

Notsecia

svecia

RVS
SI
A

GERMA
NIA

Moldaui

GALLA

HISPANI
A

HARIA
SIA

EGYPTVS

TARTA
RIA

ARMENIA

Alapo
Gerusalem

babilonie

.PERSIA

TVrchiton

A s i a

Mangi

Caraia

Cambalu
Tangut

CVS

Tabala

china

INDIA

ORIEN
TALIS

AER

I

NV
BI
A

ARA
BIA

Terra
bena

Roma

MAR ICA
Maricago

RA
MELIN

DESERT

s. lucia

ATAT
SVE
42

bana

java

CORNI

ROVTE DE RETOVI

schalla

nicola van sipes

arte veuce et corige par le dict siegneur drach

hameutabla description du naviere du
dit signeur drack eschoue et hurtant cotre
le rock le passe de 20 heures mais
a la fin par la grace de dieu fust
diture dudit peril

again. The sailing community knew what had happened, but only through professional talk. One of the rarest gems of the Drake collection is a letter written by Gerard Mercator to Abraham Ortelius in 1580, in which Mercator speculates about the route that Drake must have taken. Even the two greatest mapmakers in the world at the time were looking for information and material on the matter.

Ultimately Kraus put together sixty items that included the deed for the manor that Drake sold to raise money for the voyage, rare maps of the Spanish ports he raided, reports on Drake's successful destruction of the Armada, and the books and pamphlets that ultimately appeared about the circumnavigation in the decade following the event. When Kraus finally handed his treasure over to the Library in 1980 (Kraus was seventy-three), he said it had been "a labor of love." He had parted with it because the Library was the right place for it, "it is a pleasure to have it here," and he added with a smile, "It is still my collection whether it is under my roof or here."

Another personal collection—and one the very least likely to be found in Congress' Library—is the Avrich Collection of Anarchist Books, Pamphlets, Periodicals, Manuscripts, and Memorabilia which was received in 1986.

Dr. Paul Avrich is Distinguished Professor of History at Queens College, New York, and he originally built his reputation as the country's foremost historian of radicalism through three books on the anarchists of the Russian Revolution. In recent years, he has turned his attention to the United States, and the result is this unusually comprehensive collection of rare anarchist materials accumulated through a lifetime of study and writing in the field.

Scholars have characterized Dr. Avrich's approach to his topic as a view of "anarchism not as an extreme ideology but rather as a point of view that originates in a natural human reaction to rebel against authority perceived to be politically and economically repressive."

The works found in the collection are almost by definition rare (frequently unique) since it is not a topic normally accumulated by libraries and even less by copyright deposit. The holdings are especially rich in materials relating to Emma Goldman, writer and leader in radical activities up to her death in 1940. It includes such pamphlets as her *Love Among the Free* and *Trotsky Protests Too Much*, and contains massive correspondence to and from her intimate friends after her 1919 deportation from the U.S. These texts are filled with her outrage and disappointment with many labor and socialist groups in the 1920s and '30s.

Many of the most surprising (essentially underground) materials came from aging anarchists who gave Avrich their own libraries hoping to explain to history what their movement was trying to accomplish in the early years of this century. Professor Avrich in turn passed the materials to the Library of Congress so that they might continue to be available for research.

While Avrich's subjects directed their efforts toward destroying government, during the decade we're examining here the Library received two rare gifts of those who would build government into a more perfect instrument: Thomas Jefferson and Alexis de Tocqueville.

The Tocqueville treasure is the only known set (in their original paper bindings) of his first edition of *Democracy in America*. This classic was first published in French and, somewhat surprisingly, was a bestseller on the Continent as quickly as it became available. It first appeared in 1835 following his year's travel across New York state to Green Bay, Wisconsin, and then journeys in a giant arc from Quebec to New Orleans. His reflections on life in America were not only acute at the time, but have probably held up better than those of any other social historian before or since. (The Library has innumerable translations of the work in almost every written language including a 1917 Russian version printed in the early days of the Bolshevik revolution.)

The Jefferson trove were volumes that he bought, not wrote. After Jefferson sold his Monticello library to Congress in 1815, he found he could "not live without books." He thus began to buy again but while his original collection ran heavily to politics, history, and science, the new library centered on the classics, with many of the Greek and Roman authors represented in their original languages. The forty-four Jefferson volumes which were given to the Library by the Machen family were the largest bloc of Jeffersoniana received since the 1800s. These rare volumes had been purchased by Lewis Henry Machen in 1829, when many of Jefferson's chattels were sold to settle estate debts after the President's death. The forty-four books had been passed from generation to generation in the Machen Family into our own time, when the current family decided to give them to the Library so they might rejoin the original Jefferson library being reassembled in the Rare Book Room.

Two rare Venetian globes designed and built by Father Vincenzo Coronelli. The nearer shows the land masses of the world as known in 1688; the farther is a celestial sphere showing constellations and major stars and was produced in 1693.

It took 160 years for the Jefferson books to get back with their peers; the two magnificent Coronelli globes received in 1983 required nearly three hundred years to go full circle and rejoin the gores we saw earlier on page 105. Father Vincenzo Coronelli had engraved the land masses in 1688, and until now, the Library owned only this flat, unmounted form of the map. The second, celestial image with its major stars and constellations was engraved in Venice in 1693, and the two printings were then pasted on to their respective gypsum and papier-mâché balls and dedicated to the then current Doge, Francesco Morosini. The two completed scientific instruments stand over four feet tall and were among the largest globes in existence up to modern times (tradition has it that they had been in the homes of the noble Contarini family for most of the past three centuries). With their acquisition, the Library's holdings of Coronelli's lifetime output is virtually complete.

The other extreme from these giant globular maps is a flat one that is barely a foot wide and six feet long: the Library's newly acquired map of the original Mason-Dixon line. To our generation, the Mason-Dixon line is shorthand for the division between The North and The South, and it is understood to be essentially the southern border of Pennsylvania. In fact, the Mason and Dixon line was surveyed between 1763 and 1767, and was laid down to resolve a savage dispute between the Calvert Family, proprietors of Maryland, and the Penn Family, proprietors of Pennsylvania. When the King of England gave the two families their lands in the New World, his charter was so loosely drawn that Lord Baltimore claimed all of Philadelphia, and the Penns claimed well into northern Maryland. The argument began in the mid-1600s, and became so acrimonious that in 1750 the Lord Chancellor decreed a new and official line must be run between the two colonies. Two English astronomers, one Charles Mason and Jeremiah Dixon, were hired and they set out with transits and surveyor's chains.

According to the early charters, the north end of Delaware was supposed to be a circle drawn twelve miles around Newcastle, and the Penn-Calvert line was supposed to take off from this circle at 39 degrees 43 minutes. Mason and Dixon re-surveyed the circle and then headed west, setting cut stones

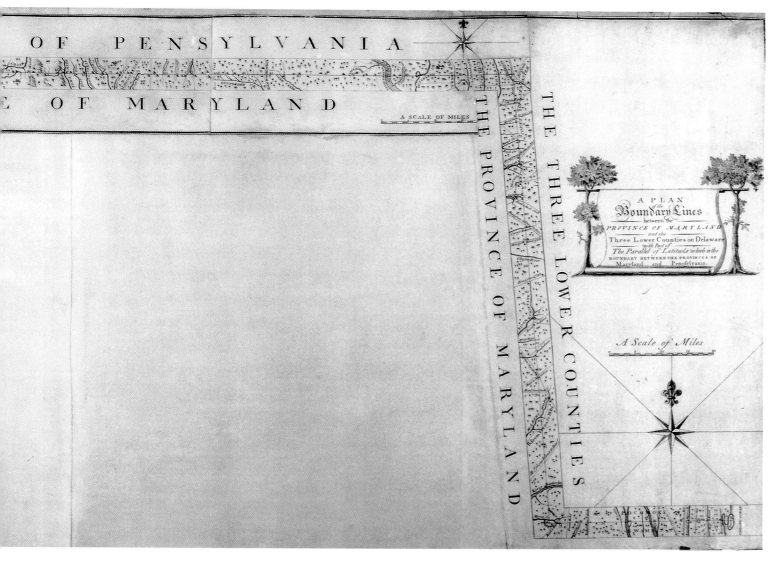

OF PENSYLVANIA

OF MARYLAND

A SCALE OF MILES

THE PROVINCE OF MARYLAND

THE THREE LOWER COUNTIES

A PLAN
of the
Boundary Lines
between the
PROVINCE OF MARYLAND
and the
Three Lower Counties on Delaware
with Part of
The Parallel of Latitude which is the
BOUNDARY BETWEEN THE PROVINCES OF
Maryland and Pensylvania

A Scale of Miles

This is the official map of the Mason-Dixon Line, certified by the British Crown in 1769. The copy (which was originally owned by a member of the 1768 survey commission) was given to the Library of Congress by the publisher Malcolm Forbes.

they'd brought from England after each mile. Every fifth marker was called a crown stone, and bore the arms of the Penn Family on the north and Lord Baltimore on the south. They surveyed away for 233 miles and got so involved in the task that they overshot the north-west corner of Maryland by 30 miles. The local Indians stopped them, pointed out their error, and headed them back to where they came from. The project was finished in 1768, and was ratified by the crown in 1769.

The Library's engraved copy of the famous line is one of the original, official documents produced in 1768, and was personally given to the Library by Malcolm Forbes, the publisher. The Forbes engrav-

ing was in turn one of those owned by a member of the commission that oversaw the original project.

Footnote: the idea of the Mason-Dixon line meaning the divide between slave and free states occurred during the Missouri Compromise debate of 1819 and 1820. It came to stand for a line drawn across the states from Delaware to the Ohio River, and as the Civil War approached, got involved in the Bleeding Kansas argument since Mason and Dixon's Line, if theoretically extended, would have fallen within mere miles of the border which divided Nebraska and Kansas (a thousand miles to the West). The latter application would have been incredible to the original surveyors of 1763–67.

A costume design sheet from the Sergei Diaghilev Collection. The personal materials, which go back to Diaghilev's founding of the Ballets Russes, contain set designs, annotated scores, letters from Otto Klemperer, Sergei Prokofiev, and others—and costume instructions like the above for his many ballets. The rare collection came to the Library from the working materials of Serge Lifar, Diaghilev's protégé.

Let's turn for a moment to sight and sound. As the volume of words preserved on paper has steadily shrunk in our own time (the number of books received by the Library has dropped 35 percent in the past decade), the holdings of computer deposits, motion pictures, compact disks, and recording tapes have risen dramatically. There are those who believe that the authors and playwrights who would have written the books and dramas of the past are now investing their time and energy in television dramas, documentaries, and educational tapes and videodisks. The Library has always received and kept these forms, too, only now it is big business, and a major element of its activities.

Under the Copyright Law of 1976, the Library is now the designated repository for off-air archival recording of the total television production of the five major networks; thus hour-by-hour coverage of what the nation sees as televised news goes directly into the Library's vaults. Massive blocks of information such as the complete Public Broadcasting Service coverage of the Watergate Hearings comes in as single deposits. Gavel-to-gavel Congressional television coverage of the Senate and House of Representatives sessions is received daily to be preserved by the Library in perpetuity giving total, unedited documentation of Congressional proceedings. The British Broadcasting System deposits the best of its dramatic and documentary productions throughout the year, while the Library is receiving similar transfers from international television companies throughout Europe and Asia.

For the purposes of our scan of individual treasures here, let's note some of the individual sight and sound blockbusters. I presume we should start with treasures blessed by legislative fiat: The National Film Registry decreed by the National Film Preservation Act of 1988. Under the terms of this law, the Library of Congress must choose and preserve up to twenty-five "culturally, historically, or aesthetically significant" films in the National Film Registry each year for three years.

The purpose of the program is to recognize motion pictures as an American art form and to emphasize the need for their preservation. (Over half of all films made before 1950 are already lost; 80 percent of those from before 1930 are gone; and, with the spread of automated, colorized reconstruction and versions shortened to fit television time requirements, even recent, still extant titles are being changed.) The Library is required to get archival quality versions of the titles chosen, and preserve them for scholars and historians in perpetuity. Once the initial seventy-five have been selected, it is anticipated that the program will extend to narrower genres such as ethnic and documentary filmmaking to increase the awareness and archival insurance of these as well. As an example of the present scope of the program, the initial twenty-five films selected were: *The Best Years of Our Lives*, 1946; *Casablanca*, 1942; *Citizen Kane*, 1941; *The Crowd*, 1928; *Dr. Strangelove*, 1964; *The General*, 1927; *Gone with the Wind*, 1939; *The Grapes of Wrath*, 1940; *High Noon*, 1952; *Intolerance*, 1916; *The Learning Tree*, 1969; *The Maltese Falcon*, 1941; *Mr. Smith Goes to Washington*, 1939; *Modern Times*, 1936; *Nanook of the North*, 1922; *On the Waterfront*, 1954; *The Searchers*, 1956; *Singin' in the Rain*, 1952; *Snow White and the Seven Dwarfs*, 1937; *Some Like It Hot*, 1959; *Star Wars*, 1977; *Sunrise*, 1927; *Sunset Boulevard*, 1950; *Vertigo*, 1958; *The Wizard of Oz*, 1939.

How does an ordinary citizen get access to all 75,000 films the Library now owns? Recognized scholars can get screenings or can use Movieolas for detailed analysis, but the ordinary interested movie goer was given a new window into film making in 1983 when the Mary Pickford Theater was opened on the third floor of the Library's Madison Building. The Mary Pickford Foundation gave a half million dollars to support "screening and related pro-

grams, including seminars, lectures, publications and other educational activities to further the study and awareness of the history and development of the motion picture." The theater was dedicated in person by Miss Pickford's husband, Buddy Rogers, and their friends and fellow actors Lillian Gish, Douglas Fairbanks, Jr., Blanche Sweet, and others were in joint attendance. Following the dedication, Mr. Rogers gave the Library a hoard of rare, and in some cases unique, Pickford films from the 1910s and '20s. The new theater offers free, weekly showing of films from the Library's vaults, and the programs became an almost instantaneous major part of the Washington theatrical scene.

Speaking of theater, consider The Mystery of the Secaucus Trunk (or trunks, to be precise—eighty of them).

Oddly enough, many complete scores of Broadway musicals by Jerome Kern, George Gershwin, Rudolf Friml, Sigmund Romberg, Victor Herbert have disappeared—we know the shows, but the music is gone. How is this possible? Because it was not until the 1940s that complete musicals were recorded, and only the most popular songs were published of the shows of the 1920s and '30s. Fur-

In a rare photo, two giants of the twentieth-century musical world appear together, probably in the late 1920s: Maurice Ravel is at the piano, and George Gershwin is standing at the far right. The photo is from the Moldenhauer Archives at the Library of Congress, a bequest of Dr. Hans Moldenhauer on his death in 1987. The collection of autograph music manuscripts, letters, and documents spanning the history of musical creativity from the twelfth century to modern times had been assembled by Dr. Moldenhauer and his wife since the 1950s. The Archives have been called one of the greatest collections of primary source materials in music ever assembled.

ther, the songs that were published were usually in simple transcriptions for home use, and thus musicologists have no knowledge of how the original (usually highly sophisticated) arrangements sounded. Indeed we have lost even the melodies themselves of most of the songs in Gershwin's *Primrose* (1924), *Tip-Toes* (1925), and *Pardon My English* (1933). Similarly, complete scores were missing of Jerome Kern's *Very Good Eddie* (1915), *Leave It To Jane* (1917), *Sitting Pretty* (1924), *Sunny* (1925), and *The Cat and The Fiddle* (1931). His masterpiece, *Show Boat* (1927), premiered in Washington, and the performance began at 8:30 and ran until 12:40, past midnight. By the end of the following week, an hour and forty minutes of songs and production numbers had been cut out and discarded. What were they? No one knew.

Then in 1982, a Yale music theater historian by the name of Robert Kimball got wind of an odd sequence of events that supposedly occurred in the 1920s. He learned that with the advent of sound in motion pictures, the Warner brothers decided that they should get control of music publishing houses, and they bought up the entire files of such companies as Harms, and Witmark and Remick. They combined these into a single firm, and closed down their individual offices. Warner collected all the files and paper and moved it into a warehouse in Secaucus, New Jersey, and...forgot about everything.

When Kimball finally traced the packing crates to their dusty preserve, in the words of John McGlinn, the leading Kern scholar, "It's like opening the tomb of King Tut. There are major works here that had been presumed lost forever, shows that were never revived and were assumed to have vanished off the face of the earth."

The whole story of what was found would require a complete book, but thanks to long-standing relationships with the Gershwin and Kern families, hundreds of the treasures were passed on to the Library of Congress. Rare and "lost" manuscripts of Gershwin's two-piano arrangement of *An American in Paris*, the complete manuscript of *Blue Monday*, Gershwin's first extended composition; the missing portions of Kern's *Show Boat*, the complete manuscript of *Very Good Eddie*, and *Leave It To Jane*, et cetera, et cetera. Oddly enough, musicologists are as excited about getting the stage orchestra transcriptions of well-known pieces as they are of the completely missing songs. As one explains, "Only now do we know how Porgy and Bess sounded to

Gershwin. The reason that *Rhapsody in Blue* sounds the way it does is that Paul Whiteman substituted saxophones for the supporting string sections—that the melody line was passed to a single banjo. There are dozens of examples like this in the musical theater classics of the so-called Jazz Age. The Secaucus discoveries will keep us busy for years." The Gershwin and Kern families rushed these treasures to the Library's Music Division so they could be easily and broadly available to music scholarship everywhere.

(Ferde Grofe was Paul Whiteman's and George Gershwin's arranger, and much of what we have known about the latter's music up to now came from the Library's holdings of Grofe's manuscripts. During the decade we're looking at, another large collection of Grofe material was given to the Library, including the holograph copies of his *Grand Canyon Suite* and literally hundreds more unique, unpublished materials.)

Let's conclude this sampling of the 1980s treasures with a demonstration of that Principle of Librarianship we met at the very beginning: If a library is to achieve its purpose it must do three things equally well—acquire the materials, organize them for use, and *use* them. The Music Division's work with the film *Intolerance* is a dramatic example of using its materials and making them more useful for its users.

Intolerance was D.W. Griffith's masterpiece of film making, with many aspects that have never been improved on, and even more that have been copied so many times that over the next seventy-five years they became a part of the protocols and standards of motion pictures as we know them. By 1915, Griffith had completed his highly successful *Birth of a Nation* and he began what he intended to be the epic film to top anything ever done.

Intolerance was in fact four different stories which would play in and out of the single showing, intercut back and forth with increasing tempo to build to a crashing finale. One plot involved the splendor of Babylon and its destruction by the Persian armies; another was "The Modern Story" about a labor striker who is unjustly imprisoned and his child taken away from him; a third was a story about a Huguenot persecuted in sixteenth-century France and ultimately swept into the St. Bartholomew's Day massacre; with the final "Judean Story" recounting the last years of Jesus Christ. The completed film was premiered in September 1916, ran three-and-a-half hours, and involved a full orches-

Copyright stills and a Library of Congress score used in the reconstruction of the D.W. Griffith film masterpiece **Intolerance** *for the New York Film Festival.*

tra for the background music. (We usually think of silent film music being a theater organ, but in the 1910s and '20s there were over 500 live theater orchestras supporting the films on the screens. The famous conductor of the Philadelphia Symphony, Eugene Ormandy, got his start in the back of the Capitol Theater pit, playing "silent film" music for three years.)

The monumental *Intolerance* was neither a financial nor performance success. Its primary thesis that Pacifism was Truth, and that Good and Right always triumphed, played increasingly poorly as the United States became involved in World War I. Griffith tried to salvage some profits from the wreckage by first cutting the film down to two-and-a-half hours, and then cutting snips from the full script and making two stand-alone movies of "The Mother and the Law" and "The Fall of Babylon," the two stories that had proved to be most popular of the interlaced four. He continued to cut, introduce new scenes, and create new silent titles until no one knew what the original had looked like. (He had only one copy of the film, so he was actually cutting and splicing the original negative.)

Thus the original *Intolerance* whose editing techniques, staging, and cinematic devices have affected so much of the mature industry became a lost Grail for motion-picture historians. In 1981, Peter Williamson, the film curator at the Museum of Modern Art, set out to reconstruct the original.

He found scraps of the film in the most unlikely places. MOMA had pieces in 16mm and 35mm; The Danish National Film Archive had a substantial chunk from 1917; UCLA had the most extensive running footage of the captions. Et cetera. Williamson got all his pieces together, but it became immediately clear that no one knew where the parts fit, which were original and which post-premier, and certainly not how they were cut back and forth in the original. At this point, the Library of Congress became involved.

Williamson had worked with a musicologist in the Library's Music Division, Gillian Anderson, in an earlier reconstruction of Griffith's *Way Down East*. He asked Anderson if the Library had anything that might help with the *Intolerance* puzzle. As it proved, it did indeed. When Griffith had copyrighted the film in 1916, he had someone on his staff cut the first frame out of every scene in the movie and staple it onto pages of a scrapbook to prove authorship. The scrapbook, deposited with the Library of Congress to satisfy registration requirements, had

2,203 individual film frames in their proper sequence. Further, the Music Division found the complete, original music score by Joseph Carl Breil with several sets of orchestral parts (over 1,000 pages of music) in its collections, and it secured access to the piano score which was at the University of Minnesota. End result: the copyright frames provided the sequence of scenes, the music provided the length of time of the scenes (the music was annotated to link it to the action and events playing on the screen above), and thus they knew how long most of the scenes would run. (There were a few scenes—frequently the most dramatic ones—that the score declared were to be absolutely silent.) Annotations for a metronome appeared on occasion, and Anderson ultimately identified 5,757 measures of music.

By the end of the project, Williamson and Anderson had spent eight years putting the final product together, and the completed motion picture was featured at the 1989 New York Film Festival. The performance was staged in Lincoln Center with Anderson directing the Brooklyn Philharmonic Orchestra and Chorus. The purpose of the effort was to provide a base for musical scholarship which would in turn be studied for years. A side benefit was what the press described as a once-in-a-lifetime, emotional event shared by several thousand viewers.

And with this, we must end our hurried walk through the treasures of the 1980s, and indeed the Library's treasures in general.

There are only three more thoughts to be expressed or underlined.

The first is the most obvious and need not be labored. We have been searching through all this trip for the rare, the unusual, and the unique—but what we found can never be more than the proverbial tip of the tritest iceberg. Everything we have seen must simply represent ten or a hundred things beside it or behind it of equal significance. We must hope that in coming years these can be made more familiar to the nation.

Second, we should restate the fact that all of these materials are here to be *used*. The time and energy that it has cost the taxpayer for acquisition, processing, and housing can never be justified unless the contents of these treasures are kept in the current flow of ideas and values and judgments of the nation. To consider the trove as a hoard or even a time capsule for future use is questionable at best. The librarians who care for the materials are obligated to keep them alive and known about, and the subject specialists working with them are equally obligated to see that the riches are mined and made useful.

But finally comes a slightly different thought. One of the anomalies about the Library is the paradox between its outer reality and its inner workings and personality. Looked at from the street or from Congress or from the nation, the Library appears to be one of the great symbols of our continuity. It seems to sit in quiet repose, maintaining consistent streams of taste and value and purpose, and generally being a vault full of enduring, rational links with the past as well as fairly predictable guides to the future.

The irony is that within the granite walls nothing could be further from the truth. In the past there have been violent shifts in what was collected, what was sought, how it was treated—how it was used. Abrupt turns seem to appear about every twenty or thirty years and the Library's future is sure to be as unpredictable as has been its past.

There are so many unknowns and unanswered questions: What materials will it hold? Will they be deteriorating paper? Short-lived film? Vulnerable digital blips? In a world where communication is instantaneous and everywhere, is there indeed any need to have all the world's literature or pictures or music in *one* place? (An Australian librarian told me that he can get a facsimile from the British Library in London faster than he can borrow a book from one of his own branch libraries.) And such a volatile future therefore affects every accumulation of treasure we have sampled here. What will we consider treasure a generation from now? What will be sought and how will it be preserved?

Thus there are so many delightful unknowns! We hope you have found the story intriguing thus far.

The above is a sheet from the work pad of the famous industrial designer Raymond Loewy. The Library received over a thousand pieces from his files, revealing his creative thought throughout his career. The sheet above shows the trials and rejections as he created a new logo for Standard Oil Company. He has given his final choice the official Loewy okay.

Foreword to the First Edition

After visiting your Library of Congress in this handsome book, you will feel richer than you could imagine any citizen to be. At the other end of Pennsylvania Avenue, another building, facing the White House, is called the Treasury of the United States. But here on Capitol Hill, facing the Congress, is where you can discover the spiritual, traditional wealth of our nation, the wealth we inherit from all the world.

Here the treasures of civilization have been collected in ways peculiarly American. The Library of Congress tells us some things about ourselves and our country that we may not have noticed, or may simply have taken for granted. Charles A. Goodrum, versatile author of this book, knows the Library from his many years of service to members of Congress and our other readers. With lively wit and ranging scholarship he has garnered and served up a scintillating sampler of the world's greatest library. He has shown us how much more than a "library" a great library can be. And we could want no better guide to the treasures that belong to all of us.

In this Foreword I will try only to remind you of what is most remarkably American about this kind of national treasury.

When you walk casually into the Library of Congress and ask to see one of these treasures you may not realize that you are doing something which you could not do in other national libraries of the world. Here you need no credentials. I often receive letters from scholars and librarians abroad vouching for the character and scholarly qualities of some particular person, who, they request, should be allowed to use the Library of Congress. The other day as I walked through the Main Reading Room I met a young scholar from England who was deep in our books—even before his "letter of recommendation" had reached me!

This is your Library. The citizens of other countries cannot feel quite the same way about their national library. Even in the free world, admission to use the collections of the national library is commonly limited to advanced scholars properly recommended. In the unfree world, the use of the national library is restricted even further—to people who are politically "reliable." There, numerous books are shown only to people who would not be apt to harbor "dangerous thoughts."

The welcome you receive today in your Library of Congress is rooted in American history. Other great national libraries grew out of private collections of kings, nobles, and aristocrats. For example, the magnificent Bibliothèque Nationale in Paris originated in the collections made by early French kings, from the time of Charlemagne. The libraries of Charles V and the House of Orleans were enlarged by Francis I, transferred to Paris by Charles IX, and then expanded by Louis XIV. Of course this explains their treasure trove of early manuscripts and old books, but it also explains an enduring tradition of collecting for the wealthy, the powerful, and the learned. The British Museum (now the British Library) in London has a similar history. It was founded in the personal collections of Sir Hans Sloane (physician to George II) and a few other learned aristocrats, and especially in the personal libraries of George II and George III. You still need a letter of introduction to be admitted to their elegant Reading Room.

The Library of Congress enjoys a more democratic lineage. As the name reminds us, our national collections grew out of an effort, at our nation's founding, to gather knowledge for the people's representatives. To call this the Library of *Congress*, then, is more than a mere matter of nomenclature. And, although it is not widely noted, our name also reveals that the role and the reach of our national library is wider and more open than libraries elsewhere which purport to serve their nations. Our national library remains a possession of the people, made by the people and for the people, and open to the people.

If this Library had its roots in any one personal collection, it was the library of Thomas Jefferson, citizen of the whole world of science, prophet of an expansive representative democracy, and advocate of universal education. "There is, in fact," Jefferson explained, "no subject to which a member of Congress may not have occasion to refer." "Enlighten the people generally," he urged, "and tyranny and oppressions of body and mind will vanish like evil spirits at the dawn of day." An open national library, taking all knowledge for its province and a whole nation as its audience, is a symbol and an instrument of a free people and their own government. When you consult any book in your national collections, you speak volumes about our nation and ourselves.

Most other great national libraries are primarily collections in the official language or languages of their nation. But here in the Library of Congress, as Charles A. Goodrum explains, nearly three-quarters of the books and a large proportion of other materials are in languages other than English. This is no accident—nor is it an extravagance. On the contrary, this too expresses the special character of our nation.

Recently at an international meeting of national libraries, I was taxed by a librarian from France with the American "megalomania." Why should the Library of the United States, alone among the world's libraries, set about collecting in *all* languages? Other nations have substantially satisfied themselves with materials in their own national languages or about their own country. Why should not the USA also be reasonable, and confine its major collections to works in the "American" language or about the United States? The answer, of course, again lies in our past, and in the unique character of American civilization. If the history of the United States had been like that of France, then we too might have been satisfied with a national stock of books in our own "national" language.

Our history has been radically different. Even English, our official language, has been an import. Our country has been peopled (and, fortunately, continues to be peopled) with immigrants from all over the world. For most of the comers to the United States, English (or "American") has been a second language. Our history bears vivid witness to the fact that people can learn all sorts of new ways of life—including a new spoken language. How, then, could we pretend to make a truly national library for our United States unless we collected in the languages that millions spoke when they arrived—and still arrive—on these shores? And unless we gathered materials on all the civilizations of the world from which Americans have come, and out of which our American civilization has been made? In the United States, of all nations on earth, our *national* library (like our people) must be *international*. This is our proud national paradox, dramatized here in our Library of Congress.

Most other national libraries consist of printed matter and manuscripts. But the Library of Congress' eighteen million volumes are only one-quarter of our items. As the reader of this book will discover, some of our most valued and most remarkable treasures are not manuscripts or books at all. The wonderful miscellany that comprises three-quarters of our inventory includes maps, musical recordings, lithographs, posters, photographs, motion-picture films, computer tapes, microforms, and numerous other formats. The Copyright Law of 1976 made this Library our national archive of radio and television broadcasts.

Yet, when the first Library of Congress building was completed, the Library was expected to collect only books, maps, prints, and manuscripts. As our technologies have grown, so has our Library. Television and the computer are not the last, but only the latest American technology that will enrich our nation's library. If we are to provide a continuous, up-to-date record of our astonishing American civilization, we cannot stay stuck in the old pigeonholes. Of course, we must be grateful for the Book, which the Library's Center for the Book celebrates. We must remain the world's greatest treasury of books. But this technological nation's library must be alert to all the new expressions of civilization. We must seek the whole experience—whatever has filled the consciousness of Americans past and present. And we cannot understand the meaning of the new unless we know what life was like before. Other nations, whose experience has not yet been so transformed by technology, may be satisfied with a library of manuscripts and books. But not the USA!

Our kind of nation thrives not only on Gross National Product but on Gross National Happiness. We are the only nation, so far as I know, that has included among its declared purposes, "the pursuit of happiness." A library which gathered only the materials of instruction and of high culture would not be true to our heritage. Our national birth certificate, the Declaration of Independence, not only declares that the pursuit of happiness is one of man's "inalienable rights," it goes much further and says that whenever any government ceases to secure those rights, it is the right of the people to alter or abolish it. In the United States the pursuit of happiness is everybody's business, and any American institution which forgets that is failing in its mission.

The Library of Congress recently mounted an exhibit of a half-century of animated cartoons. On that occasion we rendered to Mickey Mouse and his fellow creatures of the animated world honors which other nations reserve for their priests, potentates, and soccer players. Satisfying and stimulating the American desire to pursue happiness has created a few heroes, a host of celebrities, and countless prosperous businesses. These are more reasons why we must provide and report on all formats—old and new—photographs, motion-picture films, art prints, musical recordings, radio, and television, among others. Collecting, preserving, cataloging and diffusing information about all these materials, as Charles A. Goodrum shows so well, is serious business. Still, we must avoid being solemn, for while we increase knowledge, it is also our duty to increase happiness.

On a scale unequaled by any other library, the Library of Congress opens avenues to knowledge and amusement for those who need special formats. Our service for the blind and physically handicapped, by publications in braille and talking books, and by research into new technologies, opens our treasures to millions more.

The growth, variety, and modernity of the Library is revealed in our three magnificent buildings on Capitol Hill. The first Library of Congress building (illustrations of which open this volume) is itself a unique treasure. The sculpture, painting, and eloquent inscriptions you see here still provide a delightful architectural encyclopedia of the meaning of civilization in 1897. The second Library of Congress building, completed in 1939, larger in capacity than the first, was designed to hold more millions of books and manuscripts. The new Madison Memorial Building, even larger than both the earlier buildings together, now provides services and houses materials never imagined when the first building was opened. In addition to the Congressional Research Service, it offers unexcelled facilities for the storage, preservation, and study of manuscripts, motion-picture films, and musical recordings. Here are three grand monuments to the American people's awe and reverence for their national treasures. The expanding collections, the multiplying media—and the new Madison Building—have given us the opportunity to arrange our collections into a grand Multi-Media Encyclopedia. Technologies, old and new, will help us make the nation's riches more visible, more accessible, and more usable.

These treasures of the Library of Congress, as Charles A. Goodrum reminds us, did not drop from the sky into their present locations. They were all acquired for us from authors, or composers, or artists seeking copyrights or from somebody else at one time or another. Two remarkable women helped make possible the Library's music collections and performances. Mrs. Elizabeth Sprague Coolidge, herself a noted concert pianist, gave us the Coolidge Auditorium, an acoustical gem unexcelled for chamber music. Mrs. Gertrude Clarke Whittall gave us our five splendid Stradivari instruments (and for each a Tourte bow) requesting that the instruments be played regularly for public enjoyment. Some of our rarest books (illustrated in this volume) were the gift of the inspired and generous bibliophile Lessing J. Rosenwald, who not only loved books but loved all who loved books.

The keepers of the treasury, those who have attracted, collected, cataloged, cared for, and served up the nation's treasures, must not be forgotten. Here is the harvest of devoted thousands of men and women, past and present, who have worked in the Library of Congress. With our other benefactors, they have built this treasury and they keep it alive and growing.

Daniel J. Boorstin
The Librarian of Congress

Acknowledgments

I have been asked by so many people, "Out of nearly a hundred million items, how did you decide which ones to talk about?" that I thought you might be interested in a bit more methodology than is usual on an acknowledgments page. There is no value/grading system for the holdings of the Library, so the question of which pictures to take and which items to discuss was the most important element in the creation of the book. It was done thus:

My long-time collaborator, Helen Dalrymple, and I began by "making a card" on every object in the following categories: 1) all the Library's materials that had been moved to Fort Knox for safe-keeping during World War II; 2) all the items that had been displayed in special exhibits since 1946; and 3) all the items that had been the target of special press releases since 1950. We then searched the annual reports of acquisition, the divisional lists of special collections, and the articles in the *Quarterly Journal of the Library of Congress* since its inception. From this cumulation of entries, we selected items that seemed to meet the criteria of the rare, the unique, or the unlikely. All these objects plus interviews with some two dozen curators resulted in approximately two thousand items for consideration. We reduced these nominees to one thousand items by dividing the materials into two groups: the exceptionally important vs. less important or duplicated-by-equivalent examples.

We then grouped the one thousand into broad areas of subjects (which became the twelve chapters) and within these tried to select individual objects that would represent the *types* of materials within the subject categories. This distillation reduced the nominees to something over five hundred items and, after consultation with the curators, these were photographed.

The photography was done by Michael Freeman and Jonathan Wallen. Each of the photographers took some of the architectural elements of the building. I would specify what features I wished to show and Freeman and Wallen would then compose them into artistically graceful scenes. Jon Wallen did the pictures of the rarities and he had to struggle with worse constraints: I would note on each object card precisely what I wanted photographed, what portions of the object were to be emphasized, and what specific details I wished to reveal, and then Wallen had to provide a technically accurate reproduction of the piece in an artistic setting—without doing damage to the rarity through handling, weights, bending, heat, or too much light. Wallen took over one thousand exposures working with a high degree of professionalism in a difficult environment. Once I had decided what items I wished recorded, Mrs. Dalrymple assumed all responsibility for the photographing activity, meeting with the curators, setting up space, seeing that the materials were brought to the cameras on schedule, and collecting the necessary data for later captioning. I then withdrew from the photography and concentrated on writing the text of the book. The two efforts ultimately came back together when we shared the task of writing captions at the end of the project.

Obviously there are dozens of people to whom both Helen and I are deeply indebted for their patience, their assistance in selecting and explaining their treasures, and in general making the whole project possible.

A few of the specialists went so far beyond what we had any right to hope for that we cannot resist mentioning a few names, but curators in every division gave us marvelous cooperation. We would like to express our special gratitude to Jon Newsom in music for his imaginative understanding of what we were trying to do in the book, and for his wide professionalism that covered such a broad range of his varied subject. We want to express our delight and gratitude to John Wolter and Richard Stephenson of maps for the wonderful enthusiasm they show for their area of expertise, and the eagerness their whole division shows for making its materials available to everybody. Karen Beall, curator of fine prints, was marvelously patient and understanding in making the selections from the tens of thousands of masterpieces she cares for, and her good-humored ability to explain the significance of her treasures made her area a special delight to work in. Finally, the skilled enthusiasm of Kathleen Mang, and the patient professionalism of William Matheson and Dan Burney in rare books were a joy to watch. Indeed patience—even tolerance—pervaded the experience as we used up people's time, disrupted work areas, and generally distracted so many people from their ordered days.

We want to express our gratitude to several people for their overall impact on the book. Dana Pratt, the Library's Director of Publishing, was splendidly supportive in listening to our endless choices ("we can take this or that…, go this way or that way…, talk about this or that… which way do you lean?") and in general giving us the benefit of his long experience in the publishing field. We want to thank Ruth Boorstin for her lively interest and skilled suggestions about the text, and Janet Chase for her many devices for making our way smooth.

The experience of working with art director Nai Chang and editor Edith Pavese was particularly delightful, as were all of our contacts with the imaginative Abrams staff.

And I want to express my special gratitude to Daniel J. Boorstin, not only for his incisive Foreword to the first edition, but for his support of the book in general. Although he rigorously held back from the planning and writing of the volume itself, his enthusiasm for the project and his general signals of endorsement made it possible to bring it off within the exceedingly tight time frames set by modern publishing schedules.

Lastly, these acknowledgments usually express appreciation for "permission to reproduce" certain writings. In this case, I am in debt to fifty years' worth of Library specialists writing about their divisional treasures in Library publications. Such skilled and graceful words as Walter Ristow's map articles, John Cole's interesting and scholarly historical pieces, and the Prints and Photograph Division's *Viewpoints* were essential to the book and made "research" a pleasure.

Further Reading

If you wish to read further about the Library of Congress, we would recommend the following sources:

For a statement of how the Library is organized and what each unit does, candor forces us (!) to recommend our own: Goodrum, Charles A. and Helen W. Dalrymple, *The Library of Congress*. Boulder, Colo., Westview Press, 1982. For a working how-to-use the Library's many reading rooms and specialized units, the Library of Congress's *Guide to the Library of Congress* is inexpensive and available either at the doors of the Library or from its Publishing Office. The Guide is updated regularly.

If you are using your local public library, the following materials should be easy to obtain:

Fitzgerald, Randy. "America's Amazing Treasure Chest," in *Reader's Digest,* v. 134, no. 806, June 1989: 47–49, 52.

King, Seth S. "The Nation's Book Trove," in *The New York Times,* Jan. 15, 1984: 20, 34.

The Bowker Annual of Library and Book Trade Information. New York, R.R. Bowker, has a section on Library of Congress activities written by various authors each year.

Simpson, Andrew L. *The Library of Congress*. New York, Chelsea House Publishers, 1989. (Know your government series, for young people.)

The best description of the Library's architecture (with profuse illustrations) is: Small, Herbert. Edited by Henry Hope Reed. *The Library of Congress: Its Architecture and Decoration*. New York, W.W. Norton, 1982. (The Classical America series in art and architecture.)

If you are interested in the Library's history, the best single source is John Y. Cole's *For Congress and the Nation: A Chronological History of the Library of Congress*. Washington, U.S. Govt. Print. Off., 1979.

In addition, each of the Library's many specialized divisions publishes guides to its collections and explanations of its services and purpose. These are constantly being up-dated, and the best means of finding out what is presently available (either free or inexpensively) is to request a copy of the current "Library of Congress Publications In Print" from Office Systems Services, Printing and Processing Section, Library of Congress, Washington, D.C. 20540. At any given time, this catalog will list approximately 500 titles. A substantial number of these can be seen at your nearest Government Document Depository usually located in your local public or college library.

Information on new programs and future plans can be found in the two hearings held each Spring by the Legislative Subcommittees of the Congressional House and Senate Appropriations Committees. These documents record the testimony of the Librarian of Congress who will not only describe his current services and the state of the Library, but his plans for the coming years. These hearings (and the resultant instructional reports by the Committees) will also be available in your local depository library.

Index